Learn Windows IIS
in a Month of Lunches

JASON HELMICK

MANNING
SHELTER ISLAND

For online information and ordering of this and other Manning books, please visit
www.manning.com. The publisher offers discounts on this book when ordered in quantity.
For more information, please contact

> Special Sales Department
> Manning Publications Co.
> 20 Baldwin Road
> PO Box 261
> Shelter Island, NY 11964
> Email: orders@manning.com

♾ Recognizing the importance of preserving what has been written, it is Manning's policy to have
the books we publish printed on acid-free paper, and we exert our best efforts to that end.
Recognizing also our responsibility to conserve the resources of our planet, Manning books
are printed on paper that is at least 15 percent recycled and processed without the use of
elemental chlorine.

Manning Publications Co.
20 Baldwin Road
PO Box 261
Shelter Island, NY 11964

Development editors: Renae Gregoire, Susanna Kline
Copyeditor: Corbin Collins
Proofreader: Alyson Brener
Typesetter: Dottie Marsico
Cover designer: Leslie Haimes

ISBN 9781617290978
Printed in the United States of America
2 3 4 5 6 7 8 9 10 – MAL – 19 18 17 16 15 14

*To my wife Michelle, my daughter Devon,
and my parents Faith and Jim.*

*Your love, support, and patience
have made this book possible. I love you.*

brief contents

contents

preface

I sat in a darkly lit restaurant with Don Jones and Chris Gannon having a great conversation about the importance of Don's latest book in his "Month of Lunches" series—and how no one until him seemed to be trying to help the working administrator—the guy or gal in the trenches. As an IT pro teacher and speaker, his concepts of how to best help admins is important to me and I wished other authors and teachers would take up the charge. After venting my profound appreciation of his work, I noticed a smile on Don and Chris's faces. I was about to be set up. I was about to be tricked by my two friends.

Chris pointed out that I had written a book for admins about 15 years ago on IIS 4.0—in fact it could possibly be the first book written and published on IIS. He asked why I hadn't published another one—especially since I was so passionate about helping the working administrator.

I responded with the usual–no time, I have a wife and kid, too busy to sit down and spend the long hours on writing—every excuse in the book. Don looked at me, smiled with that snarky look that usually means I lost the argument before I even got a chance to litigate. Don said, "Stretch yourself." Before I could respond, he turned my initial argument against me. How could he? I thought we were friends. He said, "You have experience and knowledge about administrating IIS that could help thousands of admins, and you refuse to share it because you don't want to be inconvenienced to work a little harder?" Yup, he won the argument.

Later I found out that they had planned this little argument—ply me with a good steak and a couple of martinis—but regardless of the set up, the truth still hit me. I was just as passionate about trying to help my fellow working admins as he was. So I looked at Don, then Chris, smiled and said, "Yes sir—count me in."

This book was written during the week at night, and on every weekend, until completion. There was always something that had to be done, something changed, something that needed to be dropped and replaced, research, experimentation, and just learning to write better. When you're almost finished writing a book, the publisher asks you to write a preface. I'm surprised that they don't get, "I'll never do this again!" I have to say that I'm the opposite. I will always stretch and push myself to do everything I can to help. In other words, I'm glad I wrote this book and I hope you are too. If you like it, let me know and I'll write another one. In the end, the only thing that kept me driving forward on this book and from giving up was my desire to help working admins get through their daily job in the best way possible.

I hope you find this book worth the effort.

about this book

Almost everything you need to know about this book and how best to learn from it is in Chapter 1. There are a few things I want to point out before you get started.

First, this book is written for the IT pro that needs to learn about managing Microsoft Internet Information Services (IIS). To best experience the book, work through the labs at the end of each chapter so you can try the concepts discussed. You should build the lab environment described in Chapter 1 and try these labs out while you are reading the other chapters. In other words, you should be in front of your computer, ready for action.

Second, you should read the book from the beginning to the end. After having gone through the book, you can use it as a reference, flipping to the chapters you need. The first time through, start at the beginning. I wrote the chapters in a logical flow of working with the IIS product, building on each chapter to form a complete picture. Don't miss these pieces by flipping to the end.

Third, I use the graphical IIS Manager to demonstrate how to install and configure each subject discussed. I also show how to manage IIS using the preferred management tool from Microsoft called PowerShell. The PowerShell information I provide is so that in the future you can automate the management of IIS and scale to larger environments. This is important as your career with IIS progresses, however if PowerShell is not currently a tool you work with, you don't need to focus on that in the book. Again, everything I describe I will demonstrate in the IIS Manager. I can't teach you how to use the tool PowerShell in this book—the focus stays on IIS—so if you want to learn more about PowerShell, see Manning's *Learn Windows PowerShell 3 in a Month of Lunches, Second Edition* by Don Jones and Jeffrey Hicks.

Author Online

Purchase of *Learn Windows IIS in a Month of Lunches* includes free access to a private web forum run by Manning Publications where you can make comments about the book, ask technical questions, and receive help from the author and from other users. To access the forum and subscribe to it, point your web browser to www.manning .com/LearnWindowsIISinaMonthofLunches. This page provides information on how to get on the forum once you're registered, what kind of help is available, and the rules of conduct on the forum.

Manning's commitment to our readers is to provide a venue where a meaningful dialog between individual readers and between readers and the author can take place. It's not a commitment to any specific amount of participation on the part of the author, whose contribution to the AO remains voluntary (and unpaid). We suggest you ask the author challenging questions lest his interest stray!

The Author Online forum and the archives of previous discussions will be accessible from the publisher's website as long as the book is in print.

About the author

Jason is a 25-year IT veteran and Senior Technologist at Concentrated Technology. He's an avid supporter of the PowerShell community as board member and CFO of PowerShell.org. He is a contributing author to Manning's *PowerShell Deep Dives,* and a columnist for *TechNet Magazine* and other industry publications. He's a frequent speaker at many conferences and can be contacted on Twitter: @theJasonHelmick.

acknowledgments

Stop! Books don't write themselves and there are many people responsible for what you hold in your hands. I want you to take a moment and join me in thanking them for their hard work, late nights, and tenacious effort to make this book possible.

To the entire staff at Manning Publications—from the editors, the copyeditors, the technical reviewers, the graphics guys and gals—thank you for hard work. Special thanks to my development editors Renae E. Gregoire and Susanna Kline. Renae, you started me down the path, you taught me how to write better, when to ask myself the right questions, and to keep the reader in mind. The knowledge you taught me will serve me well for the rest of my writing career. Susanna, you took me to the end of the process with an extremely high level of professionalism and poise. Thanks to your encouragement and focus, the book is a better product. Both of you should be coauthors because of all your hard work. Thank you!

To the folks from the Author Online forum who took the time to point out my mistakes, both in grammar and missing information—you made me think and try to improve the book. This book is a product of your help, so pat yourselves on the back.

To the technical reviewers listed below, and especially to Alexsandar Nikolic, my technical proofreader—after spending long days at work, then writing at night, I would make stupid and silly technical mistakes; sometimes I would forget entire pieces to the puzzle. So thank you for finding those mistakes and pushing me to think about how to present things better. You gave me ideas through your constructive criticism and helped make this a much better book.

The technical reviewers were: Alexander Esser, Andrew Westgarth, Bay Phillips, Brian Young, Chad McAuley, Daniel Headley, Francis Setash, Glenn Swonk, Irfan Patel, Jason Varisco, Jerry Warner, Margriet Bruggeman, Mick Wilson, Mike F. Robbins,

Nick Brattoli, Nikander Bruggeman, Patrick Curry, Richard Fieldsend, Sau Fai Fong, Shane Beacom, and Victor Onate Acosta.

To Microsoft, specifically the IIS Team and PowerShell Team—thank you for making excellent, high-end products that IT pros can rely on. Your dedication to the success of the business and the IT pro in this ever-changing world is truly amazing. Thank you for the hard work.

My warmest thanks to Don Jones, the extraordinary author of too many books to count, and the editor of the *Month of Lunches* series. You have been my mentor and my friend. Without you providing the opportunity, the encouragement, and the late-night bar talks, this book would not have been written. Your passionate belief in reaching out to help the admins of the world has helped us all.

Before you begin

Are you an inadvertent IIS administrator, or even a reluctant one? I used to be and still am on occasion. I understand the life of a systems administrator—it's all about time management. We spend our days putting out fires, bringing new services online, and keeping the network always available for our users and the business. As an administrator I may have known IIS was lurking in my servers, waiting for me to install it and build a website, but I didn't want to use my time for that stuff. IIS wasn't that interesting to me, and I wanted to play with sexier technologies like Microsoft Exchange and SharePoint. I chose to ignore IIS and left it to the other system admins.

But my reluctance to spend time learning IIS started to interfere with my job in a surprising way, because IIS is more than a product to make websites; it's a primary communication gateway for many other products. Have you worked with Exchange, SharePoint, SQL Server, or some other Microsoft enterprise product? If so you've noticed that almost all of the enterprise servers have IIS as a software prerequisite. Consider this: any application you want to use via the internet—whether it's Outlook web access for Exchange, a portal system such as SharePoint, or management applications such as System Center—uses IIS for that communication. To be an expert at those technologies, the person who can troubleshoot problems (and increase your value to the company), you need to be an IIS expert.

In addition to hindering my abilities with enterprise server products, my avoidance of IIS became an even larger business issue. My company started a new product initiative and needed someone who could set up and manage the websites for the new product line. Don't get me wrong, they didn't need me to develop the new websites—I'm not a developer—but to configure, secure, and manage them. To be of better service to my company and to give in to my slight but growing fascination with this intriguing product, I chose to learn IIS.

As soon as I dove into IIS, my understanding of and management abilities for those other products soared. I could troubleshoot problems and manage the communications products better. I enjoyed working with IIS so much that I became the primary "go to" web guy. I began building highly available web servers, taking developer-written web applications, putting them into secured websites, and launching new applications for the business. IIS proved to be as sexy and exciting as any other technology and has become my favorite web server product today.

Throughout this book I do everything I can to open your eyes to the allure of IIS while providing you with the best information to manage, deploy, secure, and troubleshoot it—even if you don't find it as sexy as I do. I show you how to work with IIS using traditional Microsoft graphical and downloadable tools. Because I'm reluctant to spend more time than necessary on management, I also show you time-management techniques I've found that use PowerShell to manage and automate processes in IIS. Being proficient with IIS has increased my understanding of many technologies, including the web, and elevated my career. Whether or not you're an inadvertent IIS administrator, you'll find that learning to use the IIS tools covered in the pages of this book will help you do your job better.

This chapter starts with a high-level tour of IIS and then launches into the prerequisites you need before you begin your next lunch. You'll also learn the best ways to use this book, as well as how to set up your lab environment. To best understand and get the most from this book, you'll experience IIS as you manage and support a small-town bicycle shop with a basic website called WebBikez that will grow to a worldwide bicycle distributor. Let's begin with a closer look at IIS itself.

1.1   Introducing IIS

It helps to relate IIS—and web servers in general—to something you already know. In most cases IIS performs the same job as a file server, serving web pages as files to a network client across the internet. The client uses a browser that displays and runs those files as a useful application.

The same concerns you have about file servers regarding security and performance still apply, and in many cases IIS is configured similarly. But there is much more to IIS and its architecture, mainly due to the security challenges that impact any server connected to the internet and the need to be able to run many different types of web applications.

Figure 1.1 is a simple description of how IIS works. It provides a good starting point to get a handle on what to expect.

IIS contains a time-proven architecture that's fast and highly secured. Flexibility helps developers who are implementing modules—IIS allows for quick additions to

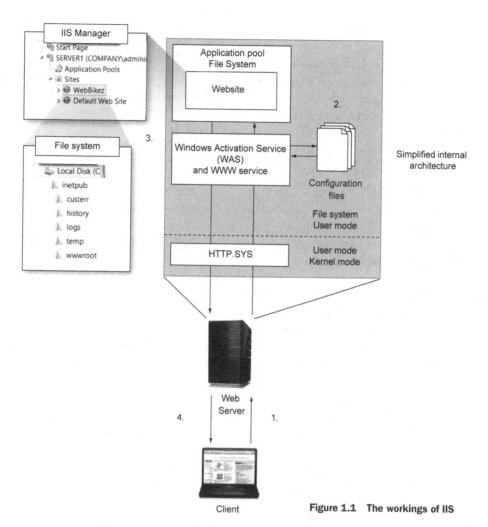

Figure 1.1   The workings of IIS

support new applications—and IIS gives web administrators a web platform that will grow into large-scale web farms for redundancy. Throughout this book you'll dive into this architecture from the perspective of a web administrator to design, configure, secure, and maintain a web environment. But before all that, let's look at the basics of how IIS delivers web content:

1   The process begins with clients who request a website or other resource by typing a URL into their browser, such as www.WebBikez.com. The URL is resolved into an IP address by DNS, and clients connect to the web server using the IP address.

2   A component in the web server architecture called HTTP.SYS intercepts the incoming request. HTTP.SYS calls the Windows Activation Service (WAS) and WWW Service to determine the location and configuration of the website or

resource. This process launches a w3wp.exe worker process that handles and responds to the client request.

3   The web pages of the website can be physically located on the local web server or on a remote share. This information, along with all the configuration settings for the website, is made accessible through the graphical IIS manager or a command-line tool such as PowerShell.

4   The client's request is processed by the worker process, and the web page contents are sent to the client, where the browser runs the web page code to display the web application.

Look beyond this simple description and you can envision the challenges that this book covers—from the installation of the web server, to the creation and configuration of websites, to configuring and maintaining security, and finally to scaling into a web farm for best performance and high availability. Let's take a look at what you'll need to complete this journey.

1.2   *What you need before you start*

I assume that you're an IT professional and not someone off the street reading this book because you enjoy my entertaining prose. As an author who wants you to be successful with IIS, I want to define what you need to know and have in hand *before* you start so you can decide whether you should brush up on any weak points. As you use this book, you may find some areas where you need some additional information or training. That's not a bad thing; it's how most of us have been successful in our careers with constantly changing technology—we find out what we're missing and get that information. I assume that's why you're holding this book. Congratulations—it gets easier from here.

This section covers what you need to know to begin this book—including how to work with PowerShell and which versions of IIS will work with the "lunches" in this book.

1.2.1   *Prerequisite knowledge*

IIS is a technology that reaches throughout your company network and onto the internet. To be an effective administrator for IIS, you need a lot of infrastructure knowledge. You probably have most of it already in your head, and you can pick up the missing parts as you go. Here are the things you should have basic to intermediate knowledge of before you get started:

- First, you *don't need* to know any development language such as ASP, ASP.NET, Java, or anything else. Surprised? This book isn't about developing web applications; it's about managing IIS servers and websites. Have no fear, you'll be fine.
- You *do* need an intermediate level of knowledge about TCP/IP and how to properly configure the protocol for the network addressing of your web servers. You don't need to know how to subnet an IP address, but you should be comfortable assigning an IP address, subnet mask, and default gateway. And you should be

comfortable using commands such as `Ping` and `Tracert` to troubleshoot IP communication issues.

- You need a basic understanding of routers, firewalls, and NAT (network address translation). You may have engineers to configure this specialized equipment, but you should understand the basics of how they work so you can request configuration changes to the devices depending on your environment.

- You need to understand the basics of DNS and name resolution. In this book, as in real life, you'll need to request changes to DNS when you set up URLs for your websites. Although you may not be the person who normally makes this change, you'll need to make the request to the folks who do. I show you how to make the changes so you know exactly what to do.

- As an IT professional with Windows, assigning NTFS file system permissions and share permissions should already be a comfortable process. You'll need this skill when we examine website security.

- You also need a basic understanding of Active Directory—nothing over the top like group policies or replication troubleshooting, but the basics of creating a user and a group.

1.2.2 IIS versions 7.0, 7.5, or 8

What version of IIS do you need? Fortunately for administrators, IIS versions 7.0, 7.5, and 8 have similar configuration settings and management tools. No matter which version you're using, this book is for you. I use IIS 8 for the screenshots in this book, but I also point out differences between IIS 8 and versions 7.x.

What do you do if you're using IIS 6? Consider upgrading to the new IIS 8 platform. IIS 6 is similar in many respects to the newer versions, but you're missing many new features and capabilities. This book is still useful to you, though, and will help you with IIS 6, but I don't address specific issues with IIS 6.

> **Upgrading may be easier than you think**
>
> If you're concerned that your web applications running on IIS 6 won't run on IIS 7/8, you may have an option that will still allow you to upgrade. IIS 7/8 have a series of components called "IIS 6 compatibility mode." This option may permit those older applications to run and allow you to upgrade. I discuss IIS 6 compatibility mode, along with other options, throughout the book.

I also don't go back and address management and architecture changes. I understand that updating can be a challenge, particularly if your web applications don't support the new versions. Remaining on the old version and not updating those web applications will prove to be more costly in the long run and much harder to secure. I recommend you update to IIS 7.5 or IIS 8. You don't want to miss out on what you can do with the most current products.

1.2.3 *Windows PowerShell*

In addition to the prerequisites I've mentioned, you also need to know how to use PowerShell to get the most out of this book. I spend a lot of time showing you how to use PowerShell for IIS to automate and manage your web environment. In fact if you have more than one IIS server, you need to use PowerShell to make your management faster.

Can you use this book and manage IIS without knowing PowerShell? Yes. I show you how to perform the necessary tasks using graphical tools. But as your web server environment grows, PowerShell can make your job much easier. Knowing PowerShell also improves your management of other technology areas you're responsible for.

If you don't know PowerShell, how do you learn it quickly? Check out Don Jones's *Learn Windows PowerShell 3 in a Month of Lunches* (www.manning.com/jones3/). Before you dig into the next lesson in this book, I recommend you pick up that book and work through the first 18 chapters. Yes, it will delay your learning IIS by 18 days (or two full weekend days if you're a masochist), but you won't regret the time investment.

1.3 How to use this book

As an IT professional, I'm sure you've read countless books and scoured each page for that one gem you need to complete your knowledge quest. This book is different, so let me explain. This book is designed for the busy IT professional who never seems to have enough time. I know you can't plop down on the sofa for a week and curl up with this book. In fact even if you do have that kind of time and want to curl up with it, you shouldn't. I need you to experience IIS, not merely read about it. With that in mind, this book has been designed to be digested one chapter at a time, one hour at a time, and provides labs and "ideas for on your own" to gain additional experience.

1.3.1 *One hour at a time*

I've written 24 chapters for you to digest along with your sandwich during lunch. As you're munching you can read one chapter in about 30 minutes. That leaves another 30 minutes to wash up and practice what the chapter showed you. The practice part is the most important for understanding the concepts of the chapter. Each chapter builds on the next, so get in the practice time to be sure you're ready to move on.

Some chapters don't take the full hour, so spend whatever extra time you have to practice cementing the concepts or returning to work. Don't rush to the next chapter; make sure you understand the current one. Try to stick with the schedule, and you'll be administering IIS in a month of lunches.

1.3.2 *Completing the labs*

To help you get the practice you need, the chapters also include short practice labs for you to complete before moving on. This is a great way for you to test the information you've learned while it's still fresh in your mind. You'll install, configure, and manage the WebBikez web servers and sites as they grow, so don't skip the lab part of your lunch. Each lab gives you a set of instructions and some hints, but no answers—not within the book, anyway. Try to complete the labs without any additional assistance. If you get stuck or want to see how I did the labs, the answers are online at More-Lunches.com.

1.3.3 MoreLunches.com

Other than lab answers at MoreLunches.com you'll find additional supplemental content, such as the latest on new updates to IIS and demonstration videos for some of the chapters to help make your journey with IIS a pleasant one.

I want you to have access to new ideas and resources. I'll be adding blogs of my favorite IIS resources and connecting you to great people to follow on Twitter. Learning IIS is a continuous process, due to ever-changing environments and web applications. I want to continue to help.

1.3.4 Ideas to try on your own

When I first learned IIS, back when dinosaurs roamed the internet, I found it a difficult task. I had much to learn, not only about the IIS product but about the internet and how things such as DNS worked. I found that as soon as I'd learn something about IIS, it'd spark some question or fascination in my mind that I'd quickly go off and explore. At first I thought this was a curse that slowed me down and distracted me from the important matters at hand, but it turned out that I gained a much deeper understanding of both IIS and how websites worked on the internet.

Now, many years later, when I sit down to learn a new product or some enhancement in IIS, I still go off on these tangents and go beyond the surface of administration into the deeper regions. Because you may be as much of a technology geek as I am, I include a section at the end of every chapter with some ideas to explore on your own. With these ideas for exploration, I include additional information about how things work at a deeper level. If you're someone who wants to stay focused on the administration of IIS and you don't want the distraction, then feel free to check out these ideas at a later time.

1.4 Setting up your lab environment

Learning a new technology is always a challenge—particularly a technology that reaches to the internet—without a place to practice. I want you to do a lot of practicing with IIS as you work through the book. That means you need an environment you can safely practice on that won't cause any disruption. Your company's production environment isn't that safe place. Please *don't* experiment on your company and friends. I have a better, safer idea.

I suggest that you create a virtual environment to work on for the month. Using your laptop, desktop, or a spare computer at work, pick your favorite virtualization software (Hyper-V, VMware, Parallels) and build the environment I describe in the next section. Keep in mind that you want to be able to access this environment during your lunch; you'll be doing a lot of practice, so create the environment wherever you're going to eat.

If you can't create a virtual environment on your laptop, another option is to use one of the available cloud technologies, such as Vaasnet (www.vaasnet.com), Cloud-Share (www.cloudshare.com), or Microsoft Windows Azure (www.windowsazure.com). These aren't free, but they're a good alternative because you don't have to set up anything. You log in and tell them what you want. If you don't want to deal with building virtual machines, you can try this option.

The next section provides details and instructions for creating both the basic and extended setup environments needed for the labs in this book.

1.4.1   The basic environment

To get the most from this book, I recommend two different lab environments, beginning with this basic lab environment. You'll need the basic lab environment for chapters 2 through 12. The basic environment is a single virtualized server (see figure 1.2) running DNS and Active Directory.

You may be tempted to use a client operating system such as Windows 7 or Windows 8 because they both run IIS. I don't recommend this because you'll miss part of the configuration process without DNS and Active Directory. Here's all you need to get started:

- *A single virtualized server*—You can use either Windows 2008 R2 or Microsoft Server 2012. If you don't have a copy of the software available, you can always download the trial from Microsoft. Currently, Windows Server 2008 R2 is located at http://mng.bz/2zqT. The best part about the trial is that it lasts for 180 days—5 more months than you need for this book.
- *A domain controller*—You need a domain controller so you have access to Active Directory and can look at security permissions later in the book.

If you don't have the server software, you can use the trial software from Microsoft at: http://technet.microsoft.com/en-us/evalcenter/dd459137.aspx

Virtual Window Server 2008 R2 or Server 2012 with Active Directory

Figure 1.2   The virtual server setup you need for the labs

BUILDING THE DOMAIN CONTROLLER

I realize that building a domain controller isn't something you probably do every day, so this section outlines the basics of installing Active Directory. The process is similar whether you use Windows Server 2008 R2 or Server 2012.

Need more help?

If you find that the instructions provided here aren't detailed enough, please go to MoreLunches.com, where you'll find a more detailed lab setup guide.

1 In your virtual software, create a new computer and install Windows Server. You don't need much memory for this—512 MB to 1024 MB is sufficient. You can name the computer whatever you like and assign a password of your choosing to the Administrator account.

2 Install the ADDS role and a domain controller. You do that in Server Manager for Windows Server 2008 R2 and Microsoft Server 2012.

3 Install Active Directory. When asked for a Fully Qualified Domain Name for your forest root domain, choose something simple. For this book I chose Company.loc.

4 Supply the Windows NetBIOS name for the domain. I'm using Company in my environment.

5 When prompted to choose the forest and domain functional level, choose the highest level, which will be Windows Server 2008 R2 or Microsoft Server 2012.

6 When prompted for Additional Domain Controller Options, select the option to install DNS. Not only does Active Directory need DNS, but you'll be using it for your websites.

NOTE If you set up your virtual computer with a dynamically assigned IP address, you'll receive a warning message saying that this isn't good practice. You can quit the installation and set the IP address, but this is only a test environment, so it's okay to select "Yes, the computer will use a dynamically assigned IP address." If you receive a warning about a DNS delegation creation problem, click "Yes" to continue.

7 When prompted for the file locations of the Active Directory files, accept the default locations.

8 When prompted for a Restore Mode password, use the same password that you set for the Administrator account. It's okay because this is a test environment.

9 When the installation of Active Directory is complete, reboot.

10 Using Active Directory Users and Computers, create three or four users. Nothing special. It can be John Doe1, John Doe2, and so on. You'll need them in the security sections.

Virtual Windows Server 2008 R2
or Server 2012 with Active Directory.

The extended setup adds two additional servers,
each with a minimum of 512MB RAM, to the
initial setup. If you're extending right now, name
those additional servers Web1 and Web2.

Figure 1.3   The extended virtual environment for labs

At this point you're ready to get started with the next lunch in your month of lunches.

Feel free to enhance and add to your environment at any time. But keep in mind that I'll use this basic environment in my examples so that we stick together. One enhancement you may want to make now is to extend this environment to a couple more web servers. Take a look at the next section on how to extend the basic environment.

1.4.2   *Extending the basic environment*

Many of the concepts discussed in chapter 13 and later involve multiple web servers—topics such as load balancing and high availability. To be able to practice those concepts, you'll need to build an extended virtual environment. Although you don't need this environment to get started, you can save time by setting it up now and using it for the labs.

You'll need two additional virtual servers, as shown in figure 1.3; the hardware requirements are minor because each VM only needs 512 MB of RAM and will perform limited processing. You should install the VMs on the same virtual network as the domain controller. You'll turn them into web servers later, so I suggest naming them something like Web1 and Web2.

If you have some IIS experience already, I recommend starting with the extended environment now. Although you don't need the extra servers for the first part of the book, it's a more accurate representation of the real world and will be better for your overall experience. In a test environment like this one, I do my testing and management from the domain controller as if it were a client computer. You could even go so far as to add a Windows 7/8 client computer to your virtual environment and use that for management, but I find the concept works fine without the extra virtual computer.

1.5   *Taking immediate control over IIS*

As an inadvertent and busy IIS administrator, the last thing I wanted to do was write a book that had you spend countless hours on theories and background instead of immediately starting to use IIS. In fact, *taking immediate control* is a phrase that I've made my primary goal for this book.

The original designer of the Month of Lunches series, Don Jones, is passionate about getting readers to be "immediately effective" with technology in the workplace. I'm a firm believer in this practice. I'm paraphrasing Don from his *Learn Windows PowerShell 3 in a Month of Lunches* book when I say I'll do my best to focus each chapter on something you need to use in your production environment right away. This means that sometimes I may gloss over details when we're starting a new chapter, but I promise to circle back and hit those areas in depth in later sections. Like Don in his book, I had to choose whether to write several chapters of architecture and theory or dive right in and accomplish some administrative tasks with IIS. In almost every chapter I chose to dive in so you can take immediate control over IIS.

I explain all of those other nuances and theories at some point in the book or in articles on MoreLunches.com, where they can be more effective. I won't let you miss anything important. Using this approach means you can start creating solutions with IIS immediately.

Now, wasn't your first lunch good? I'll see you back here for your next lunch, where you'll find a juicy "IIS deployment" on the menu.

Deploying the web server

I remember my first IIS server deployment. Back in those days it was a lot more difficult than it is now. Walking miles to the data center from my desk, in the snow, uphill both ways. Those were the days. You younger administrators have it easy.

Well, in fact, you don't. Sure, the initial default installation of IIS is simple, and you may have already done that, but you probably didn't get all the software components and configuration you needed. In fact for many years most administrators would click a button to install IIS and walk away, leaving the rest of the installation and configuration for an imaginary "someone else." This method doesn't result in a successful web server. In this chapter I help you get your install right. As an added bonus I also show you a few tricks I doubt you've heard of that can turn a deployment into an enjoyable task.

I also explore the placement of the web server in your infrastructure in this chapter and in the rest of the book. The physical location can affect website configuration, access to back-end applications such as databases, and firewall settings that in turn affect your security. Your infrastructure will play a large role in the success of your production web environment, so you need to think about where to locate the web server and how it will be protected. In this book's labs you'll install and begin to manage the WebBikez web server in Smalltown, U.S.A.

In this chapter you'll learn about how the physical location will impact your web server and then move on to installing your first web server. You'll learn how to install IIS to both a GUI-based server and Server Core. When the installation is complete, I show you how to test and verify that your installation was successful.

Let's start at the beginning by locating IIS in your infrastructure.

2.1   Locating and protecting the physical web server

Location, location, location. The first rule of buying a home or starting a new business applies to your web servers as well. You should have your virtual environment ready to go for the labs in this book, but at some point you're going to need to put a real web server into production.

The location of the web server in your infrastructure will impact how people from inside and outside your network access your websites. This will affect configuration settings on firewalls, the Network Address Translation (NAT) device, and DNS. The network team will make many of these decisions for you, but you'll need to investigate your infrastructure so you can determine whether it meets the best security and performance strategy. As we dive deeper into performance and security, you may discover that you need to request changes to the infrastructure. Perhaps *you're* the network team, and if that's the case, as we move forward, I'll take you through all of the concerns, configurations, and troubleshooting problems that might occur. I start gradually and *add infrastructure information* as we go. In this section I work through some basic infrastructure concepts:

- Where to locate your server and why it matters
- How to protect your server with a single firewall
- How to create and work in the middle tier with multiple firewalls

As you install and work with IIS during the next few chapters, I recommend you think about your infrastructure and what configuration impact may occur.

2.1.1   Server location matters

Imagine connecting a web server directly to the internet with no protection of any kind. Wow! It's a fun experiment that I don't recommend. Several years ago I did that as a demonstration and it took less than an hour for it to be script-hacked. You protect your internal network with a cascade of devices, most commonly known as firewalls.

Properly locating your web servers requires an understanding of your network environment. I find it helps to have a picture of the network structure and devices. This picture should contain the following:

- The location and type of network devices
- The location of your clients and servers
- Most importantly, the communication path from the servers to the outside internet

You can start by hand-drawing your network on a piece of paper, as shown in figure 2.1. I often do this for a quick visual guide.

For larger and more complicated networks I prefer to use a good visual-diagraming tool such as Microsoft Visio. Figure 2.2 shows you what a complex network diagram looks like. Don't worry about all the pieces right now—this complex network resembles what you'll build up to as you work through the book.

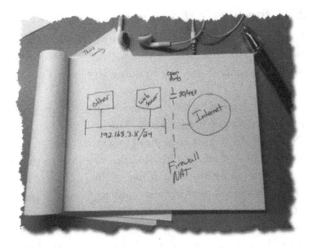

**Figure 2.1   Hand-drawn
representation of a small network**

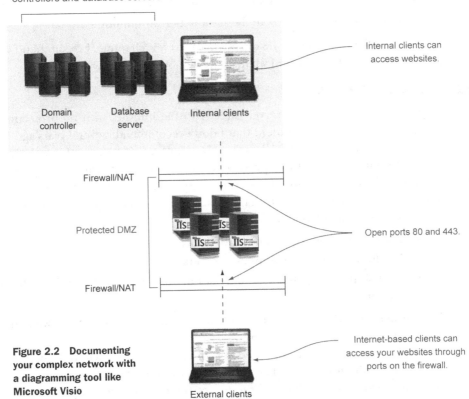

Back office servers like
Active Directory domain
controllers and database servers

Domain
controller

Database
server

Internal clients

Internal clients can
access websites.

Firewall/NAT

Protected DMZ

Open ports 80 and 443.

Firewall/NAT

**Figure 2.2   Documenting
your complex network with
a diagramming tool like
Microsoft Visio**

External clients

Internet-based clients can
access your websites through
ports on the firewall.

Once you've completed your network diagram, you'll be able to decide the best location for the web servers and make corrections to your network to best protect them. For the first part of this book, your lab environment will be fairly simple to diagram, but I want you to start thinking about your production environment. You can diagram your network later on; I remind you to do so in the "Ideas to try on your own" section. For now I give you a couple examples of the kinds of diagrams and decisions that you'll need to consider, starting with a basic network environment with a single firewall.

2.1.2 Protecting the web server with a single firewall

Perhaps you want to install a web server with some websites at home or in a small office. Placing even a simple firewall between IIS and the internet will help reduce your attack surface. Starting with a simple network diagram like figure 2.3 will help you make decisions about the best location of the web server and security considerations.

In a network with one firewall, the web server is located behind the firewall for best protection. The decision becomes how to best configure the firewall based on client traffic to the website.

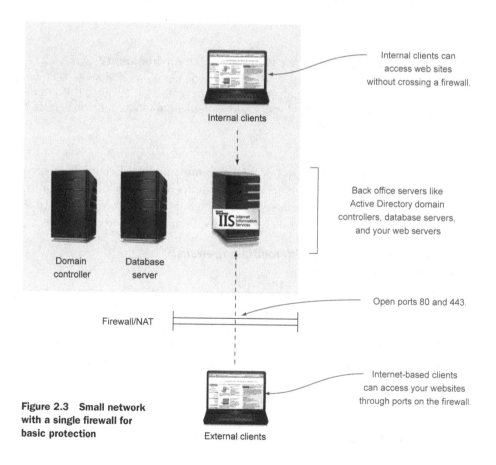

Figure 2.3 Small network with a single firewall for basic protection

- If the web applications you run on the web server are for internal clients only (common with a product such as SharePoint), then you can block almost all inbound traffic to the web server at the firewall.
- If you want folks from the outside to have access to your web applications, you'll need to carefully open up holes in that firewall to permit access.

NOTE Each manufacturer of firewalls has its own method of configuring port access. You'll need to review documentation for the one you choose for configuration specifics.

In most situations you want clients to be able to access your websites from the internet. The goal then is to open as few ports in the firewall as necessary to accomplish that goal. Common ports for websites are port 80 for HTTP traffic and port 443 for HTTPS. These may not be the only ports needed for your web applications, but I'll cover that as we progress through the book.

Whether you're building a new network environment as a test lab or for a small office, having the firewall protection in place before you deploy IIS is important. The risk of being attacked is too great.

What about the firewall for your virtual lab environment?

Keep in mind that in the virtual lab machine you set up for this book, Microsoft Windows Server has already enabled a firewall for protection by default. Don't turn this off. In the next few chapters, you'll work with this firewall to open up access to your websites when needed.

If a simple single firewall is good, then two must be great, right? Web servers often need access to back-end servers such as Active Directory domain controllers for authentication and database servers for storage. Many network teams add additional protection for these back-end servers, so let's discuss that protection next.

2.1.3 *Protecting the back-end with multiple firewalls: Working in the middle tier*

Back-end servers such as domain controllers and database servers are precious and contain confidential information. Many network teams add an additional firewall between the web servers and those back-end servers. This creates a middle tier in which to place servers such as publicly accessible web servers. This middle tier enhances security for the back-end servers and is one of the most common infrastructure designs.

It's always a physical firewall. Most firewalls today come with three network segments:

1 *Internal network*—For the prize back-end servers

2 *Dirty demilitarized zone (DMZ)*—The dangerous unprotected segment that connects directly to the internet

3 *Clean DMZ*—A middle tier between the internal network and the dirty DMZ

These segments are protected by firewalls that block unwanted traffic. IIS is usually placed in the middle tier if outside access is desired. The firewall closest to the internet needs to have several ports open to accommodate public access to your various websites. The firewall closest to the back-end servers will be much more restrictive, preventing anyone from hacking past the web server into your internal network environment. Figure 2.4 displays a typical network design for this approach.

With this setup you have firewall configuration considerations in both directions. You may be wondering which ports need to be open to support outside access to your websites. (Hint: It could be more than ports 80 and 443.) Or which ports need to be open so IIS has access to the domain controller and the database? I answer these questions and more in the coming chapters. For now I want you to get an idea of the

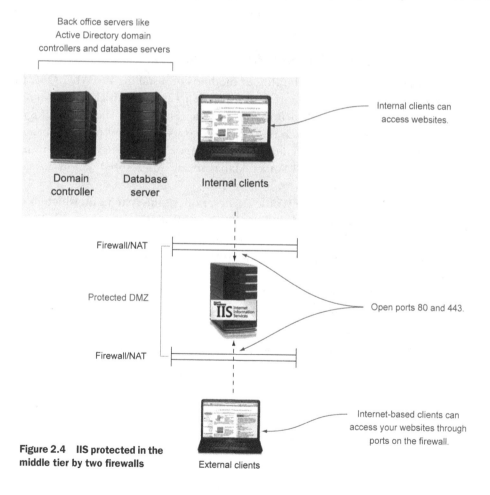

Figure 2.4 IIS protected in the middle tier by two firewalls

current infrastructure you have in place. Remember, you don't want to deploy IIS into an unsecured location. With your virtual lab machine, the Windows firewall is providing some protection for your deployment. In the future you'll need to address the full infrastructure.

Should I set up a firewall now?

Keep in mind that the virtual machines you're using for the labs in this book already have a Windows firewall protecting them, so you're good to go for the labs. When you begin to deploy IIS in your own network environment, you should verify your firewall protection. If you're the person that configures this, you probably already know the answer, but if you're part of a network team that performs this operation, check with them.

Because your lab environment has protection enabled, and you've started to think about a secured production environment, let's look at how you can get IIS deployed so you can start to see how all this works.

2.2 *Installing IIS on Microsoft Windows Server*

You can choose from several different methods of installing IIS. Why? Over the years, Microsoft has tried to find more efficient ways to accomplish IT tasks. A quick search on the internet is bound to turn up command-line tools such as Pkgmgr.exe and ServerManagerCMD.exe. Each one of these has its own set of parameters and syntax. Instead of reliving old commands such as these, we're going to install IIS using the two best methods: the graphical Server Manager and Microsoft's standardized management tool, PowerShell.

You also have a choice of Windows Server operating systems on which to install IIS. Most administrators start by installing IIS on a typical Windows Server 2008 R2 or Windows Server 2012. The other option is to install IIS on Windows Server Core. My favorite, and the one I think is the most powerful way, is Core, but I'm saving that for last because you may not have started using Core in your company yet. In this section, I walk you through two installations:

- Installing IIS using the graphical Server Manager, which is great for single-server installations and configurations
- Installing IIS using PowerShell for rapid deployment (my favorite way)

We'll start with the single-server installation method.

How big does your server need to be?

I teach IIS to both budding administrators and highly experienced enterprise administrators. It's interesting that at the point of our first deployment, without fail, the first questions I get concern server hardware. For example, "How big does my server need to be?" Translation: how much RAM, processing, and disk space will I need to support my web applications?

At this stage, early in learning about IIS, this is like asking, "How many MPGs does this vehicle get?" without knowing whether the vehicle in question is a car, truck, motorcycle, or bicycle. You can't determine this until you understand more about what the vehicle is, what you need it to do in your environment, and what's under the hood.

Hold on to those questions about capacity planning. I promise I'll get to them as you progress through the book. For now, let's get IIS installed and start figuring out what's under the hood.

2.2.1 Installing IIS with Server Manager

When you first install a Microsoft server, you get a simple server that can perform basic file sharing. All the other software features must be added, including IIS. This is a good practice Microsoft uses, and it's called *secured by default*. It's a practice you'll apply to IIS as well. You don't want to install software you don't need: less to update, less to secure.

> **IMPORTANT** Although I'm walking you through the how-to-install steps here, don't try the installation until you reach the lab. As we move through the chapter, I walk you through two installation methods that you can use for Windows Server 2008 R2 or Windows Server 2012. When you get to the lab at the end of the chapter, you'll be able to choose which method works best for you.

Microsoft loosely categorizes additional software into roles and features. *Roles* are services that affect the entire network, such as Active Directory. *Features* only impact the server, such as clustering. IIS has network impact, so it's considered a role.

LOCATING THE IIS ROLE BY NAME ON SERVER 2008 R2

IIS is a role that can be added using Server Manager. In figure 2.5 I've opened Server Manager and selected the Add Roles link in preparation for installing the IIS role.

If you've run Server Manager before, and I assume you have, you know that from here you only need to select the role you want to install, click the Next button, and install the software. Installing IIS is no different, except for one challenge: what's the role called?

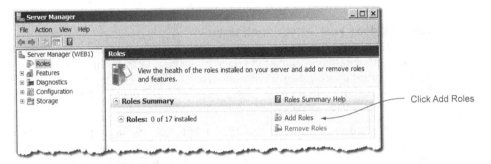

Figure 2.5 Using Server Manager to install a new role

If you installed IIS in Windows NT, 2000, or 2003, the name of the software went through a series of changes. In Microsoft Server 2000 it was named Internet Information Server (IIS), and in Microsoft Server 2003 it was called Application Server. Take a look at figure 2.6 and notice both—the dilemma and the solution.

Bingo. We have both Application Server and Web Server (IIS). So which one is it? You probably guessed correctly that the role you need to install is Web Server (IIS).

INSTALLING IIS ON MICROSOFT WINDOWS SERVER 2012

Fortunately most of the administrative tasks between IIS on Windows Server 2008 R2 and Windows Server 2012 are similar if not identical. The installation is no exception. You'll notice some visual screen differences between the two versions of Server Manager, but adding the IIS role is virtually the same. In figure 2.7 notice that the Add Roles and Features selection is located in a slightly different place. After selecting Add Roles you'll be able to select IIS and its additional services as we did earlier.

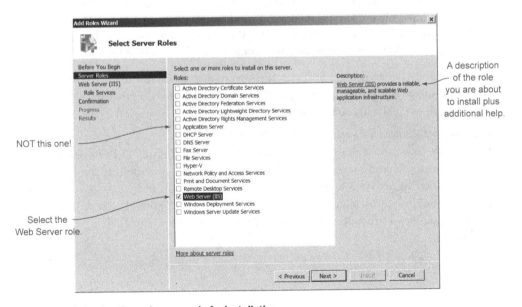

Figure 2.6 Selecting the web server role for installation

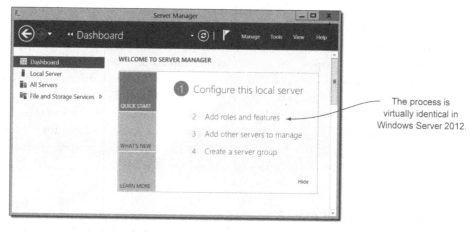

Figure 2.7   Using Server Manager in Windows Server 2012

THE DEFAULT SOFTWARE COMPONENTS

After selecting the role and clicking next, you're confronted with a long list of additional software components that you can add to IIS. Those selected by default are the minimum components you need to run a static web page (figure 2.8).

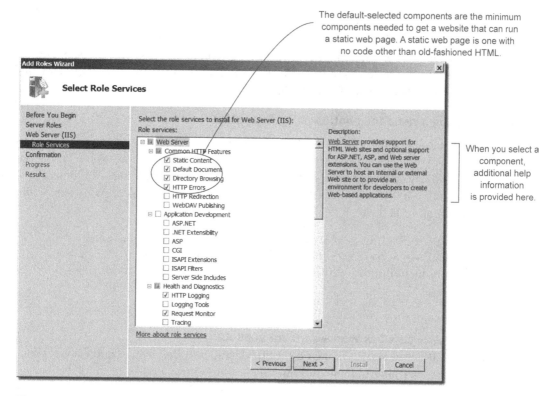

Figure 2.8   Viewing the default components

This is where the phrase "Don't install it if you don't need it" comes in handy. You only want to install the additional services you need for your web applications. By not adding components you don't need, you reduce the attack surface for hackers. Think of a firewall— you don't open ports that you don't need because it's risky.

How do you know what components you'll need for your environment? You should base most of your additions on the needs of your web applications. An example would be that you're using a web application that uses ASP.NET, in which case you'll need to install ASP.NET. In most cases the application vendor's documentation describes the necessary services you need to add. You'll be installing (and removing) various components throughout your month-of-lunches journey.

Removing the IIS role

You can remove roles as easily as you add them. You may need to remove a web server for a variety of reasons, such as moving a web application to another server or if a failed install occurs. To remove a role, open Server Manager and select Remove Roles.

Later in the book we'll be working with the file system and the storage of your websites. Note that when you remove the IIS role, the file system stays intact. This means when you remove the IIS role, it won't delete any of your files and web pages.

The graphical installation of IIS is fairly quick and straightforward. Many administrators in smaller environments use it exclusively. I want to show you a faster and, as you'll see later, better method that will work on a single server or hundreds. Time for a rapid IIS installation with PowerShell.

2.2.2 *Performing a rapid installation using PowerShell*

I hope you spent some time getting familiar with PowerShell as I suggested in the first chapter. Now you can put what you learned to work. The techniques you learn in this chapter will pay off as you move forward through the book. We'll start with PowerShell v2 that ships with Windows Server 2008 R2 and then we'll look at Windows Server 2012 and PowerShell v3.

> **NOTE** PowerShell v3 is now available as an update to Windows Server 2008 and Windows Server 2008 R2. Although you should update to the new version, I'm including the v2 instructions for those who haven't performed the update.

First I'd like to show you some slight differences *before you do the installation in the lab.*

USING POWERSHELL V2 ON WINDOWS SERVER 2008 R2

The capabilities of Server Manager, specifically the part that installs and removes roles and features, are also available in PowerShell. Microsoft added three cmdlets:

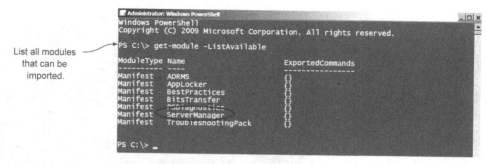

List all modules that can be imported.

Figure 2.9   Finding the list of modules available for import

- `Get-WindowsFeature`—Displays the roles and features available to install or remove and displays the name of the software for the next two cmdlets
- `Add-WindowsFeature`—Installs one or more roles and features; you must use the name of the software as it's displayed by `Get-WindowsFeature`
- `Remove-WindowsFeature`—Removes one or more roles or features

These three cmdlets aren't part of the core PowerShell commands that are loaded when you open the shell. Instead they're part of a separate module. *Modules* hold a collection of cmdlets that can be loaded and unloaded as needed. The module you want, called the ServerManager module, is shown in Figure 2.9. Use the following command to see a list of available modules on your system:

```
PS> Get-Module –ListAvailable
```

A reminder about PowerShell modules

Often PowerShell needs additional cmdlets to manage products and perform tasks. These cmdlets are stored in modules that can be imported when needed. To install additional Windows and IIS components, you need the ServerManager module.

To get access to the cmdlets in a module, you must first import the module with the `Import-Module` cmdlet. You can get a list of cmdlets that are in a loaded module using the `Get-Command` cmdlet (see figure 2.10):

```
PS> Import-Module ServerManager
PS> Get-Command –Module ServerManager
```

At this point, you can also use `Get-Help` to learn about the cmdlet parameters and see examples of how to use them. But because that's what I'm here for, I'll show you how to add IIS with the default installation using the `Add-WindowsFeature` cmdlet (see figure 2.11):

```
PS> Add-WindowsFeature Web-Server
```

Get-Command -Module
ServerManager will list all
the cmdlets in the module.

```
Administrator: Windows PowerShell                                          _ |□| x|
PS C:\> Import-Module ServerManager
PS C:\> Get-Command -Module ServerManager

CommandType        Name                      Definition
-----------        ----                      ----------
Cmdlet             Add-WindowsFeature        Add-WindowsFeature [-Name] <...
Cmdlet             Get-WindowsFeature        Get-WindowsFeature [[-Name] ...
Cmdlet             Remove-WindowsFeature     Remove-WindowsFeature [-Name...


PS C:\> _
```

Figure 2.10   Using Get-Command to list the cmdlets in the module

Add-WIndowsFeature
Web-Server will
begin the installation.

```
Administrator: Windows PowerShell                                          _ |□| x|
PS C:\> Import-Module ServerManager
PS C:\> Add-WindowsFeature web-server

Start Installation... |

     [oooooo                                                          ]
```

Figure 2.11   Using Add-WindowsFeature to install the web server

Above and beyond

In PowerShell v2 the cmdlet that adds roles and features to a server is named
Add-WindowsFeature. In PowerShell v3 this has been changed to Install-
WindowsFeature. If you're using PowerShell v3, you can still use the Add-Windows-
Feature name because it's now an alias to the Install-WindowsFeature cmdlet.
I wanted to give you examples that worked for both versions of PowerShell, so I'm
using the Add-WindowsFeature cmdlet instead of the v3 only cmdlet Install-
WindowsFeature.

It's truly that simple and fast. Later in the book you'll see examples of how to install to
multiple servers at once using this same cmdlet. If you haven't started working with
PowerShell, this is a good time to start.

Three tips and a "gotcha"

Tip   You can add additional services, roles, and features by separating the names
with a comma:

```
PS> Add-WindowsFeature Web-Server, Web-ASP
```

Tip To use `Add-WindowsFeature` you need to look up the name of the component you want to install. The names of all roles and features are listed in the Name column when you run `Get-WindowsFeature`.

Tip In PowerShell v2 you need to launch modules every time you launch a new shell. A feature in PowerShell, called a Profile, can automatically load the modules for you. But because you won't need the ServerManager module that much, it's best not to put it in a Profile and waste environment memory.

Gotcha In Windows Server 2012 the GUI management console isn't installed by default when you use PowerShell. Add the management console component using the `Install-WindowsFeature Web-Mgmt-Console`.

USING WINDOWS SERVER 2012 AND POWERSHELL V3

One of the coolest and most convenient features of PowerShell v3 is the ability to dynamically load modules when they're needed. In short, you don't have to import the module to use its cmdlets.

This is a feature of PowerShell v3, so if you've installed v3 on Windows Server 2008 R2, you can perform an IIS install even faster. In figure 2.12 I'm using Windows Server 2012 and PowerShell v3. Notice that you don't need to import the ServerManager module:

```
PS> Add-WindowsFeature Web-Server
```

The preceding alias cmdlet works, or you can use the name of the new cmdlet, as follows:

```
PS> Install-WindowsFeature Web-Server
```

Huzzah! It takes the graphical Server Manager utility longer to initially load than it takes to fire off that PowerShell command.

WARNING If you search Help for the `Install-WindowsFeature` cmdlet, you'll notice a switch parameter called `-IncludeAllSubFeature`. You may even see someone on the internet using it. To use it yourself, do the following:

```
PS> Add-WindowsFeature Web-Server -IncludeAllSubFeature
```

Don't use the `-IncludeAllSubFeature` when you're working with IIS. Doing so will install all of IIS, including every available service. Remember what I said earlier: you only want to install what you need, for security reasons.

Notice in Server 2012 you do not need to import the module.

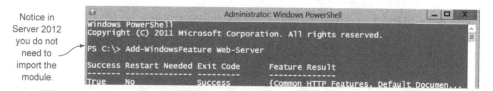

Figure 2.12   Installing a web server role on Windows Server 2012

So far I've walked you through an IIS installation using the GUI-based Server Manager and the ServerManager PowerShell module. I'll bet you're ready to get to the lab and get IIS installed, but I want to show you one more operating system option—one that you'll need to consider in the near future if you want the best performance from IIS.

2.3   Installing IIS on Server Core

Microsoft Server Core is my favorite installation option for Windows Server when working with IIS. Its performance, ease of updates and management, and performance are amazing. Yes, I said performance twice. You may not have had a chance to experience Server Core, but you should if you're the IIS administrator.

> **NOTE** I recommend that you use only Windows Server 2008 R2 Server Core or Server Core on Windows Server 2012. The prior version, Windows Server 2008, didn't support ASP.NET, and it was hard for most administrators to configure. Starting with 2008 R2, adoption of PowerShell has made Server Core much easier to use.

Server Core has been performance-optimized by removing the entire graphical desktop. As you can see in figure 2.13, it has no start bar, no icons, and no graphical components. The desktop is a blue background with a command prompt. You perform the initial configuration of the Server Core at the command prompt using PowerShell or a utility named SConfig.exe. Once it's installed, you can manage IIS remotely using the graphical tools or PowerShell.

In almost every case placing IIS on this lightweight version of Windows Server is the right choice. The stumbling block for most administrators is the command line. Without the GUI, they feel lost. If you've been paying attention to the PowerShell cmdlets I've been demonstrating, you'll excel at using Server Core.

In this section you'll prepare a Server Core for an IIS installation and install IIS using PowerShell. Server Core requires a little more initial configuration than the graphical server before installing IIS. The configuration utility SConfig.exe will help, so we'll start there.

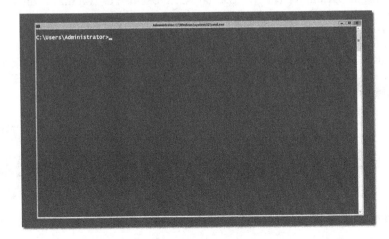

Figure 2.13   Using IIS on Server Core

Why no desktop on Server Core?

Having a graphical desktop slows down the server, preventing it from accomplishing the task of "serving" efficiently. The removal of the graphical desktop also means fewer components to update and service pack.

Don't let the lack of a graphical desktop keep you from using Server Core. You can perform management remotely using graphical tools installed on your local computer or through PowerShell.

In chapter 11 I show you how to configure IIS on Server Core for remote management with both the graphical tools and PowerShell. You'll find no differences in the management tasks you need to perform.

2.3.1 *Preparing Server Core for IIS*

Windows Server 2008 R2 made configuring Server Core much simpler with the introduction of the SConfig.cmd (SConfig) utility. This utility lets you change the computer name, set an IP address, and join a domain. It also permits you to enable PowerShell and remote management.

Before you can install IIS on Server Core, you need to first enable PowerShell. As figure 2.14 illustrates, you do that by selecting option 4 and then enabling options 1, 2, and 3. This turns on PowerShell and gets you the ServerManager module you'll need for the install.

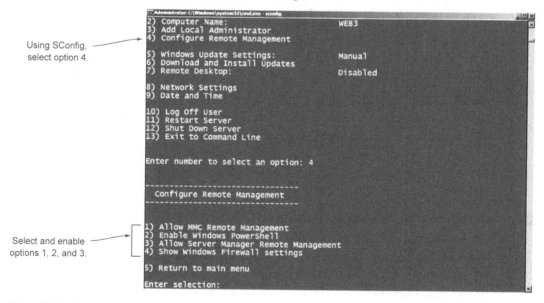

Figure 2.14 Enabling PowerShell on Server Core

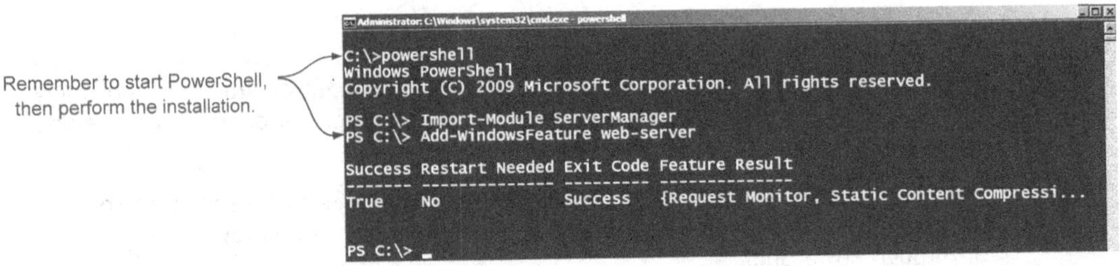

Remember to start PowerShell, then perform the installation.

```
C:\>powershell
Windows PowerShell
Copyright (C) 2009 Microsoft Corporation. All rights reserved.

PS C:\> Import-Module ServerManager
PS C:\> Add-WindowsFeature web-server

Success Restart Needed Exit Code Feature Result
------- -------------- --------- --------------
True    No             Success   {Request Monitor, Static Content Compressi...

PS C:\> _
```

Figure 2.15   Installing IIS on Server Core

Once you've enabled PowerShell you'll be able to install IIS easily. How are you going to perform the install without a graphical tool? I'll bet you already know the answer: PowerShell. Let's dive in.

2.3.2   *Adding IIS to Server Core*

This is one of those times when you might search the internet on how to install IIS on Server Core and see a lot of old and bad stuff. Commands such as ocsetup.exe and oclist.exe are the wrong direction—they're unnecessarily complex and have been replaced by a better tool: PowerShell. The only stumbling block is that when Server Core boots initially, it runs the old CMD.exe.

The fix is simple. Type PowerShell at the command prompt to load PowerShell. After it loads, the process to install IIS is the same as I described in the preceding section: import the ServerManager module and add the web server (see figure 2.15).

That was easy. In fact, with PowerShell managing, Server Core is faster and more efficient than the GUI-based installation. As you move through the book, all the PowerShell commands will work on Server Core.

> **TIP**   If for some reason you can't find the ServerManager module on Server Core, open SConfig, select option 4, and then select option 3 (Allow Server Manager Remote Management) again. This will get the module installed.

As we move along in the book I talk more about Server Core and why it might be the best installation option for your server operating system and IIS. After completing any IIS installation, it's best practice to test the web server to make sure it's operating normally.

Our last stop before running the lab will show you a quick method of testing the web server.

2.4   *Verifying a successful installation*

After every installation of IIS, before I start configuring the containers that will hold websites and web applications, I check to make sure IIS is installed properly and working normally. It's rare for IIS to have problems during installation, but it's good practice to always check. In this section you'll learn how to test the web server using the default website and check for error events in the logs. To assist in the testing process, Microsoft created a default website container that contains a simple HTML web page.

2.4.1 Testing the default website

During installation of IIS, a default website container and web page is created. In your next lunch you'll dive into the details of this default website, but this is a perfect chance to use this website to make sure the web server is functioning as it should.

Default web page for IIS 7

After you install IIS, open your favorite web browser and type the URL of the web server. If you're physically sitting at the new web server, you can use any of the following URLs:

- http://localhost
- http://<ServerName>
- http://<IP Address>

If your test is successful, in your browser you'll see one of the welcome pages shown in figure 2.16.

I prefer testing from another computer because it tells me that the web server and all its networking components are working. I also recommend that you test in this way when you do the lab for this chapter.

Speaking of the lab, I want to cover one last thing before I turn you loose on it. It's always best practice to check for errors in the logs after an installation, so let's examine that. Then you can dig in to the lab and try it yourself.

Default web page for IIS 8

Figure 2.16 The default web pages displayed in a browser after a successful installation

2.4.2 Checking for problems

Most network administrators check the Event Viewer for errors after an installation. I don't like the Event Viewer. It takes too long to load, and I have to surf through hundreds of entries to locate a possible error message (see figure 2.17). You can filter and sort the views in Event Viewer in other ways, but I have a still better way. Again, it's that "inadvertent administrator" thing, and I don't want to waste time.

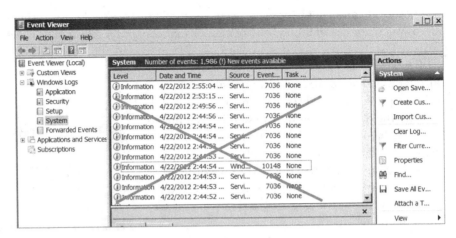

Event Viewer is too slow!
A better, faster way - Get-Eventlog -Logname System -Source IIS*-EntryType Error.

Figure 2.17   The graphical Event Viewer is a slow method of checking for errors.

A more useful way to quickly check for events regarding IIS is to use the PowerShell cmdlet Get-EventLog (figure 2.18). This cmdlet searches any of the logs you have. Let me show you how to focus it on IIS and errors in the system log:

```
PS> Get-EventLog –LogName System –Source IIS* –EntryType Error
```

I added the –EntryType parameter so that the cmdlet would only search for error messages. This is much more efficient than dealing with Event Viewer, and if you know a little about PowerShell, you can now export this information to a CSV, HTML report, or text file for future reference. In the following example I export my results to a CSV file:

```
PS> Get-EventLog –LogName System –Source IIS* –EntryType Error |
    Export-Csv c:\IISErrors.csv
```

You now have all the information you need to try out this lab. Are you excited? Go wash your hands after your delicious lunch and get started.

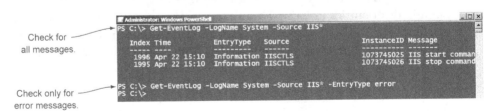

Check for all messages.

Check only for error messages.

Figure 2.18   Using PowerShell to check the system log for installation errors

2.5   Lab

Now it's your turn. I want you to install IIS to support the future WebBikez website on your lab computer. The bicycle shop has a network environment similar to your virtual computer: a web server using Windows Firewall plugged into the internet. This lab will only take a few minutes but will help ensure that you understand the concepts discussed in this chapter.

If you get stuck on a task and need help, go to MoreLunches.com for a complete walk-through of the lab. Open up your virtual environment and let's get started.

TASK 1

For your first task go into Control Panel and verify that your firewall is turned on. Remember, you don't want to deploy IIS to an unprotected environment.

TASK 2

Install IIS with only the default components and services. For this installation you get to choose the installation method—graphical or PowerShell. When the installation is complete, move on to task 3 to test the web server.

TASK 3

After IIS is installed, test IIS to see if it's working. On the web server open a browser and type http://localhost in the address bar. You should see the default test page.

I prefer to test a new installation on a different computer. If you created the multi-VM environment described in chapter 1, open your domain controller and attempt to access the new web server from a browser. The URL will be the IP address or hostname of the new web server.

TASK 4

To make sure you had no errors during the installation, check the Event Logs for IIS errors. Do this on the new web server using PowerShell and the `Get-Eventlog` cmdlet.

TASK 5

Here's a challenge before you put down the book and go back to work. If you installed IIS using the graphical Server Manager, consider trying the installation again using PowerShell. If you have the extended environment, you can install IIS on the remaining virtual machine. If you have only the one virtual machine, I want you to remove IIS and reinstall it using PowerShell. Yup, do the install again.

After you've successfully installed IIS, to double-check it test it again by opening a browser and typing http://localhost. You should also use PowerShell to check for any errors in the system log.

2.6   Ideas to try on your own

When you get a chance in your busy schedule, I have two ideas for you to try out. This won't be easy, but it's something you should consider trying before you finish the book.

First start diagramming your own network environment. A hand-drawn picture is fine, but if you already have a network schematic in something like Visio, that's even better. Diagramming will help you to decide how you may want to implement IIS in your own environment.

Try to install IIS on Server Core. If you haven't worked with Server Core, this may seem like a daunting task, but I'll help you. I've posted a full installation on More-Lunches.com, but let's look at the highlights to get you started:

- Install Windows Server 2008 R2 Server Core or Windows Server 2012 Server Core into a virtual environment with your existing lab computer. We'll use your existing domain controller.
- Using SConfig change the computer name to something like Web1.
- Using SConfig assign a static IP address.
- Using SConfig assign an IP address to your DNS server. This should be the IP address of your virtual domain controller.
- Using SConfig join your existing domain.
- Using SConfig enable PowerShell.
- Using PowerShell install IIS with its default components.
- Test your installation and check for errors.

Exploring and launching a website

It doesn't matter if it's a personal blog on your own IIS server at home or a new corporate commerce site for your company's newest product, there's a certain amount of joy in a successful website launch. The process has a lot of moving parts, usually involving a team of people including the developers who wrote the website to the web admins and network engineers who configure the communication and security to the internet.

One of my favorite launches was for a large customer that had warehouses all over the world. They had been taking customer orders over the phone for many years and wanted to move their order processing to the web. After the development team completed the new order process application, I completed the web server infrastructure, security, and all the configuration changes and testing that had to be done to launch the site on the internet (the same things you'll do in a month of lunches).

Seeing that first order get placed and processed through the new website was pretty cool. The customer had a new communication line with their customers for order processing, and I got to be a part of building the solution.

Now I'll take you through the process. Open up that lunch sack and start munching, and let's begin by creating a better test page for the default website, exploring the options on the site, and creating new folders and applications for the site. When you've completed that, I'll show how to open the website to the real world and which DNS settings to make.

3.1   *Locating website configuration settings*

I want you to remember something I mentioned back in chapter 1: in most cases a web server is very much like a file server serving web pages like files to a network client across the internet. The client uses a browser to display and run those files like a useful application.

Don't let the overly misused term *website* confuse you when working with IIS. In IIS a website has two parts: the website container for configuration settings such as security and reliability (configured in the IIS manager) and the actual web pages themselves on the filesystem, whether written by you or a development team.

As a web administrator you'll often create websites and web applications in the IIS Manager or PowerShell. Think of these as containers that hold the web pages and applications that a developer has written. You'll configure the website container properties and configuration and then fill those containers with the developed web pages.

When you installed IIS for the bicycle shop, it created a default website container and placed a simple web page on your hard drive in a specific folder structure. You'll start adding containers to hold the bike shop's website applications throughout this chapter.

First I show you how to find the default website and its configuration settings using IIS Manager and PowerShell. Currently the bike shop is using the default website to store pictures and building instructions, so you'll need to make some simple "testing" web pages until the development team has finished the "live" (real) web pages.

3.1.1   *Locating website configuration settings using the IIS manager*

The primary management tools for IIS are the graphical Internet Information Services (IIS) Manager and the WebAdministration module for PowerShell. I'll mention other tools from time to time, but these are the main ones.

The IIS manager graphical tool, installed during the deployment of IIS, is used to display and manage the configuration of your web server, websites, and web applications. This tool has a unique interface, different from most other graphical tools on the server, and is the primary graphical tool you'll use for most of your administrative tasks. There's always PowerShell as well, but we'll get to that later.

When the IIS manager is first opened, it displays a Start Page with common and useful information displayed in two panes, one for navigation and one with extra information, such as the web server that you connected with and the latest news about

---

Above and beyond

The IIS manager tool can be opened on a server under Administrative Tools in Server 2008 R2 or the Tools menu option in Server Manager for Windows Server 2012. Many admins prefer to run the IIS manager from their client using the Remote Administration Tools. You can download and install those tools for either Windows 7 or Windows 8 (Windows 7 at http://mng.bz/I21g and Windows 8 at http://mng.bz/YGH9.)

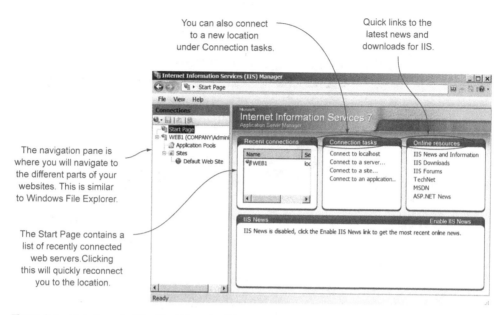

You can also connect to a new location under Connection tasks.

Quick links to the latest news and downloads for IIS.

The navigation pane is where you will navigate to the different parts of your websites. This is similar to Windows File Explorer.

The Start Page contains a list of recently connected web servers.Clicking this will quickly reconnect you to the location.

Figure 3.1 Main layout of the Start Page for IIS manager

IIS from Microsoft. Although the Start Page (see figure 3.1) isn't normally the place you'll perform most of your management, you should still become familiar with it.

In the left navigation pane, the Sites folder contains all your websites and applications. IIS can host multiple websites on a web server, and as the new admin for the bike shop, you'll be adding several websites in the next few chapters.

When you click an element other than the Start Page—such as your web server, application pools, or the Sites folder—the entire view changes to a management view with three panes of information, as illustrated in figure 3.2.

The center pane contains a list of the components installed with IIS. Remember back in chapter 2 when you installed the default components for IIS? As you add more components (throughout this book), this list changes, adding additional icons for each component. Each icon has a set of configuration settings that will affect your web server, website, and web applications. Some of these components are application-specific and configured by the developers of the application, and some you'll need to modify. Over the course of the next several chapters, you'll discover how to configure these components as they're needed.

The rightmost pane is where you find *actions* that can be performed on whatever you selected in the navigation or center pane. The cool trick about the actions pane is that it removes the need to right-click for additional options so prevalent in other utilities.

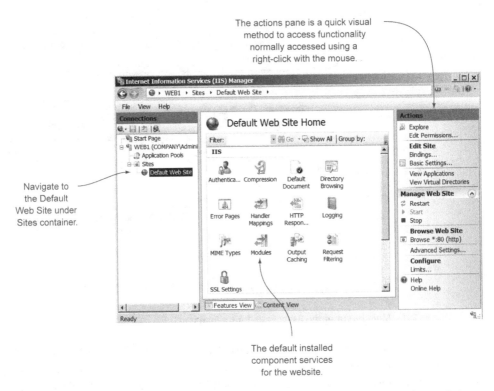

The actions pane is a quick visual method to access functionality normally accessed using a right-click with the mouse.

Navigate to the Default Web Site under Sites container.

The default installed component services for the website.

Figure 3.2   The graphical IIS management tool is segmented into three parts. The left pane is for navigating to your websites, the center pane is to access additional components and features, and the right pane is for actions.

The default website gives you a quick method of verifying (testing) the web server to make sure it works. In production you may even decide to host your real website in the default container. Most of Microsoft's products that use IIS do this, such as Exchange, SharePoint, RDS, and so on. In chapter 2 after the deployment, I had you "test" your web server by typing the URL http://<servername>. Your browser connected to the web server and opened this default website container and the web pages contained inside. If it hadn't opened you would have known that something had gone wrong during installation.

The graphical tool you've just been exploring displays the website configuration settings, not the actual web pages that make up the website. To see those pages, and to add pages to your default site (which you'll do later), you need to find out where they're kept in the filesystem. Before you look for that, let's make sure you can find the default website's configuration settings using PowerShell.

3.1.2   *Locating website configuration settings using PowerShell*

You have a choice when managing the bike shop (and your real websites) in the management tool you use, so I want to show you PowerShell whenever I can. When IIS is installed on a server, an additional module for PowerShell is added, called WebAdministration. The WebAdministration module contains cmdlets and PSProvider WebAdministration which exposes the IIS: drive. You can view and change configuration information using either the IIS cmdlets or the provider. In general most admins prefer to use cmdlets (like me!), but as you'll see throughout the book, there will be instances when an IIS cmdlet just doesn't achieve the goal, and that's when the provider can be useful.

To manage the bike shop in this book (and your own production sites in real life), load the cmdlets and WebAdministration provider by importing the module. Once it's imported, get a list of the available IIS cmdlets using Get-Command:

```
PS> Import-Module WebAdministration
PS> Get-Command -Module WebAdministration
```

> **NOTE** The WebAdministration module doesn't need to be imported manually if you've updated to PowerShell v3. PowerShell v3 dynamically loads the module when you attempt to use any of the IIS cmdlets. If you haven't upgraded your management client to PowerShell v3, you should stop right now and do it. This feature alone will make your life easier using PowerShell.

There are a couple of other ways to find the cmdlets for IIS that may prove faster at times. The cmdlets for IIS have the prefix *Web* in the noun portion of the cmdlet name. Using this prefix you can use Get-Command or Get-Help to search for the cmdlets. I use Get-Help so much that it's become natural for me to search for cmdlets this way. Take a look at the two examples:

```
PS> Get-Command -Noun web*
PS> Get-Help *web*
```

The following are two examples of using cmdlets to get basic information about the default website. The first uses an IIS cmdlet from the WebAdministration module; the second uses the IIS: drive:

```
PS> Get-WebSite -Name Default*
PS> Get-ChildItem -Path iis:\sites
```

To locate the files for the website, use Get-ChildItem or the alias Dir:

```
PS> Get-ChildItem -Path c:\inetpub\wwwroot
```

> **TRY IT NOW** On occasion I ask you to put down your sandwich and try something immediately. You may be tempted to keep eating and forgo this, but now is a great time to reinforce the idea. So here is what I want you to do in preparation for working with the bike shop: on the server where you installed IIS, locate the default website using both the IIS manager and the WebAdministration PowerShell module.

Now that you've had a chance to locate the default website in the IIS manager and PowerShell, it's time to build some better web pages for testing before we begin adding components for the bike shop.

3.2 Creating new web pages for testing and troubleshooting

As an IIS administrator, one of your primary goals is to verify and test websites that connect to the outside world. Imagine that your company is getting ready to launch a new product. It will be your goal to create the website container, open access to the outside world, and test for performance and security. In the lab you'll experience this with WebBikez—the company wants to launch a new site in the next two weeks to support the local shop.

Sometimes you have the actual production website that you can load for testing, and other times the web pages may still be in development, meaning you need to create your own. I always start with my own test web pages before I load an actual developed site so I have a chance to verify the configuration. That way if something goes wrong after adding the developed site, I can isolate and troubleshoot the problem better.

Before I can show you how to launch the default site to the internet, you need some better web pages to use for testing. The default web pages that IIS installed into the wwwroot folder don't provide enough information to be useful for troubleshooting. In this section you'll create two different web pages to use for testing every time you create a new website.

You may be wondering, "Do I need to become a developer to make great web pages for testing and troubleshooting?" No, but you do need a little code to make the web pages work. It's nothing you can't handle. Who knows? You might find that making web pages and applications is something you enjoy and decide to learn more about web development. (See manning.com for additional resources, such as the book *ASP.NET 4.0 in Practice* by Scott Hanselman, Manning Publications, 2011.)

You'll make a simple test page for easy and quick testing and then a more complicated one that produces useful information for troubleshooting website issues.

3.2.1 Locating the website pages in the filesystem

The web pages (files) for the default website are located on the filesystem. These files are what you saw displayed in the browser in the previous chapter when we tested the web server.

You can access the IIS folder structure using File Explorer. Another method to access the structure (and faster in my opinion) is to click the Explore option in the actions pane of the IIS manager. Anytime you select a website in the navigation pane, you can quickly get to the filesystem this way.

The default folder C:\inetpub is created during the installation of IIS. It contains folders that hold the web pages for the default website, as shown in figure 3.3. Additional folders in this structure contain custom error messages and connection logs that we'll examine later.

Several default web pages make up the default website—a few more of them for IIS 8—and they're located in the wwwroot folder, shown in figure 3.4. Notice the file extensions .htm and .png in that figure. By default Windows hides the extensions, and

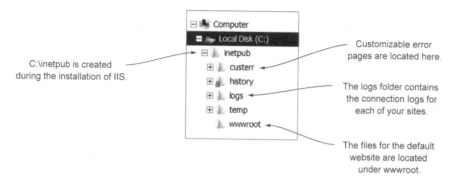

Figure 3.3   The default folder structure created during the IIS installation. Future websites can be located here, in other folders created by yourself, or on network shares.

you may not be able to see them. If that's the case, open Control Panel or File Explorer and turn this feature off so you can see the extensions.

I prefer to avoid deleting these files unless absolutely necessary so I can have them around for testing the website. These are simple HTML pages that under normal situations should always work. They'll assist in troubleshooting problems later as you add additional web pages that use components that need to be added to IIS, such as ASP.NET.

If you're testing new web page content, and it's failing to load, try checking these default pages. If they work, you know the website is functioning but may be missing a needed component.

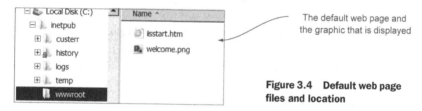

Figure 3.4   Default web page files and location

Above and beyond

You may be wondering: "Do all my websites have to go into the inetpub folder?" The answer is no—not all of your websites have to be located there. When you add additional websites and applications, you can choose where to locate them. You can create your own folder structure on the local server, such as C:\Sites, or use a network share. We look at these options in Chapter 5.

3.2.2   Making an easy web page for testing a website

The default web page that's displayed when you access the default website is far too generic for most of the troubleshooting you'll need to perform. WebBikez bike shop will grow to a complex, multi-website environment, and you'll need specifically labeled web pages to test the website communication and display useful information before the developed website is loaded. The simple web pages you'll make to test the bike shop will provide information about the name of the web server and the specific website you're connecting to. This not only proves the website and its applications are working, it prevents you from becoming confused if you have more than one application or website. (In this chapter you're going to add applications.)

To remove future confusion between your websites, you'll create your own web page (figure 3.5). This simple HTML test page will work on a default installation of IIS without any additional components. Now, you may be tempted to modify the existing default web page or even replace its graphic with one of your own, but don't. These default pages serve as a good safety net. No matter what additional pages you add, even if they don't work for some reason, these default ones should always work.

To create a simple web page that contains unique information is a simple process. Notepad or your favorite text editor will work. The goal is to add a simple sentence that describes the name of the website and the name of the web server that hosts the website. This sentence needs to be surrounded by an opening and closing HTML paragraph tag, like this:

```
<p> This is the default website located on server Web1 </p>
```

The next step is to save the file in the default website folder C:\inetpub\wwwroot, as shown in figure 3.5. The text file needs a filename and extension so the website can load it as a web page. In this case, because this is simple HTML, the extension will be .htm. In my example I named the file Default.htm. IIS understands how to load this file automatically without any additional configuration. If you name the file differently at this point, it won't load. In the next section I show you how to fix that.

Once the file is saved, you can test the web page in a browser by typing HTTP:// <webserver> into the address bar (see Figure 3.6).

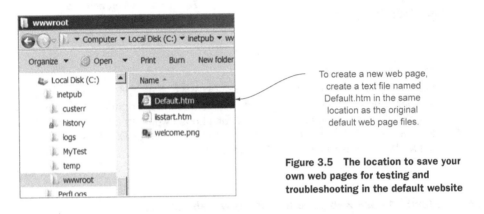

To create a new web page, create a text file named Default.htm in the same location as the original default web page files.

Figure 3.5   The location to save your own web pages for testing and troubleshooting in the default website

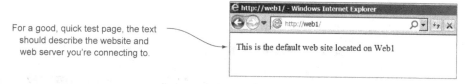

For a good, quick test page, the text should describe the website and web server you're connecting to.

This is the default web site located on Web1

Figure 3.6 A simple, quick test page for your websites and applications

TRY IT NOW In the wwwroot location, create a text file using Notepad. Name this file Default.htm. Edit the file and add the following HTML tag and text:

```
<p> This is the default website for WebBikez located on my Web1 server </p>
```

Save the file. If your web page doesn't load, one of the problems may be the name of the file. Check to make sure you have extensions displayed and that the file ends with .htm. Also, make sure you named the file Default.htm.

Congratulations! You just created a simple web page for testing. Make sure to test the page using your browser too.

3.2.3 *Creating a web page using server variables for better results*

The simple web page you created in the last section is one I use all the time when preparing to launch a website or web application. It's very useful and is much better than the Microsoft default web page because it identifies the website or web application and the server where the page is hosted. This prevents me from getting confused when I have multiple websites or applications. The other benefit of the simple web page is that it runs with a default installation of IIS. It only uses HTML, so I don't need to add any components.

The problem with the previous solution, though, is that you must edit and change the web page for every new website, web application, and server you need to test to uniquely identify the new site properly. There's a better way, but it requires an additional component installed into IIS. Besides the new component, you'll also need a little more code under your belt. Again, it's nothing you can't handle. The code for our new web page requires the additional component ASP or ASP.NET, so let's get that installed first.

INSTALLING THE ADDITONAL COMPONENTS ASP OR ASP.NET

You can install ASP.NET or ASP using the graphical Server Manager (see figure 3.7).

You can also install using PowerShell, which is easy and fast. Here is how to install ASP as an additional component:

```
PS> Add-WindowsFeature WEB-ASP
```

With the addition of ASP or ASP.NET, you can make a new test page that has more intelligence. The new test page won't require editing every time you copy it to another site or application and it will contain much more useful information.

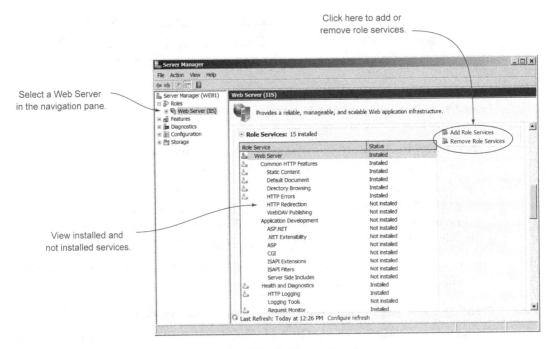

Figure 3.7   Installing additional components into IIS using Server Manager

TRY IT NOW   Before we go any further, go to your web server and add the component ASP. You'll need this to test the new test page you'll make in the next section. Feel free to use either Server Manager or PowerShell for the task.

THE NEW TEST WEB PAGE

The ASP and ASP.NET components provide the ability for a web page to display information about the website or web application that's hosting the page. The information about the web server, site, application, and more can be displayed in your web browser. This information is dynamically built, so you only need to create the web page once and copy it to each new website or application container.

The dynamic information this new web page displays (see figure 3.8) is gathered

Above and beyond

Server variables are pieces of information about the client, website, and web server—such as IIS version and website location—stored in memory on the web server. You can open these variables and look at the information or display it on a web page. A complete list of all server variables that can be used for a custom testing page is available at http://mng.bz/J05R.

At that site, you'll find other variables that may be useful to developers when they're working on their applications. You might consider expanding your test page to include some of those if you have an in-house development team. Make them buy you lunch for helping them!

The URL contains the name of the test page with the .aspx extension.

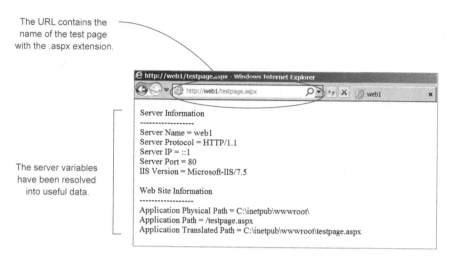

The server variables have been resolved into useful data.

Figure 3.8 New web page with dynamic information using server variables

from server variables. Server variables hold a tremendous amount of useful information, and as you progress through the book you'll examine and use most of it.

To gather the information from the server variables, you need a little more code. The code in ASP or ASP.NET that I'm using has no official name but is often called expression syntax or data binding. You don't need to remember this, but what kind of author would I be if I didn't at least tell you what it was? The code you're interested in looks similar to the example in Figure 3.9.

Notice the syntax between <%...%>. Everything else is just text I use to label the information. In this example, instead of my hand-writing the server's IP address into the web page, the server variable populates it for me. See how this is going to save time? I can easily copy this page to different websites and servers without modifying it again.

Using several server variables you can create a great dynamic web page that will remove confusion by correctly identifying each and every new website and application you create. The following listing shows the code for a new and improved web page.

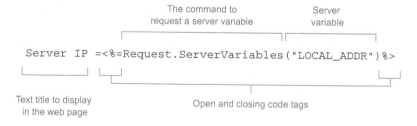

The command to request a server variable

Server variable

```
Server IP =<%=Request.ServerVariables("LOCAL_ADDR")%>
```

Text title to display in the web page

Open and closing code tags

Figure 3.9 Sample code requesting a server variable to retrieve the local IP address

Listing 3.1   Dynamic web page using server variables

```
<html>
Server Information<br>                                    <── Create line break
------------------ <br>
Server Name = <%= Request.ServerVariables("SERVER_NAME") %> <br>
Server Protocol = <%= Request.ServerVariables("SERVER_PROTOCOL") %> <br>
Server IP = <%= Request.ServerVariables("LOCAL_ADDR") %> <br>
Server Port = <%= Request.ServerVariables("SERVER_PORT") %> <br>
IIS Version = <%= Request.ServerVariables("SERVER_SOFTWARE") %> <br>
<br>
Website Information<br>
-----------------<br>
Application Physical Path = <%= Request.ServerVariables("APPL_PHYSICAL_PATH")
    %> <br> #C
Application Path = <%= Request.ServerVariables("PATH_INFO") %> <br>
Application Translated Path = <%= Request.ServerVariables("PATH_TRANSLATED")
    %> <br>
<br>
</html>
```

Variables with specific info ⊳

Variables with application info ⊳

I know it looks a little scary, but there really isn't much here. The server variables I'm using list basic information about the website and application, such as name, location, IP address, and IIS server version. When you create this text file, save it with a filename and special extension. This is very important or it won't work correctly:

- If you installed the component ASP, the extension is .ASP
- If you installed the component ASP.NET, the extension is .ASPX

I usually name the file TestPage.asp or TestPage.aspx, which won't automatically load when you make a request to the website or application. You'll need to include the name in the URL:

```
http://web1/Testpage.asp
```

TRY IT NOW   Take a moment and make your own version of this web page to test the bike shop. Put a copy of the new web page into the default website C:\inetpub\wwwroot and try the page to make sure it works. Remember to save the file as TestPage.asp—you'll need to include that as part of the URL.

If your page doesn't automatically load, it's probably because the page isn't part of the Default Document list in IIS. Each website and application can have its own list of documents that it will load when you request them. This is why the Default.htm document you created earlier automatically loaded—it was in the list. In the next section, I show you how to modify this list so that you can automatically load your Testpage.asp if desired. Most of the time I don't add it to the list because I only want it to load when I specifically request it through the URL. You may find it more convenient to have it automatically load, so I'll demonstrate that at the same time as showing you how to control the Default Documents.

I like to save this test page to an easily accessible folder such as C:\TestPage so I can copy it to new websites and applications when needed. For a later lunch I show you how to deploy your test pages to multiple servers all at once, but for now you can just copy it when needed using Windows Explorer.

Throughout this book I add variables to this test page to make it even more useful later. As an example, this page will evolve to the point where it will help you trouble-shoot everything from improperly configured websites to a misbehaving network load balance with multiple servers (yes, you'll do that in chapter 7!). Keep this file handy because you'll use it often.

3.2.4 *Default Documents*

IIS automatically loads documents (files) that have specific names and extensions. It "knows" that it can load them for you automatically. This improves the end-user experience. How ridiculous would it be to be forced to type a URL with a document name for every website or application you visit (http://web1/Default.htm)?

In the preceding section you created a great web page for troubleshooting called Testpage.asp. I want to show you how to have it automatically load so that you don't need to type it in the URL.

In the center pane of the IIS manager, when you select Default Document, a list of currently automatically loaded documents will appear, and you can add your own to that list (figure 3.10).

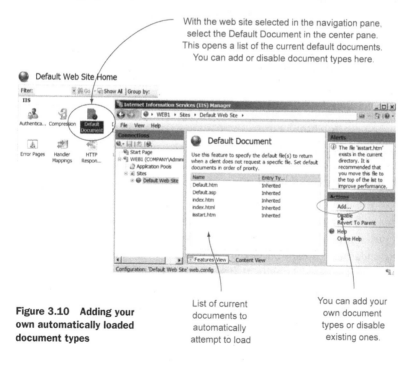

Figure 3.10 Adding your own automatically loaded document types

TRY IT NOW   Open the Default Document list for the default website and add your new TestPage.asp file to the list. Make sure you move it to the top of the list so it's the first page loaded. Try it by typing the URL into your browser's address bar, but this time without specifying the page name: http://<servername>.

Now you have a test page for your sites and applications. Let's put it to use and start creating additional folders and applications to customize the default website. Once these are working we'll launch the website to the outside world.

3.3   Adding new folders and applications in the default website

A website may start out small, meaning a few files (web pages) comprise the entire site. As the needs of our bike shop grow, so will the desire to increase the size of the website by adding new products and features for customers. This will dramatically increase the number of web pages and make it harder and more confusing to keep track of all those files.

Think of your hard disk for a minute and all the files it contains. What if you didn't have any folders and stored all the files in the root of your hard disk? Can you imagine the problems? Files with the same name overwriting each other, trying to find a single file in the enormous list—security management would be almost impossible. The same goes for your website.

The bike shop website will contain files that the end-user can download, it will have multiple web applications, and it will contain pictures of WebBikez's latest bikes. You'll need to organize these files and make them available to users. There are three primary methods to do that, and you'll try each one of them:

- Adding normal folders
- Adding virtual directories
- Adding new web applications

Let's get started with normal folders.

3.3.1   Adding normal folders and content

You need to create additional folders for organizing pictures and files for the bike shop website. The first type of folder, a *normal* folder, is in fact just a regular file folder (directory) that appears in IIS. Normal folders are the easiest to create, but they have no special IIS features or capabilities, so they're the least used. (A better solution is virtual directories, discussed later in this section). Normal folders do what any folders do—store files, but without any special features, such as redirection to network storage, they can be limiting in larger environments. You should be aware that these exist, but you won't use them much.

When you create a new folder off the root location of your website, it becomes part of the website and its URL. The default website is located in C:\inetpub\wwwroot.

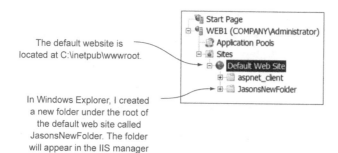

The default website is located at C:\inetpub\wwwroot.

In Windows Explorer, I created a new folder under the root of the default web site called JasonsNewFolder. The folder will appear in the IIS manager after a screen refresh.

Figure 3.11 Creating a normal folder with files for your website

When I create a new folder such as JasonsNewFolder off of wwwroot, it's displayed in the IIS manager (see figure 3.11).

Any files placed in the new folder will be available to any browser. You can put downloadable content here or even new web pages.

TRY IT NOW Create a new folder under the location of the default website C:\inetpub\wwwroot. Name the folder something like BikeShopDocs. Once you have the new folder, view it in the IIS manager. It's now become part of the website. (Hint: you may need to refresh the IIS manager to see the folder.) Next copy the test page you made in the preceding section to this folder. See if you can display the page in your browser. Remember, the URL should contain the new folder name and the name of the test page: http://<server>/BikeShopDocs/TestPage.aspx.

Although using normal folders seems like a nice way of organizing multiple web pages and files in your website, it's limited to only local storage on the web server. This is great for single-server websites, but when you need to load balance (provide fault tolerance) for a website, you need a better option that will permit you to store the web pages off the local server and on a network share.

3.3.2 Adding virtual directories for better content control

Virtual directories provide better configuration options than normal folders for the location of stored files or web pages. Virtual directories are the type you'll want to use for the bike shop files. For example, a virtual directory has an *alias* (a shortcut name) that will become part of the URL. This alias should be short and memorable. Most administrators like to name the physical folders that contain the files very descriptively, but that's generally not a good idea for the URL, especially if it has spaces. As an example, I can name a folder "This is where I store bike pics," which is very descriptive, and give it the alias BikeImages. When an end user attempts to access the location, they'll use the alias name in the URL:

```
http://<servername>/BikeImages
```

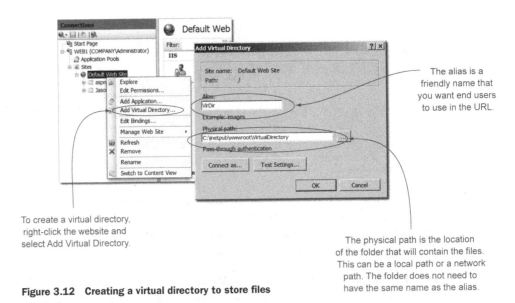

To create a virtual directory, right-click the website and select Add Virtual Directory.

The alias is a friendly name that you want end users to use in the URL.

The physical path is the location of the folder that will contain the files. This can be a local path or a network path. The folder does not need to have the same name as the alias.

Figure 3.12   Creating a virtual directory to store files

Creating a virtual directory is as simple as specifying the alias and the physical path you want to store the files in, as shown in figure 3.12.

There's another reason why virtual directories are better than normal folders. The location of the folder can be *virtual*. The folder doesn't need to be a physical location on the local hard drive—it can be a network share on another server. Later in the book when we start to look at multiple server deployments, this will become a very useful feature.

TRY IT NOW   This is a great time to create a virtual directory. Use the alias name BikePics and the physical path C:\inetpub\wwwroot\PicsOfWheel-Spokes. Copy your test page into the virtual directory and see if you can load the page using a browser: http://<servername>/BikePics/TestPage.aspx.

3.3.3   *Adding application folders to the website*

So far I've described two methods of creating an organizational structure to the bike shop website: normal and virtual directories. These are great for images and file downloads. But the developers of the bike shop website have informed you that they need to add web applications to the site for a shopping cart. A web application container is different than a normal or virtual folder.

Don't let the term *web application* confuse you. A web application is a collection of files that contain HTML, ASP, ASP.NET, or other code that a browser can execute. The test page you created earlier can be considered a web application. In IIS you need to treat applications differently than just image or download files by adding them to application pools.

What's an application pool? For now, think of an *application pool* as a separate memory location for your application, similar to the virtual machines you built for labs in

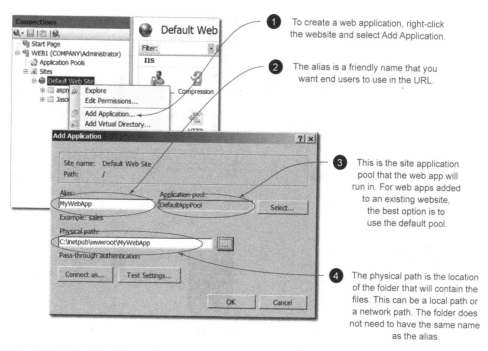

Figure 3.13 The steps in creating a new application in the default website

chapter 1. In chapter 4 I cover how to configure and control application pools for your web applications.

Placing a web application into its own self-contained pool of memory protects other web applications and the IIS server in case something goes wrong with the application. Remember the old computer days when applications would "hang"? Most often you'd need to reboot your computer. That's what an application pool protects you from—bad applications crashing your entire system. Figure 3.13 demonstrates how to create a new web application in the default website.

TRY IT NOW Try to create a new application for yourself as part of the default website. Use the alias name BikeShopApp and the physical path C:\inetpub\wwwroot\BikeShopApp. As you did with the virtual directory, copy your test page into the physical path and try the URL in your browser: http://<servername>/BikeShopApp/TestPage.asp.

Now we have the default website and multiple folders and applications. It's time to launch this website to the outside world.

3.4 *Opening your first website for business*

In the virtual machine environment you've built for the labs in this book, accessing and testing a website from any one of the VMs is pretty simple: open the browser and type the name of the server or its IP address.

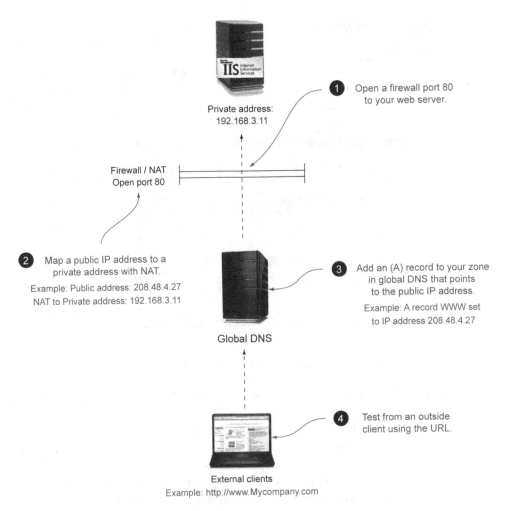

Private address:
192.168.3.11

❶ Open a firewall port 80
to your web server.

Firewall / NAT
Open port 80

❷   Map a public IP address to a
private address with NAT.

Example: Public address: 208.48.4.27
NAT to Private address: 192.168.3.11

❸ Add an (A) record to your zone
in global DNS that points
to the public IP address.

Example: A record WWW set
to IP address 208.48.4.27

Global DNS

❹   Test from an outside
client using the URL.

External clients
Example: http://www.Mycompany.com

Figure 3.14   Opening a website to the outside world

When you want to open a site to the public, or to people outside your network, there's more to the process. You need to check the firewalls and possibly open ports, get an outside public IP address, and configure DNS. Figure 3.14 shows the process of opening a website to the internet.

Let's give people access by opening holes in the firewall.

3.4.1   *Opening the right ports in the firewall*

The default website will respond to browsers making requests on port 80, which is the default port for all browsers. It's possible to specify other ports for your website, but I cover that in chapter 5.

On your firewall closest to the internet, port 80 must be opened to your web server. Everyone uses different firewalls, so you'll need to contact your firewall specialist to figure out how to open yours. You probably have this port open already, because it's a common and normal port to have open. But if something isn't working when you test, don't forget to check this port.

> **TRY IT NOW** Open Control Panel on the virtual machine you use for labs and check the Windows Firewall advanced settings. Do you have port 80 open for HTTP traffic?

3.4.2 Getting an outside IP address

Along with the firewall port opened, you'll need a public (outside) IP address for your web server. This confuses many administrators, especially if they're not familiar with how TCP/IP addressing works. See, a long time ago, in an internet far, far away, we ran out of IP addresses. Every computer needs one, so a special set of new IP addresses was created.

Basically, you have an IP address scheme inside your office. In fact it probably begins with the number 10. or 192. or 172. These are private IP addresses that can't be used for the internet. The internet uses *public* IP addresses. You need one of these public addresses, and it must be mapped through a network device known as NAT to the private address of your web server.

You'll need to contact your network team for an outside IP address that's "NAT'd" to your web server. If you're the network team, you'll contact your internet service provider if you don't already have a list of your public addresses.

3.4.3 Configuring internet DNS for your website

People on the internet find your websites using name resolution from the internet's DNS provider. Your company probably already has its own internet domain (as does the bike shop), and if you want people to see your new website, you need to add a new record to your DNS zone.

The record you need to add is called an *(A) record* or *Host record*. The name you use in the (A) record will become the first part of the URL people will use to access your website. In figure 3.15 I'm adding a new record to my corporate zone called MyCompany.com. The (A) record has the name WWW and points to my web server's external address of 208.48.4.11.

If everything has been correctly configured, the last step is to test from outside your network to make sure your website works.

> **TRY IT NOW** There's no way for you to test this using internet DNS without the huge risk of breaking something important. The closest thing you can do— and I want you to try this—is to modify the DNS on your VM. Pretend it's the internet DNS and add a www record to your zone.

3.4.4 Testing from the outside

To test your configuration, you need to go to a computer that's outside your office network. This can be a home computer or my favorite: an iPad or phone over 4G. The phone option is handy because you don't have to leave the office to get an outside test.

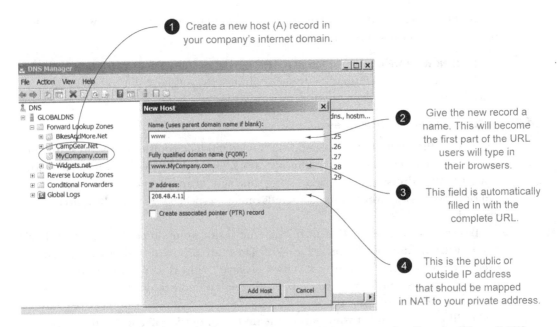

Figure 3.15   Configuring internet DNS for your new website. For this demonstration, I'm using Microsoft DNS. Your actual public DNS will have its own unique screens and layout, but the concepts are the same.

The URL you used inside your office won't work from the outside, so now you need to use the proper URL created when you configured the internet DNS. In my example the correct URL is http://www.mycompany.com.

You can also test any additional web applications or virtual directories you create under the default website by extending the URL. Here are a few examples from folders I created in this chapter:

```
http://www.mycompany.com/TestPage.aspx
http://www.mycompany.com/VirDir/Testpage.aspx
http://www.mycompany.com/MyWebApp/TestPage.aspx
```

Okay, go wash your hands and let's try the lab!

3.5   Lab

If you've been following along and performing the Try It Now sections, you already have several test pages running under your default website. You can keep these if you like, but I need you to start building the website structure that we'll use throughout the book. As you move on to later lunches, you'll add more websites and applications to your web server.

Begin by building a website structure for the WebBikez bicycle shop. The owner of the shop has hired some developers to create a simple website. You've been hired to create the structure of the website and prepare the site for launch.

TRY IT NOW If you didn't get a chance to perform the Try It Now sections, I have repeated them here for your convenience. Once complete, you can start the lab with task 1.

1 On the server where you installed IIS, locate the default website using both the IIS manager and the WebAdministration PowerShell module.

2 In the wwwroot location, create a text file using Notepad. Name this file Default.htm. Edit the file and add the following HTML tag and text:

```
<p> This is the default website for WebBikez located on my Web1 server
</p>
```

Save the file. If your web page doesn't load, one of the problems can be the name of the file. Check to make sure you have extensions displayed and that the file ends with .htm. Also, make sure you named the file Default.

3 Go to your web server and add the additional component ASP. You'll need this to test the new test page. Feel free to use either Server Manager or PowerShell for the task.

4 Take a moment and make your own version of the web page to test the bike shop. Put a copy of the new web page into the default website C:\inetpub\wwwroot and try the page to make sure it works. Remember, save the file as TestPage.asp—you'll need to include that as part of the URL.

5 Open the default document list for the default website and add your new TestPage.aspx file to the list. Make sure you move it to the top of the list so it's the first page that will be loaded. Try it by typing the URL into your browser, but this time without specifying the page name (http://<servername>).

6 Create a new folder under the location of the default website C:\inetpub\wwwroot. Name the folder something like BikeShopDocs. Once you have the new folder, view the folder in the IIS manager. Notice it has now become part of the website. (Hint: you may need to refresh the IIS manager to see the folder.) Next, copy the test page you made in the last section to this folder. See if you can display the page in your browser. Remember, the URL should contain the new folder name and the name of the test page: http://<server>/BikeShopDocs/TestPage.aspx.

7 Go out to your server and create a virtual directory. Use the alias name BikePics and the physical path C:\inetpub\wwwroot\PicsOfWheelSpokes. Copy your test page into the virtual directory and see if you can load the page using a browser: http://<servername>/bikepics/testpage.aspx.

8 Try to create a new application for yourself off the default website. Use the alias BikeShopApp and the physical path C:\inetpub\wwwroot\BikeShopApp. As you did with the virtual directory, copy your test page into the physical path and try the URL in your browser: http://<Servername>/Bikeshopapp/Testpage.Aspx.

9 Open Control Panel on your virtual machine that you use for labs and check the Windows Firewall advanced settings. Do you have a port 80 open for HTTP traffic?

10 There's no way for you to test this using internet DNS without the huge risk of breaking something important. The closet thing you can do (I want you to try this) is to modify the DNS on your VM. Pretend it's the internet DNS and add a www record to your zone.

TASK 1

Create a virtual directory with the alias WebBikezPics and the physical path C:\inetpub\wwwroot\BicyclePhotoLibrary.

Add a basic HTML web page that automatically loads and displays *This is the WebBikez Photo Library.* Include a copy of your test page.

TASK 2

Create a virtual directory with the alias WebBikezInstructions and the physical path C:\inetpub\wwwroot\AssemblyInstructions.

Add a basic HTML web page that automatically loads and displays *Download area for WebBikez assembly instructions.* Include a copy of your test page.

TASK 3

Create two additional web applications:

1 Name the first application WebBikezShopping with the physical location C:\inetpub\wwwroot\StoreFront.

2 Name the second application WebBikezCart with the physical location C:\inetpub\wwwroot\Cart.

Add HTML web pages along with your test page to both application sites.

TASK 4

Open your favorite browser and test the sites you've created. Verify that the HTML pages automatically load when you use the proper URL (http://<servername>/BikePics). Verify that your test page loads correctly (http://<servername>/WebBikezPics/MyTestPage.aspx).

TASK 5

This website should be accessible using port 80 through the firewall. On your virtual machine, verify that this port is open. (In chapter 5 I have you configure DNS for unique site names and URLs. For now, perform your testing using the name of the virtual machine: http://<servername>.)

3.6   *Ideas to try on your own*

The virtual machine environment you're using for this book is great for testing most of the concepts I'll take you through over the remaining chapters. One of the challenges in real life is testing both the web applications the developers are making and the full communication chain out to the internet.

Many web admins build a pre-launch environment for extensive testing of the applications and the network configuration settings. This full environment can be built virtually or with physical servers. They key to this environment is that it should have the least amount of impact on production—even air-gapped from production if possible. The environment should be designed to be destroyed; you should be able to easily start over with a fresh environment for testing.

Many admins have built lab environments like this for years, and if you aren't one of them, then you should consider building your own lab. If you haven't built this kind of lab environment before, don't worry. I provide some guidance and instructions on MoreLunches.com.

Managing
application pools

Let's face it, as an administrator your biggest concern with IIS is this: will it keep running your sites and applications reliably? Have you ever had a misbehaving application, one that leaks memory and starts to slow down your computer? Without dealing with the situation, your computer will eventually crash and need to be rebooted. Websites and applications are no different. Some of them are well-behaved little children running on your web server. Others are nightmares eating up memory and hogging processing. Without the ability to separate the good from the bad, you'd find yourself going to the office in the middle of the night to restart your web servers.

Application pools provide isolation to each website on a server, preventing one site from harming (crashing) another. Using them increases the web server's reliability and the availability of each website. Think of the virtual machines you're using for the labs for this book; each one has its own memory and processing allocation. If one VM crashes, it has no effect on the others, nor does it crash the host operating system.

You can use application pools to isolate websites and applications in several scenarios, such as the following:

- Isolating well-behaved applications from unstable ones
- Increasing security by preventing one application from accessing the resources of another

- Increasing security by assigning unique identities to pools
- Grouping websites and applications that have the same pool configuration settings

In this chapter I show you how to work through such scenarios, using the bicycle shop website you started building in chapter 3. You'll focus on creating and configuring new application pools, setting the best security for the pools, and managing the recycling and cleaning of the pools.

So open your lunch sack and let's get started with creating and configuring application pools.

4.1 Creating and configuring standard application pool settings

Application pools have basic configuration settings that will work for most websites and applications right out of the box. Some applications—for example, misbehaving ones that crash often—need to have their settings tweaked to increase their reliability. I show you what to look for after examining the default settings. This section focuses on the basic application pools settings, understanding which ones to use and alter for the websites, and applications that comprise the environment of the bike shop.

4.1.1 Locating application pools and settings

When IIS was installed, it created the default website we explored and began adding the bike shop to in the last lunch. Fortunately it also created a default application pool we can explore. In this section I show you where to find the application pools used for your websites and web applications, both in the graphical manager and using PowerShell.

FINDING APPLICATION POOLS IN THE GUI TO MANAGE SETTINGS AND CONFIGURATION

In figure 4.1 you can see Application Pools under the navigation pane. When you select this, the center pane lists all the currently defined application pools and the basic settings for them. You'll create new application pools for new websites and new web applications for the bike shop here. You'll view both basic and advanced settings in the actions pane.

FINDING APPLICATION POOLS USING POWERSHELL TO MANAGE SETTINGS AND CONFIGURATION

In PowerShell using the WebAdministration module, you can gather the same information. Much of the IIS information is stored under a PowerShell drive called IIS:. You can access that drive and its information by navigating the directory system or directly using the Get-Item cmdlet.

To navigate the IIS: PowerShell drive, do this:

```
PS> Set-Location IIS:\appPools
PS> Get-ChildItem
```

To access the application pool information directly, do this:

```
PS> Get-Item -Path IIS:\appPools\defaultAppPool
```

Click here to see a list
of application pools.

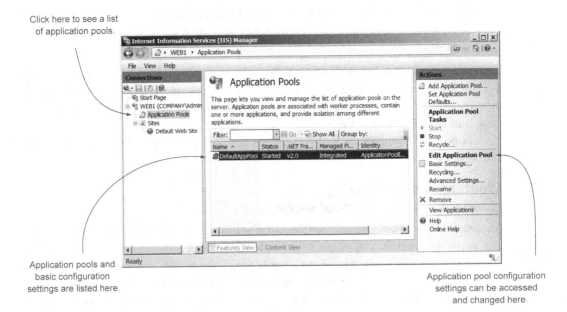

Application pools and
basic configuration
settings are listed here.

Application pool configuration
settings can be accessed
and changed here.

Figure 4.1   Locating application pools and the configuration settings

TRY IT NOW   Put down your sandwich for a minute and open the IIS manager. Navigate to the default application pool and examine the basic settings by viewing them in the center pane or selecting Basic Settings in the actions pane. While you're at it, open up a PowerShell console, import the WebAdministration module, and locate the default application pool using the filesystem.

Now that you've located the default application pool and its basic settings, let's decipher what those settings do. You'll understand those settings better if we start by creating a fresh, new application pool.

4.1.2   *Creating a new application pool*

Placing websites, and sometimes applications, in their own application pools is the most reliable and most secure option. Application pools are isolated from each other to prevent one application from bringing down another. As an added security benefit, application pools also prevent one application from sneaking into another pool and stealing information. The best practice is to place new websites into their own application pools.

CREATING AN APPLICATION POOL WITH THE GUI

You don't have multiple websites yet for WebBikez (you'll do that in chapter 5), so rather than use the default application pool, let's experiment with one of our own using both the GUI and PowerShell. You create a new application pool in IIS manager by selecting Add Application Pool from the actions pane. A menu pops up prompting for a new name for the application pool, plus some additional settings, as shown in figure 4.2.

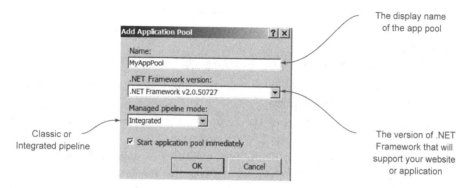

The display name of the app pool

Classic or Integrated pipeline

The version of .NET Framework that will support your website or application

Figure 4.2 Basic application pool settings

Let's look at each of these details, starting with the name.

NAME

The application pool name can be any unique alphanumeric name of your choice. The best practice is to name your application pool the same as the website or application that will run inside the pool, adding the suffix *pool*. That makes it easy to keep track of which pool goes with which website or application.

As an example, in chapter 5 you'll be creating several new websites and applications. One of the websites might be named WebBikezBags. A great name for the application pool would be WebBikezBagsPool. I prefer not to add spaces, dashes, or underscores to an application pool name. Although it may be easier to read visually, it's harder to deal with when using PowerShell or other command-line utilities.

In figure 4.2 I named the pool MyAppPool because I'm not using it for an application yet. You can always rename an application pool later.

.NET FRAMEWORK VERSION

Many of the applications and websites that you'll host on IIS require a special library called the .NET Framework. Developers use this library to provide functionality for their applications. The application pool will load the library so that the applications will work properly.

You'll need to select the correct version of the .NET Framework for your application. How do you know what is the correct version? You need to check the application installation documentation to know for sure. For the bike shop, the developers are

Above and beyond

An application pool can only support one version of the .NET Framework. All applications that run inside the pool must support the same version. If you need to have two applications that need two different framework versions, create a new web application and application pool for each.

developing the sites using .NET 4.0. Not all applications require the .NET Framework—in fact you may have several that don't. You'll explore those types of applications in later chapters.

Here are the options you'll see when you click the .NET Framework dropdown:

- *No Managed Code*—Select this if your application or website doesn't require .NET Framework support.
- *V2.0*—Use this version of the framework to support applications written with .NET Framework versions 2.0, 3.0, or 3.5.
- *V4.0*—Use this version of the framework to support applications written with .NET Framework 4.0. Note also that you may not initially see this option; if that happens, it's because the .NET Framework 4.0 has not yet been installed on your web server (this is common with IIS 7). After you download and install the latest framework version from Microsoft (our short URL is http://mng.bz/HnLw), the selection will appear.

MANAGED PIPELINE MODE

Starting with IIS 7 and IIS 8, a new method of handling requests, known as the Managed Pipeline, was developed to make ASP.NET applications faster than in IIS 6. The Integrated mode is the best selection almost every time. The only time you should change it to Classic mode is if you have an older IIS 6 application that won't use the new mode.

CREATING AN APPLICATION POOL USING POWERSHELL

To create a new pool for the bike shop, use the `New-WebAppPool` cmdlet to create an application pool with PowerShell and the WebAdministration module:

```
PS> New-WebAppPool -Name BikeTestPool
```

Then view the properties using `Get-Item`:

```
PS> Get-Item -Path IIS:\appPools\BikeTestPool | Format-List -Property *
```

The `New-WebAppPool` cmdlet doesn't provide parameters to adjust the .NET Framework version or pipeline mode. You can use the `Set-ItemProperty` cmdlet to change the properties after the application pool is created. The names, shown in figure 4.3, are a little different than in the IIS manager.

Viewing is easy, but changing the properties of the .NET Framework version or the Managed Pipeline is a little strange using PowerShell. There's no cmdlet (such as `Set-WebAppPool`) to change the properties. Instead—and this is common with IIS—you access the properties through the WebAdministration provider IIS: drive and use `Set-ItemProperty`. For the bike shop the application pools need to use .NET Framework version 4.0. To change the value, do this:

```
PS> Set-ItemProperty -Path IIS:\appPools\TestBikePool -Name
    ManagedRuntimeVersion -Value v4.0
```

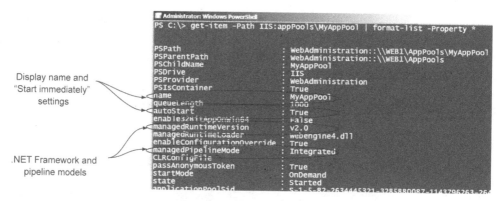

Display name and
"Start immediately"
settings

.NET Framework and
pipeline models

Figure 4.3   Viewing the application pool settings in PowerShell

TRY IT NOW   If you've been following along, you may be so excited that you've already created a new pool using PowerShell. If not, create your own application pool named WebBikezBagPool using the GUI or PowerShell. It should support the .NET Framework v4.0. Remember, if you don't see the selection for v4.0 you'll need to download it from Microsoft.

You can remove an application pool using the IIS manager or the `Remove-WebAppPool` cmdlet.

Now that we have a new application pool, let's move the default website into the new custom pool so we can work on some advanced pool settings.

4.1.3   Moving a website or application into an application pool

There will be times when you want to create a custom application pool (as we just did) and then test a website or application in that pool. Many commercial web applications get updated to the latest .NET Framework version. Even in-house built apps get updates, like our bike shop. You'll want to create a new pool with a new configuration and test those updated applications. Being able to move the website into the pool and then back to its original pool if something goes wrong is an important part of the testing process.

MOVING A WEBSITE USING THE GUI

The website or application Basic Settings link in the actions pane handles the application pool selection. To move a website to a different pool, select it from the dropdown list, as shown in figure 4.4.

MOVING A WEBSITE USING POWERSHELL

Here's what you do to move the bike shop default website to a new application pool using PowerShell and the WebAdministration module:

```
PS> Set-ItemProperty -Path "IIS:\Sites\Default Web Site" -Name
    ⇒ApplicationPool -Value BikeTestPool
```

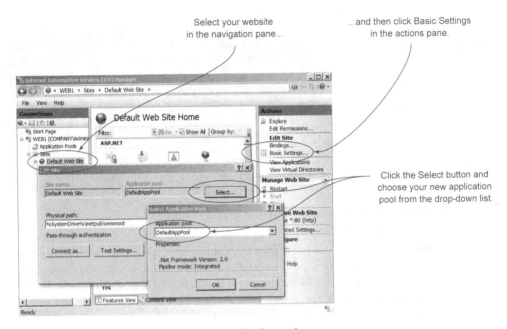

Select your website
in the navigation pane...

...and then click Basic Settings
in the actions pane.

Click the Select button and
choose your new application
pool from the drop-down list.

Figure 4.4   Moving a website to a different application pool

TRY IT NOW   Move the default website from its original pool to the new pool
you created earlier using either the IIS manager or PowerShell.

With a website in our newly created application pool, let's take a look at how an application pool keeps your websites clean and working smoothly.

4.2   *Application pool recycling: increasing reliability and availability*

Even the best websites and applications can have small problems that cause them to
become memory bloated or performance lethargic or even crash. One of the benefits
of application pools is that they isolate applications so that they can only hurt themselves and no other applications. In our bike shop example, if the WebBikezBags site
should fail, it won't crash the WebBikez site because it's running in a separate pool.

Application pools also have the benefit of being able to reset themselves, cleaning
up the fragmented memory and stalled processes of a misbehaving application and
then restarting the application in a clean environment. This process is known as *recycling*. Application pools have default configuration settings on when to recycle. But
many times you'll need to recycle a website or application immediately (on-demand)
or change the configuration settings to something that suits the application better.

Recycling can occur for three primary reasons:

- *On-demand*—You determine there's a problem and decide to manually recycle.
- *Configuration changes*—Changes to the IIS configuration can cause recycle
  events.

- *Unhealthy website or application*—IIS monitors applications, and if one begins leaking memory or causes a problem, it can be automatically recycled.

This section focuses on recycling an application pool and changing the recycle settings. Let's start by examining what's happening when an application pool recycles. Then you'll get a chance to try it for yourself.

4.2.1 Recycling an application pool

Every application pool you create has its own worker process. Think of a *worker process* as similar to a waiter in a restaurant. The waiter takes your order, goes back to the kitchen to place the order, and then brings the food to you. Similarly, the worker process in an application pool handles your request for a website ("Get me the web application"), passes the request information to the application for processing, and then gathers the response from the application and returns it to you in the form of a web page.

When a recycling event occurs, the worker process is restarted, memory gets cleaned up, and the web application is refreshed. This process helps keep problematic applications—those that corrupt memory and hang processes—running smoothly (see figure 4.5). The web administrator can force a recycle event, or the recycle can occur on a timed basis.

> ### Above and beyond
> You can see a worker process in action using the process view in Task Manager. Look for a process named w3wp.exe. This is the worker process for your application pool. Each application pool gets its own worker process.

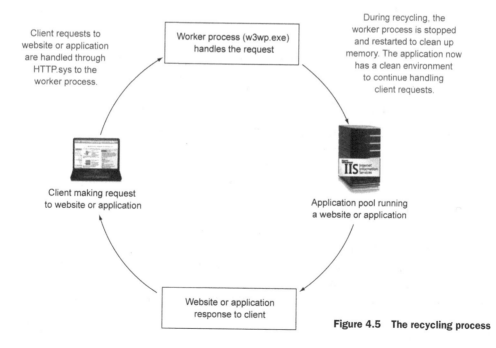

Client requests to website or application are handled through HTTP.sys to the worker process.

Worker process (w3wp.exe) handles the request

During recycling, the worker process is stopped and restarted to clean up memory. The application now has a clean environment to continue handling client requests.

Client making request to website or application

Application pool running a website or application

Website or application response to client

Figure 4.5 The recycling process

Recycling (also known as *process recycling*) can cause the website or application to appear to be offline until a new process is started. To compensate for this, during a recycle, before the old w3wp.exe process is stopped, a new one is created to handle incoming requests. This overlap of processing helps to ensure that the website appears normal during the recycle.

Overlapping recycles seem to be the perfect solution to cleaning up a bad web application, but sometimes they aren't. Some of your applications hold information about the user (such as shopping cart contents), and a recycle will lose the session state containing this information (the shopping cart suddenly clears its items). Well-developed applications tend to store session-related information so that this isn't an issue, but some applications aren't written to handle the recycle. Each application you host will need to be tested to see how it handles a recycle. I'll show you the default recycle settings that I prefer for most applications.

RECYCLING AN APPLICATION POOL ON DEMAND USING THE GUI

Suppose you're sitting at your desk when the phone rings. It's one of the bike shop managers complaining that the website isn't letting customers buy products. After checking the worker process, you determine the website has hung. Rather than reboot the server, you decide to try to recycle the website application pool. This is recycling on-demand.

You can recycle an application pool and its worker process by selecting the application pool from IIS manager and clicking Recycle in the actions pane. Figure 4.6 shows a view of the w3wp.exe process in Task Manager. For a brief moment, there will be two w3wp.exe processes listed for the application pool. This is the overlap occurring in real time to handle requests while the old process is stopped.

If you fail to see any worker processes (w3wp.exe) it's because the website has cooled down—not been accessed—for some time. Worker processes, like waiters, only need to process orders when there are customers. If a website or application has no activity (requests) for 20 minutes, the worker process stops. A new worker process starts as soon as a new request comes to the website or application.

RECYCLING THE APPLICATION POOL ON DEMAND USING POWERSHELL

In PowerShell you can view w3wp.exe processes for the bike shop and restart the application pool with certain commands.

Here's how to view a list of w3wp.exe processes running on your web server:

```
PS> Get-WmiObject -Class Win32_Process -Filter "name='w3wp.exe'"
```

You may be familiar with using Get-Process to retrieve process information. The preceding code snippet could be achieved with Get-Process -Name w3wp. The reason I'm not using that and instead using the WMI class is because I want more information about the process than Get-Process provides. The next example is one of many cases where the WMI class is more useful although a little more complicated.

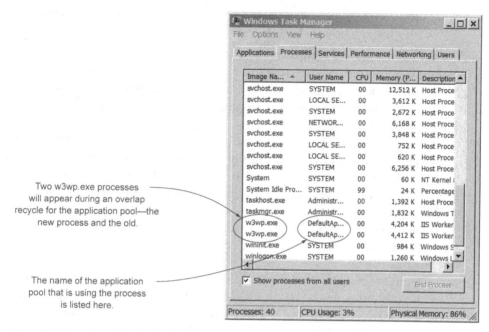

Two w3wp.exe processes will appear during an overlap recycle for the application pool—the new process and the old.

The name of the application pool that is using the process is listed here.

Figure 4.6   The overlap recycling of a worker process

Here's how you view a list of w3wp.exe processes and the application pools they're assigned to:

```
PS> Get-WmiObject win32_process -filter "name='w3wp.exe'" | Select-Object
    ➥Name, ProcessId, @{n='AppPool';e={$_.GetOwner().user}}
```

To restart an application pool, do this:

```
PS> Restart-WebAppPool -Name BikeTestPool
```

> **TRY IT NOW** Let's recycle the application pool running the default website. Start a w3wp.exe process by launching your browser and opening the default page (this could be your custom page from chapter 3). Open Task Manager or use PowerShell to view the w3wp.exe process. Try to notice the second w3wp.exe process start when you recycle the pool.

4.2.2   Modifying the default recycle settings

Remember the bike shop website that hung in the last section? Let's say it happens when you're not around—perhaps you're on vacation. Or suppose you know from your past experience with the application that it will hang after every five days if not recycled. Wouldn't it be nice to configure an automatic recycle to occur in four days—before the crash? Default settings control the automatic recycling of application pools to keep your applications running smoothly. In situations where an application becomes slow or stops responding to requests, see if a recycle solves the problem. If it does you can modify the automatic recycle settings to handle the cleanup process for you. I'll show you how to do that now.

CHANGING THE RECYCLE SETTINGS IN THE GUI

You can access the recycle settings using the IIS manager after selecting an application pool. In the actions pane click Recycling. Two screens will appear one after the other. The first contains options for configuring the automatic recycling of the application pool, as shown in figure 4.7.

These default settings are generally best left alone unless you understand how a specific application can benefit from making changes. Let me give you an example: I don't want the bike shop's application pool to recycle during the normal business day because it might cause an issue with customers connecting. I set a specific recycle time of 9:00 p.m. rather than the default of every 1,740 minutes (29 hours).

Another example is if the finished, developed web applications turn out to be well behaved and don't need to be recycled often, I set the interval to a few weeks rather than every day.

Doesn't sound like I'm being helpful, but each misbehaving application may need a different setting to keep it running smoothly. Keep in mind that most applications will be fine with the default, but you'll have a few that you'll need to customize.

The second window that appears after clicking the Next button in the Edit Application Pool Recycling Settings dialog box is the logging options, shown in figure 4.8. What do you want to log about your recycles?

I don't normally log on-demand recycles because I'm the guy that does them. But if you're in a shop with several other web administrators, you should log this to keep

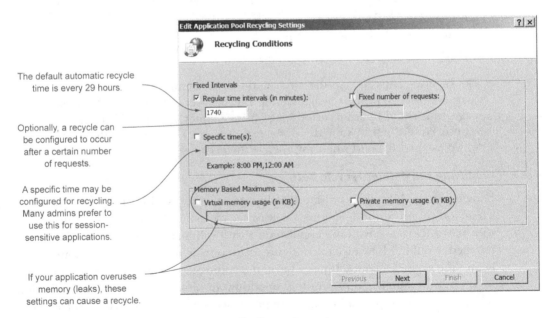

Figure 4.7   Setting the conditions when an application pool recycles

The log settings are based on the selection from the previous screen. Notice the default of regular time intervals.

You can select specifically what events to write into the Windows System log.

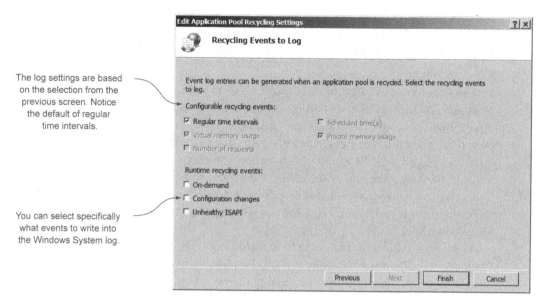

Figure 4.8 Setting the logging options for application pool recycling

track of how often others are recycling a pool. If it's happening frequently that's an indication that you should optimize your recycle settings and see if there's a fix for your application.

Configuration changes that you make to the website or its applications using the GUI manager or PowerShell will also cause recycling. I like to log these so I know whether changes are being made. Keep this in mind and it's worth repeating: if you make configuration changes to a website or application, it will recycle the application pool. For some applications recycling may make them appear to go offline for a brief moment, and that will affect your customers.

Many developers write their applications using Internet Server Application Programming Interface (ISAPI) so that IIS can monitor the health of the application. The application can look at itself, determine it isn't working well, and request a recycle event. I like to monitor for the event, so I enable the unhealthy ISAPI logging.

Jason's recycle defaults for most applications

I have a set of preferred recycle settings that I use for applications pools. I generally start with these settings and then adjust them if necessary:

1 Turn off or set Regular Time intervals to 0.
2 Turn off or set Fixed Number of Requests to 0.
3 Set the recycle at a specific time parameter to late at night or during the time of least use (such as 3:00 a.m.).
4 Enable all logging events (okay, not the on-demand if I'm the only web guy).

For a single application pool, setting the recycle settings using the IIS manager is quick and easy, but later—when you have several pools—PowerShell is the way to go. Take a look at the PowerShell commands for recycling before you try the lab at the end of this chapter.

SETTING RECYCLING USING POWERSHELL: YOU'RE GOING TO WANT TO USE THIS METHOD!

Most admins stick to the GUI when setting recycle options. The reason they avoid PowerShell is because they don't see any easy-to-use cmdlets like `Set-Recycle`. However, there's a way to configure the recycle settings with PowerShell. Let me tell you a secret: when you have 30 application pools on 15 web servers that all need new recycle settings, the last thing you want to use is the GUI. You're going to want to automate those changes with a script. Later in this book I show you how to make the script for the ever-growing bike shop. For now you should know how to make a single change using PowerShell.

This may be different from what you would expect, but most of a web server's configuration can be done through the IIS: PowerShell drive mentioned in chapter 3. Here are two examples to view and change the recycle properties.

To view and change the default interval time, do this:

```
PS> Get-ItemProperty -Path IIS:\AppPools\DefaultAppPool -Name
    recycling.periodicRestart.time

PS> Set-ItemProperty -Path IIS:\AppPools\DefaultAppPool -Name
    recycling.periodicRestart.time -Value 3.00:00:00
```

And here's how to view and change a scheduled time:

```
PS> Get-ItemProperty -Path IIS:\AppPools\DefaultAppPool -Name
    recycling.PeriodicRestart.schedule.collection

PS> Clear-ItemProperty -Path IIS:\AppPools\DefaultAppPool -Name
    recycling.PeriodicRestart.schedule.collection

PS C:\> Set-ItemProperty -Path IIS:\AppPools\DefaultAppPool -Name
    recycling.PeriodicRestart.schedule.collection -Value @{value='06:00:00'}
```

> **TRY IT NOW**   Take one of your existing application pools (or create a new one) and change the recycle and logging settings. Set the recycle interval to 24 hours instead of 29 and turn on the logging for on-demand events and unhealthy ISAPI.

VIEWING THE RECYCLING LOGS

You can use the Event Viewer to look for recycle events in the System log, but PowerShell is faster.

Here's how to check for recycle events using PowerShell:

```
PS> Get-Eventlog -LogName System -Source WAS
```

Perfect! Now you can monitor for recycling events. If an application begins recycling more frequently than normal, you'll know something is wrong with the application.

Try to configure recycle intervals to minimize outages to your customers but still clean the pools so the applications run smoothly.

There are more recycling options that you can set using the Advanced Settings in the IIS manager, and you'll get to those in later chapters as we run into them. For now let's try a lab before we break from our lunch.

4.3 Lab

I want you to prepare several application pools for the beta applications that come from the development team working on the bike shop. Normally the applications would run in the same application pool as the website, but initially, for testing, separating them is good practice.

In this lab you'll create new application pools for the applications, move the applications into those pools, and configure the recycle settings. After testing and recycling the pools, I want you to check the logs for the recycle messages.

TRY IT NOW

If you didn't get a chance to perform the Try It Now sections, I've repeated them here for your convenience. Once complete, you can start the lab with task 1.

1 Navigate to the default application pool and examine the basic settings by viewing them in the center pane or selecting Basic Settings from the actions pane. While you're at it, open up a PowerShell console, import the WebAdministration module, and locate the default application pool using the filesystem.

2 Create your own application pool named WebBikezBagPool using the GUI or PowerShell. It should support the .NET v4.0 Framework. Remember, if you don't see the selection for v4.0, you'll need to download it from Microsoft and install it.

3 Move the default website from its original pool to the new pool WebBikezBag-Pool. Again, you can use either the IIS manager or PowerShell.

4 Time to test the recycling of the new pool. Start a w3wp.exe process by launching a browser and opening the default page. Open Task Manager or use Power-Shell to view the w3wp.exe process. Recycle the pool and try to notice the second w3wp.exe process start when the pool is recycled.

5 Change the recycle settings and log of the WebBikezBagPool. Set the recycle interval to 24 hours instead of 29 and turn on the logging for on-demand events and unhealthy ISAPI.

TASK 1

Create two new application pools for the web applications you created in the last lunch. Name the first pool WebBikezShoppingPool and the second WebBikezCart-Pool. Each pool should support the .NET 4.0 Framework and an integrated Managed Pipeline.

TASK 2

Set the recycle settings for the default app pool to an automatic recycle every 48 hours. Because the applications are in beta and may quickly memory leak the environment during testing, set the automatic recycle settings for the WebBikezCartPool and WebBikezShoppingPool to 4 hours.

TASK 3

Turn on the logging for all the application pools. Make sure to log on-demand as well as configuration changes and unhealthy ISAPI.

TASK 4

While the applications are in beta, it's best to protect the environment by moving them into their own application pools. Move the Shopping application into the WebBikezShoppingPool and the Cart application into the WebBikezCartPool.

TASK 5

Time to test the application pools and the recycle logging. Verify using Task Manager or PowerShell that there are worker processes for each application pool. (Remember, they'll stop after 20 minutes of inactivity.) If you need to start a worker process, open your browser and access the site.

Perform an on-demand recycle of each application pool. After the recycle events have occurred, use PowerShell (or Event Viewer) to view the recycle events in the logs.

4.4   *Ideas to try on your own*

If you have an existing web server environment in production, carefully examine the website application pools and recycle settings. Examine the logs to see if recycling has been occurring on the configured schedule, or if an application has been recycling more often. That could indicate an issue.

Adding more websites to your server

From time to time every IIS admin will need to create additional websites for new applications that the business needs to run, including applications for new product launches and internal help desk ticketing applications. You'll create and configure websites to support many internal products like Microsoft System Center and SharePoint.

You may be wondering, "Why do I need additional websites? Can't I create more web applications in the default site? What's the big deal?" Back in chapter 3 you learned that it's best to put new applications in their own application pools for isolation purposes: if something bad happens to one application, other applications won't be affected. You get those new application pools by creating new websites.

But there's another, even more important, reason for creating new websites: it's all about the name, the URL. Often you want a unique URL—hopefully a simple one, easy for people to remember—that clients will use to access a specific web application. Here's an example: let's say you have a website dedicated to customers wanting information about cool bicycles. The current URL for these customers is www.WebBikez.com. Now consider that the business has added a new repair line called WebBikezRepair, as shown in figure 5.1. Instead of directing customers who need repairs to the original link, you can direct them to www.WebBikezRepair.com. This is one of several reasons for a new, unique site.

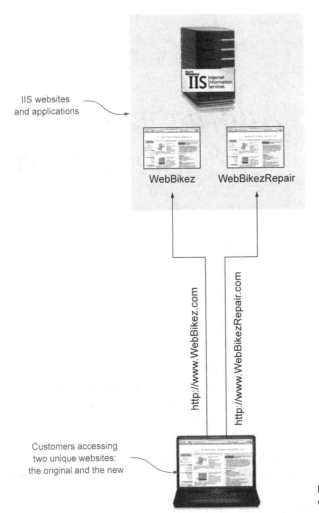

IIS websites
and applications

WebBikez   WebBikezRepair

http://www.WebBikez.com

http://www.WebBikezRepair.com

Customers accessing
two unique websites:
the original and the new

**Figure 5.1   Hosting multiple
websites, each with a unique name**

Another reason? You may want to have different customers with websites on the same server, such as www.BikeCompetitor.com. You want the unique name and the website isolation.

Creating new sites is an important part of being the web administrator and supporting the needs of the business. Also important is the way additional websites and traffic can change the performance of your IIS server. By the time you're done with this chapter, not only will you be able to create new websites, you'll be able to test their performance. You'll start off using the IIS manager to create new websites and bindings. After you've had a chance to work with the concept, I show you how to do it with PowerShell.

At first you may think that adding a new website is straightforward. And it is, for the most part—but only once you understand all the components. Many administrators

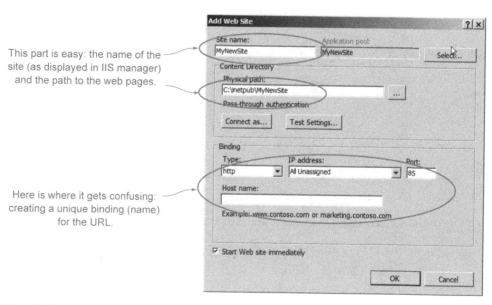

This part is easy: the name of the site (as displayed in IIS manager) and the path to the web pages.

Here is where it gets confusing: creating a unique binding (name) for the URL.

Figure 5.2 Creating a new website isn't as simple as it first seems. You'll need several pieces of information, and there are hidden traps to avoid.

attempt to create a website without understanding all the parts, and that usually ends in failure. Take a look at figure 5.2 to see why—several of the steps are rather complex. One final note before we begin: I need you to bear with me through this lunch and munch on your sandwich for the first two sections. Don't jump into your VM yet—until you finish learning the setup, you'll wind up with errors. I'll show you everything you need to know to make additional websites. Then you can try it for yourself.

5.1   Phase 1: Adding a new website using the IIS manager

You can create a new website using the IIS manager or PowerShell. PowerShell requires that you have complete understanding of the process, so I focus on the IIS manager in the next two sections so that you have all the information you need to create new websites. Then you'll be able to appreciate the ease with which you can accomplish the process with PowerShell.

When you're adding a new site, you start with the main GUI view, as shown in figure 5.3. In the navigation pane under your web server, you'll see the Sites container used to organize all your websites. This is where you'll create additional websites and see them displayed.

To get started on the first phase, either right-click Sites in the navigation pane or click Add Web Site in the actions pane. A website form will launch that's designed to make creating a new website fast and simple if you know what to do. As mentioned earlier, the form is also confusing until you understand all the little settings.

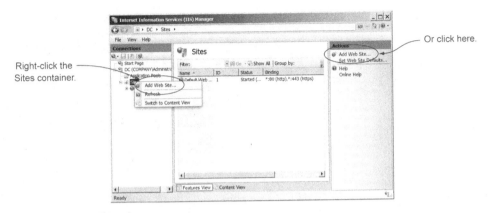

Figure 5.3   Creating a new website using the IIS manager

With this form open, you're ready to begin phase 1, which happens in three steps:

1   Enter a new site name.
2   Create a new application pool for the site.
3   Specify the physical location of the web pages.

Figure 5.4 illustrates the portion of the form we're working on now. So get that lunch sack open and let's make some websites.

5.1.1   Step 1: Enter the site name

The first step in creating a website is to give it a friendly and descriptive name. Unlike the applications you created in chapter 3, this name won't be used in the URL to identify and locate the site. It's a name for your own organizational purposes. The unique

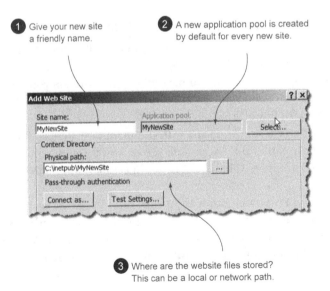

Figure 5.4   Phase 1: Adding a site name, application pool, and physical path for your new website

URL customers will use to access the website will be designated by the binding and DNS discussed later in this chapter.

I know you want to try this out, but don't open your VM yet. Let me explain what will happen when you enter the name. The GUI will take over and you may not like what it does.

When you enter the name into the form, you'll notice that a name for a new application pool is also entered for you automatically. The GUI tool is trying to help you perform both the first step and the second step all at once. I personally don't care much for this, as I explain in step 2 when you prepare to create the application pool.

The website name is fairly simple to handle, but I still need to discuss the application pool and physical path.

> **Above and Beyond**
>
> Remember that the site name is for organizational purposes. It has no bearing on the URL that customers will use to connect to the website. I prefer to use a site name that describes the contents of the website. If the website contains bicycle parts, then I might name the site BicycleParts. I prefer not to use spaces, dashes, or underscores because those make it harder to use command-line tools later.

5.1.2 Step 2: Create the application pool

When creating a new website, you may be a bit puzzled because the application pool field is greyed out by default. I get this question often: "Why is this field greyed out and how do I fix it?" The field is greyed out because it autofills with whatever name you typed for the website. When the form is complete, a new pool is created automatically for your website. This is a feature that helps you keep track of your websites and application pools by naming them all the same.

Remember back in chapter 4, when you created a new application pool for the bike shop and moved a website into it? You can do the same thing here. I prefer to create the application pool first and add the suffix *pool* to the pool name. Then later, when you're working with the site, you can use the Select button to choose the application pool that has the name you want instead of the one with the automatically generated name. This is how you'll add application pools in the lab for the bike shop's websites. For now, you can leave that default-created application pool and move on.

Next up, let's talk about how you set the physical path of the website and where it can be located.

5.1.3 Step 3: Set the physical path

The physical path of the site is where your application files are stored. Remember back to chapter 3 when you created a new web page for the default site? The path for the default site was C:\inetpub\wwwroot. When you make a new website, you can choose an existing path or create a new one to locate those web files.

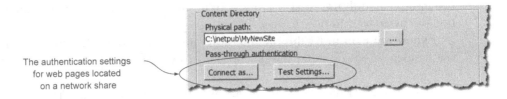

The authentication settings
for web pages located
on a network share

Figure 5.5   Pass-through authentication settings for network shares

Many administrators, me included, prefer to create a new folder structure for the web pages of new websites. I like to make a folder under C:\sites with the same name as the website—it's easier for me to keep track of the folder that way.

You may have noticed the sub-setting called Pass-through authentication, which is used to test communication to a path not located on the local server but on a remote server (see figure 5.5).

Having a website on a network share makes it easier to deploy it across multiple web servers in a load balance and faster to update with changes. We'll explore this option later in the book, when you have multiple web servers.

Above and beyond

A website's physical path to the web pages doesn't have to be located on the local server. In fact, later in this book I show you how to store and access your web pages from a network share. When you have multiple web servers running the same website to provide redundancy, it helps to have the web pages located in a single location for faster updates and changes to the web pages.

Up to this point everything seems fairly simple, but we aren't done yet. Now it's time to give your website a unique name the rest of the world can use for a URL. Time to dig into bindings and uniquely identify your sites to the outside world.

5.2   Phase 2: Uniquely identifying your websites with bindings

What if everyone in the world had the first name of John? A conversation might go like this: "John told me that John and John were going to the concert, but John didn't want to see John playing guitar, he wanted to see John." This doesn't make any sense. People have different names: John, Mary, Frank, Bob. But even that may not be good enough if too many people are named Frank. So we also have last names, and even middle names. This makes for a conversation that goes something like this: "Bob told me that Mary and Frank were going to the concert, but Bob didn't want to see Frank Alves playing the guitar, he wanted to see Frank Moore."

In the same way websites must also have different—unique—names so that servers know where to send requests. If they each had the same name, you wouldn't know which website you were going to get. To avoid that confusion you create a unique name, or *binding*, for each website so that the URLs are different.

A protocol binding is a set of communication rules that define a path between two computers so they can communicate. A simple example is the internet. Everyone in the world has agreed to use the protocol TCP/IP version 4 (that's the binding rule). Because everyone is using that rule, we can all communicate. If someone were to break that rule and use a different protocol, like Novel NetWare's IPX/SPX, they wouldn't be able to talk to anyone else. As amazing as it sounds, *binding* is one of the most important concepts of a web server, any web server, and because it's confusing it's one of the most misunderstood and misconfigured website settings, causing web admins everywhere needless heartburn.

How do you set a unique binding? Like humans, who use a first name, middle name, and last name to differentiate ourselves in the world, a binding uses four parts that, combined, uniquely identify a site:

- Type
- IP address
- Port
- Host name

Figure 5.6 illustrates the format (syntax) of the four parts. Each website on a single web server must have something in the binding that makes the website unique.

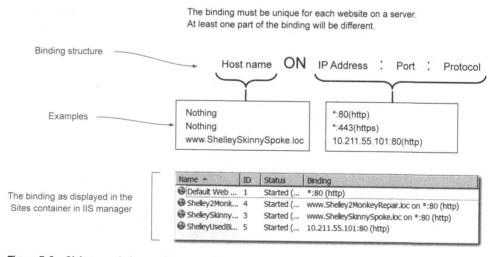

Figure 5.6   Giving a website a unique name using the four parts of a binding

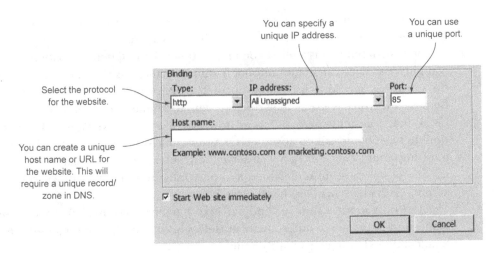

Figure 5.7 Each website must have something unique in one of these four parts to set the binding.

You configure the bindings in the IIS manager (or PowerShell). Figure 5.7 shows you where you set the bindings on the bottom half of the Add Web Site form.

Each website you create must have something different in its name from every other website you host on a server—in at least one of those four parts. Bob Smith and Bob Jones have the same first name, but unique last names. Same thing goes with websites: as long as one binding part is unique, your website will be unique.

In the next four sections, I walk you through setting the type, IP address, port, and host name for the bike website. This information will also work for every website you create in the future. I show you how to do it through the GUI first; you'll learn how to do it using PowerShell in the last section of this chapter.

5.2.1 *Defining a unique name by type*

The first part of every website's name begins with the *type*, or *protocol*, that browsers use to access it (figure 5.8). The type is most commonly HTTP or HTTPS, but you'll see others in IIS, such as FTP and WCF.

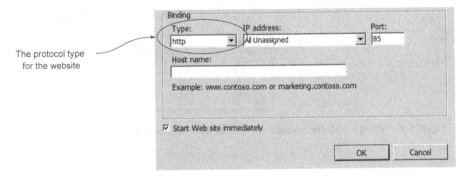

Figure 5.8 The type specifies the protocol to use for client connections.

Because several of your websites will contain the same type or protocol, type usually isn't enough to make a unique name. Let's look at IP address and see if it helps.

5.2.2 *Defining a unique name by IP address*

A common method of creating a unique name for your website is to assign it a unique IP address. In DNS, you can then create a host (A) record (such as *www*) that points to that unique IP address. This is the second best method to create a unique binding for multiple websites on the same server. The other best method is the *host name*, discussed shortly.

Most administrators ignore the IP address option because they think they have only one IP address for the entire web server. You can create virtual IP addresses in the advanced network properties of your network adapter, adding as many unique IP addresses as you like. When you create a binding using that unique address for a website, anyone that makes a request of your server on that IP address is directed to the correct site (see figure 5.9).

The virtualized IP method of making a binding unique is one of the most common, along with host names, which we'll get to. But first there's another, not-so-common option you should be aware of: ports.

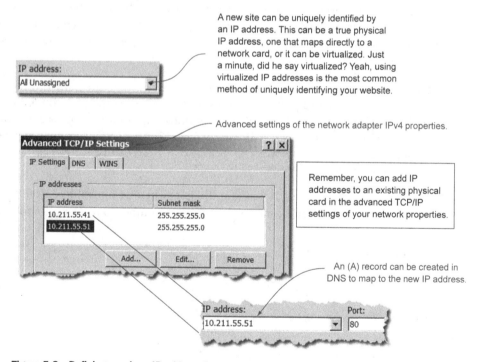

Figure 5.9   Defining a unique IP address for your website

5.2.3   *Defining a unique name by port*

The practice of using port numbers to uniquely identify a binding for a website is an old one riddled with many problems. In fact, virtualized IP addresses and host names were created to replace the old port method. Why do we still have it? There may be a rare time when you want to use it for something; it's still common for developers to use ports for internal website redirection—such as the shopping cart application switching to the credit card authorization application. Another reason we still have port numbers as part of the binding is because no one wants to get rid of them.

You can see the Port option on the Add Website form in figure 5.10. I'll only talk about ports briefly because it's not a good idea to use them for unique identification. There are two problems with using port numbers. I'll explain them, and then you can play with the port yourself.

- *The URL will be weird*—Your website is listening on a unique port, so a customer must use that port number in the URL to access your site. They must tack on a colon followed by the port number, leading to a URL like this: http://mySite:85. And this scheme assumes the customer knows to do that.
- *Every time you use a unique port number, a firewall somewhere will need to be configured for that port*—Read that again. Security folks don't like to open ports; sometimes the only way to get them to do it is to buy them dinner. There's a good reason for that; it gets harder every day to protect against hackers. The normal ports to have open are port 80 for HTTP and port 443 for HTTPS. We don't want to open more ports than we need to.

TRY IT NOW As an interesting test of ports, create a new site with the name TestSite and a physical path of C:\Sites\TestSite. Change the port to 85. Copy the test page you made in chapter 3 into the website's physical path (C:\Sites\TestSite) and access the site using the proper URL, which will be something like http://<Server>:85. See? Not a pretty URL, and certainly not one most customers will remember.

Now you can see why to avoid changing the port whenever possible. I don't want you to think that there's never a time to use the port number, but it's rare and generally

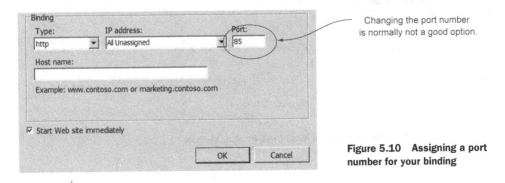

Changing the port number is normally not a good option.

Figure 5.10   Assigning a port number for your binding

only for internal sites that don't have firewalls in between them. Let's try to avoid this option altogether.

5.2.4 Defining a unique name by host name

Host name (also known as *host header*) is probably the hardest of the binding settings to understand. Host names were all the rage a long time ago, before virtualized IP addresses were big. Take a look at figure 5.11, pretending that you only have one IP address and need to have several websites.

In figure 5.11 the web server has a single IP address. To uniquely identify a binding for two or more websites using the host name, one website may contain www.WebBikez.com in the host name, and the other www.WebBikezRepair.com. In DNS both

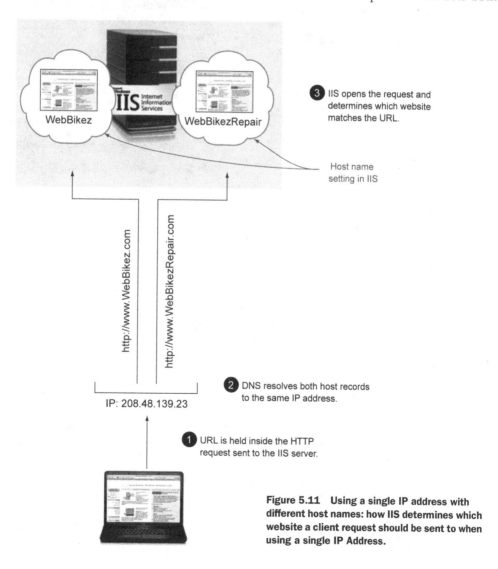

Figure 5.11 Using a single IP address with different host names: how IIS determines which website a client request should be sent to when using a single IP Address.

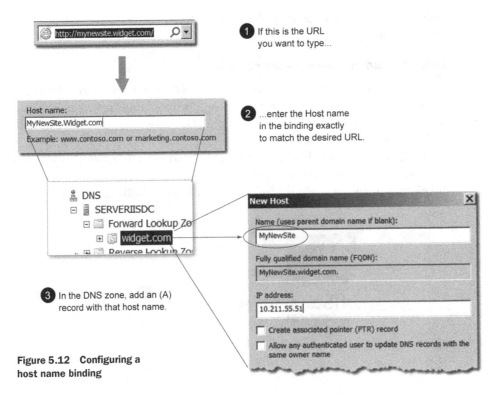

Figure 5.12   Configuring a host name binding

(A) records point to the same IP address of the single web server. When the web server receives a request, it looks at the requested URL and attempts to match it to the list of host names. If a customer typed *http://www.WebBikezRepair.com*, the web server matches it to the host name you created and sends the request to the correct website. Figure 5.12 shows how this process plays out.

Using host name and DNS, you can create bindings for websites that use entirely different internet domain names, such as www.widget.com and www.MyCompany.com, but point to the same website! As long as they're registered and you have access to DNS for the domains, you can host websites for anyone. You've started your own hosting company on a single web server!

I know at first this may seem like an overwhelming amount of information merely to make a new website. The important point is that each website needs to be uniquely identified. The site name that you type into the top of the Add Website form is for organizational purposes—it's the bindings that truly identify the website. Something in the binding must be unique. Figure 5.13 provides examples of valid bindings for several websites on the same IIS server.

Bindings can be confusing at first, so you'll want to practice creating them in the lab for the WebBikez website. WebBikez will need new websites, and you'll get a chance to try three of the four parts to create a unique binding for each website. You'll change the protocol part of the binding in a later chapter when you apply certificate security.

Notes	Protocol	IP Address	Port	Host name(host header)
Default web site	HTTP	All	80	
Site using different port	HTTP	All	85	
Site using virtual IP	HTTP	10.211.55.51		
Mysite using Host name	HTTP	All	80	MySite.Widget.Com
YourSite using Host name	HTTP	All	80	YourSite.Widget.Com
New www site in a new domain	HTTP	All	80	www.NewDom.Com

Figure 5.13　Examples of unique bindings

5.2.5　What happens if you create a website with a non-unique binding?

This may seem a little strange, but I want you to break something for me so you can see what happens when you add a new website incorrectly. The good news is that IIS is so smart that if you even try to create a website with a non-unique binding, you receive an error message, such as the one in figure 5.14, and the new site won't start.

Before we go any further, I want you to try this and see the error.

TRY IT NOW　Create a new site with the name NoGood and a physical path of C:\Sites\NoGood. Don't change any of the binding information. When you click OK, you'll receive an error similar to figure 5.14.

The error message in figure 5.14 is IIS trying to tell you that you've made a mistake. Don't confirm the creation of the site: just say no! If you jumped ahead and did confirm the creation of the site, no big deal. Delete the site from the IIS manager.

Once you know all the moving parts to making additional websites on a single server, creating them in PowerShell becomes quick and easy.

5.3　An alternate way: adding a new website using PowerShell

The GUI is a practical, useful, and protective tool for creating websites. The GUI won't let you make too many mistakes; it protects you from forgetting things. PowerShell, on the other hand, doesn't. PowerShell sometimes requires a little more work, but it's much faster and will be a lifesaver in later chapters when you'll have multiple servers to work with.

The pieces of the process for creating a new website are similar to those you follow when using the GUI:

1　Create a directory to hold the website files.
2　Create the application pool for the website.
3　Create the new website, during which you include the unique binding physical path to the files and the application pool name.

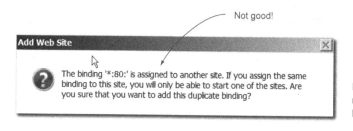

Figure 5.14　Warning message received when bindings aren't unique

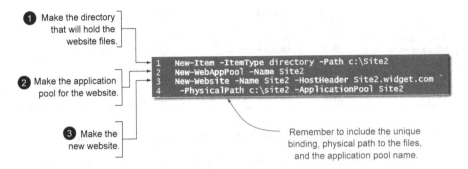

Figure 5.15   Creating a new website using PowerShell

Figure 5.15 shows an example of the entire process in PowerShell.

In this section I dive into the code for each of those three steps, breaking the individual lines apart, so you can understand what's happening.

5.3.1   Step 1: Create the directory for the website files using New-Item

The first task is to make the directory that will contain the website files. The cmdlet `New-Item` lets you create files and directories, but you can also use the aliases `md` or `mkdir`. (Believe it or not, I prefer `New-Item`; it looks longer to type, but if you use tab-completion, it goes pretty fast.)

```
PS> New-Item -ItemType Directory -Path c:\PoshTestSite
```

Remember that this directory is empty, so before you test the completed website, you'll want to place a web page similar to the ones you created in chapter 3 into the directory.

5.3.2   Step 2: Make an application pool for the website using New-WebAppPool

Unlike the GUI, with PowerShell you need to make your application pool yourself. Do you remember how I did this in chapter 4? You use the `New-WebAppPool` cmdlet.

```
PS> New-WebAppPool -Name PoshTestSitePool
```

5.3.3   Step 3: Make the new website using New-Website

Last step, time to make the website. Here are three important parameters to remember when using `New-WebSite`:

- The website's file location
- The unique binding such as IP address, port, or host name (note: if a parameter isn't specified, the default will be used)
- The application pool for the website

```
PS> New-Website -Name PoshTestSite -Hostheader Posh.Widget.Com `
  -PhysicalPath c:\PoshTestSite -ApplicationPool PoshTestSitePool
```

TRY IT NOW   You've held off for a long time in this chapter; I can't let you go any further without trying to make a website of your own. I have one simple rule for this exercise: don't modify, stop, or delete the default website. I want the default to work by typing http://<servername>. Make a test website called TestTwo using PowerShell. Put a test web page in the new site so you can make sure it works. (Hint: You need to have an idea how you'll make the binding unique. You can use a port, an IP address, or a host name.)

5.4   Lab

The developers working with WebBikez on the new site have requested that you create a new website structure. They would like the default website left intact. But they need additional website containers for the new applications. In the process of creating the new sites, they've determined the URLs they want for each. You'll create the sites, the application pools, and the bindings for each of their requirements.

You'll also create new zones in DNS and test the bindings you configured for each site. Two of the websites will use host naming, and the last one will use a virtualized IP address.

TRY IT NOW

If you didn't get a chance to perform the Try It Now sections, I have repeated them here for your convenience. Once complete, you can start the lab with task 1.

- As an interesting test of ports, create a new site with the name TestSite and a physical path of C:\Sites\TestSite. Change the port to 85. Copy the test page you made in chapter 3 into the website's physical path (C:\Sites\TestSite) and access the site using the proper URL, which will be something like http://<Server>:85. See? Not a pretty URL, and certainly not one most customers will remember.

- Create a new site with the name NoGood and a physical path of C:\Sites\NoGood. Don't change any of the binding information. When you click OK, you'll receive an error similar to figure 5.14.

- Don't modify, stop, or delete the default website. I want the default to work by typing http://<servername>. Make a test website called TestTwo using Power-Shell. Put a test web page in the new site so you can make sure it works. (Hint: You need to have an idea how you'll make the binding unique. You can use a port, an IP address, or a host name.)

TASK 1

Using the DNS server on your domain controller, create three new forward lookup zones for WebBikez Bikes:

- WebBikez.com
- WebBikezRepair.com
- WebBikezUsed.com

Hint: They should be primary zones—you can integrate them into Active Directory. No need to have them support dynamic updates.

TASK 2

Two websites will use host name headers for resolution. Using IPConfig.exe get the IP address of your web server. Using this IP address create a www record in DNS for Web-Bikez.com that points to the web server IP address. Using the same IP address, create a www record for WebBikezRepair.com.

Open your web browser and test each URL (such as www.WebBikez.com). Notice that you're redirected to the default website. That will be corrected in the next task when you create the new websites with host names.

TASK 3

Using the IIS manager or PowerShell, create two new websites based on the following information:

- *Website name*—WebBikez
- *Application pool*—WebBikezPool (.NET 4 and Integrated Pipeline)
- *Physical location*—C:\Sites\WebBikez
- *Binding: host name*—www.WebBikez.com

For the second site

- *Website name*—WebBikezRepair
- *Application pool*—WebBikezRepairPool (.NET 4 and Integrated Pipeline)
- *Physical location*—C:\Sites\WebBikezRepair
- *Binding: host name*—www.WebBikezRepair.com

TASK 4

Create a simple default.htm file for each website and copy it to the proper physical location. Here's what I did:

- *Default.htm*—`<p> WebBikez Bicycle Shop </p>`
- *Default.htm*—`<p> WebBikez Repair Shop </p>`

Now the fun part: testing! If you have everything configured correctly, you should be able to open your browser and type the two new URLs, and IIS (using host names) will redirect you to the correct website.

TASK 5

Create a third website, this time using a virtualized IP address. First, though, open your network settings and add a new IP address to use for the website. Hint: Make sure the IP address is on the same network as your original IP (for example, 192.168.0.25).

After you create the new IP address, create a new website using the following information:

- *Website name*—WebBikezUsed
- *Application pool*—WebBikezUsedPool (.NET 4 and Integrated Pipeline)
- *Physical location*—C:\Sites\WebBikezUsed
- *IP address*—The virtualized IP you created

Add a new DNS zone named WebBikezUsed.com and create a new www record using the new virtualized IP address.

Once again add a default.htm to the new site (for example, `<p> WebBikez Used Bike Sale </p>`) and test using your browser.

5.5   *Ideas to try on your own*

Creating websites and unique URLs can be confusing, and you should take some additional time to practice it in your virtualized environment. Create one or two new websites of your own using a port, IP address, and host name. Make sure to test each website you create with a custom web page.

But don't stop there! Create a couple of applications and virtual directories under one of those websites and use your browser to access them. Notice how the URL is affected by adding web applications and virtual directories. Making structure decisions becomes easier when you understand how your decisions will affect the URL.

What every administrator should know about web applications

Up to this point you've configured and tested the primary components (containers) that make up a web server with sites and web applications for the WebBikez bike shop. Now it's time for the final steps, placing the web application into those containers.

In some instances it will be as simple as copying the web pages into the folders for the website. In other situations you may be asked to make additional configuration changes for the application or add supporting components. Each situation is unique, but I've found that understanding the configuration options always helps me understand the application developer or documentation instructions for the application. In this chapter I show you the ropes for the most common configurations to watch for and some fast ways to get a variety of applications supported on IIS. Many admins aren't involved in the application deployment part of the process, in particular if they have an internal development team that performs this process. If this is the case for you, then you can use the information in this chapter to give your developers some help when things aren't working so well.

The most important (but not complicated) part of this chapter for every admin is the one about the monitoring and logging of web applications. Soon your application will go "live" to the customer, and it's important to record how your customers are accessing the websites. This information will be used for security and performance, which I address in chapter 9, but now's a great time to start with a few monitoring/logging tricks so you can help developers troubleshoot a misbehaving web application.

Hungry? Me too. Let's start lunch by talking about how IIS and web application configurations are stored and the best ways to make the most common changes that affect all applications, like compression, Directory Browsing, and customizing error pages. Then you'll add new components and platforms to your website to support ASP.NET and PHP. I walk you through the process using the web server for the bike shop. The bike shop has two websites that you need to prepare for applications, so let's get started.

6.1 Configuring the basics for all applications

The smart folks at Microsoft have already set up IIS to efficiently host your websites and web applications by preconfiguring the basics by default. Each application you install may benefit from tweaking the basic configuration, either in performance or functionality. I want you to see what Microsoft has done so you can customize or modify these basic options when needed.

It's also time to remove a layer of *black box* or abstraction from how IIS stores all these configuration settings. IIS 7/8 use an amazingly simple method of storing your configuration settings that will provide a unique (and necessary) feature, covered in chapter 17, known as Shared Configurations, for web farms that provide failover protection.

After locating those configuration files, you'll start changing them using the IIS manager and PowerShell to support specific website application requirements such as compression, Default Document settings, Directory Browsing, and customizing error pages.

6.1.1 Locating the IIS configuration files

I've been waiting to tell you something—biting my lip, in fact, for the last five chapters to stop myself until it was the best time. Now's the time. Everything, and yes I mean everything, you've done in the last three chapters and that you'll do in the rest of the book, everything from creating websites to configuring bindings to the configurations you'll perform in this chapter—all that configuration information is stored in a few text files.

What? You may have thought that all that would be stored in a huge database, and it kind of is, except the database is a handful of XML text files located on the Windows filesystem. XML (eXtensible Markup Language) is a special kind of text file that has a schema and hierarchy. IIS uses it to store everything but the web pages for an application. Think of it as the Windows Registry but in a giant text file.

The reason for storing this configuration info as text files is simple: it's quick to parse (read) an XML text file. Text files are easy to back up—you copy them—and easy to

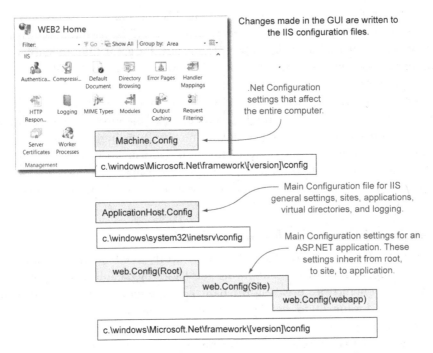

Figure 6.1   The configuration files that control IIS and your web applications

restore if something goes wrong, such as file corruption. Later you'll see more benefits, but for right now understand that every time you use the IIS manager or the PowerShell WebAdministration module—every change or new addition you make—is stored in a collection of text files. The location for these files is described in figure 6.1. Don't try to remember the location or filenames. You'll use the IIS manager or PowerShell to make changes to them. I only want you to see where they exist. In chapter 17 you'll examine the file locations again when you use Shared Configurations for web farms.

As you make configuration changes like the ones in this chapter, those changes are stored in these configuration files. Most of the settings that affect your web server, websites, and web application containers are stored in ApplicationHost.config and Machine.config. Specific settings for the developed and installed applications are controlled through the Web.config files.

Do you need to know exactly what's stored where? No. That's why you have the IIS manager and PowerShell—to make these changes and store them in the correct places. As an example, I have no idea where my bank account information is stored in my bank's database, but I trust the bank's website to show me my account information, not someone else's.

Now that you know where the configuration settings are stored, let's take a look at the basic configuration settings for IIS websites and web applications and see how to correctly make changes to support your needs. Let's get started with compression.

Above and beyond

One question I get from admins is this: "Can I edit the configuration files directly with something like Notepad.exe?" Before you run out to the filesystem and start opening up these files (and I know you will), be careful. It's true that many developers directly modify these files—for example, Web.config and the primary ASP.NET configuration files—but doing so can be dangerous. The XML text files have a specific structure and syntax. If you open one and make a small mistake, a typo, or even change some of the spacing, the file is no longer valid. That means you may have stopped the web application or the IIS server from functioning properly. You should back up (copy) these files before modifying them.

It's true that web developers generally do know the inner workings of these files and often make direct changes to them—in particular, the Web.config files that affect their application. For the most part, you'll always have a better tool—the IIS manager or PowerShell—that will safely (no typos) let you make configuration changes.

6.1.2 Applying compression to make your web pages faster

At some point in your IT career you've compressed a hard disk volume or folder. Compression removes the white space—and does other magical math—to decrease file sizes and increase available disk space. To improve performance, IIS can do the same thing to your web pages before transmitting them over the internet to the client's browser. When the browser receives the compressed web pages, it uncompresses (rehydrates) them and displays them. From the client's perspective this improves the performance of your website. For the two bike shop websites, you'll view the default compression and make some adjustments.

IIS has two types of compression, called static and dynamic, that you can configure for a website or application. You have to install dynamic compression before using it, but static compression is enabled by default and will compress your static web pages (ones that don't change like .htm and .html pages), squeezing them to be smaller and faster to transmit. The compressed versions of the files are stored in the default location (figure 6.2).

Dynamic compression is a little more complicated. Most web applications today produce content on the fly. The content on the web page changes dynamically each time the user clicks. Because the content is constantly changing, it can't be compressed once and stored for everyone to use. Instead it must be compressed as needed. Dynamic compression is a great option to install and enable in most situations, but keep in mind that the compression algorithm must be run constantly, and this causes an increase in processor utilization on the web server. Here's a tip: If your web server is already exceeding 80% processor utilization, enabling dynamic compression will create no visible gain for the client. For an example of calculating the effects of dynamic compression, see http://mng.bz/U2cV.

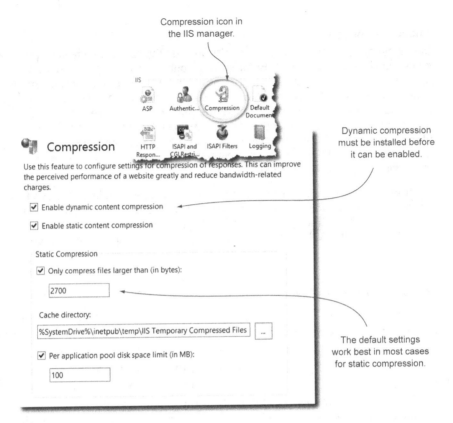

Figure 6.2 Compression settings increase the web page performance for the client.

My best recommendation is to use dynamic compression unless you know your web server is running high processor utilization. When you install dynamic compression, it's automatically enabled.

You have the hang of using the Server Manager GUI for installing additional web server components. From this point on I focus on showing you how to install components using the faster method, PowerShell (make sure you import the ServerManager module):

Above and beyond

Without a product like Microsoft System Center Operations Manager, which is dedicated to monitoring multiple servers, monitoring the processor utilization on your web servers can be challenging at best. You can configure dynamic compression to automatically turn on and off at a certain processor utilization, without the need to monitor. Using PowerShell you can view and set the attributes `dynamicCompressionEnableCpuUsage` and `dynamicCompressionDisableCpuUsage`.

```
PS> Add-WindowsFeature -Name Web-Dyn-Compression
```

TRY IT NOW   The bike shop websites will support dynamic compression. I want you to enable it for them. First install dynamic compression. Then open the compression settings for the WebBikez and WebBikezRepair websites and make sure that dynamic and static compression are enabled. Hurry back, we have more to do.

6.1.3   *Setting Default Documents to automatically load web pages*

Each web application you place on a web server will have a web page that starts the application. Default Documents let you specify which start page to load automatically so that clients don't have to include the name of the page in the URL. You first ran into this configuration option in chapter 3 when you created the custom web pages for testing.

You should verify that the start page for your application is listed in the Default Documents. In the bike shop applications that the developers are creating, the start pages are named Launch.htm. You'll add this start page in a moment, but keep in mind most web applications use a start page that's already defined in IIS, such as Default.htm, shown in figure 6.3.

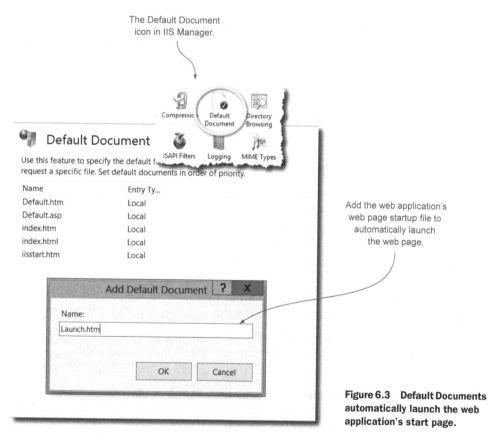

Figure 6.3   **Default Documents automatically launch the web application's start page.**

Above and beyond

Removing unused web pages from the Default Documents list will slightly improve performance and prevent errors in ordering the list correctly. This setting—like many of the IIS settings—can be set at the server level to enforce a corporate standard across multiple websites.

You can always add a new filename to the Default Documents if your web application has a different start page. Sometimes you don't know until you've copied the web page in place or checked the documentation.

The Default Documents list is also listed in the order (priority) the pages will be loaded. I make sure that the start page is ordered at the top of the priority list. If someone accidently places a lower priority file into the folder, it will never get a chance to load because mine is the number one priority.

> **TRY IT NOW** For the bike shop's two websites, set the Default Document to Launch.htm as the top priority. (Hint: You can adjust the priority in the actions pane.) Create two simple web pages as you did in previous chapters, one called Launch.htm and one called Default.htm. Using your web browser, access the website and notice that the higher-priority web page is the one automatically loaded.

After you configure the Default Documents and their priorities, it's a good time to check a configuration option that permits users to download files from your website. I consider this an important security configuration: let me show you why with Directory Browsing.

6.1.4 *Directory Browsing for file downloads*

Directory Browsing determines whether a consumer using a browser can see the files inside a website, application, or virtual directory. This feature is installed but not enabled by default, and in most cases you won't use this feature.

Directory Browsing was originally created so that if you had a virtual directory of files you wanted people to download, they could click a nicely presented file list and download files, similar to using Windows Explorer. You don't want people browsing your web application files and possibly downloading them, so don't enable Directory Browsing unless you specifically want this capability on a virtual directory.

USING THE IIS MANAGER TO CHANGE DIRECTORY BROWSING

If you do find yourself in need of Directory Browsing, you can enable it per virtual directory and select the file information that you want to be displayed, as shown in figure 6.4.

USING POWERSHELL TO CHANGE THE DIRECTORY BROWSING FEATURE

Using the WebAdministration module in PowerShell, you can accomplish the same goals of getting the current configuration and enabling or disabling Directory Browsing.

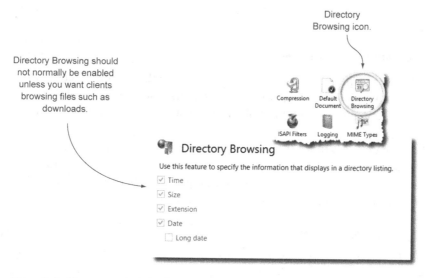

Figure 6.4   You can control the file information displayed in a directory listing.

Above and beyond

The IIS team hasn't had a chance to provide cmdlets for every possible configuration setting. Instead, they provide a set of generic cmdlets, such as `Get-WebConfiguration` and `Set-WebConfiguration`, that gives you access to the configuration files without the need to learn XML. You'll see me start to use these cmdlets in this chapter and future ones. A word of caution about the `-Filter` parameter for these cmdlets: the path is the XML configuration file path, or XPath. The / (foreword slash) must not be confused with the \ (backslash). If you're curious and want more information about XPath, see http://mng.bz/OJKT.

The second method to access the configuration is to use the IIS: PowerShell drive and cmdlets such as `Get-Childitem`, `Get-Item`, and `Set-Item`. I like to use the PowerShell drive for many things, but for configuration changes I prefer the first method.

While searching the internet or at www.iis.net, you'll also notice a command called AppCmd.exe. This has been a popular command, but it's being replaced with PowerShell, the standard Microsoft management command-line tool. I've not used AppCmd.

The following example retrieves the current setting to determine if the feature is enabled:

```
PS> Get-WebConfigurationProperty -Filter system.webserver/directorybrowse -
➥PSPath iis:\ -Name enabled
```

Here's how to disable the feature:

```
PS> Set-WebConfigurationProperty -Filter system.webserver/directorybrowse -
➥PSPath iis:\ -Name enabled -Value false
```

You probably won't use this feature often, but it's always good to check to make sure it's not enabled for your web applications.

6.1.5   *Customizing the error pages*

Have you ever typed in a URL and misspelled something? You received an error (like 404) in your web browser letting you know that there was a problem. These error pages are fairly generic and don't offer any assistance to the end user other than to say something broke.

IIS supports creating customized error pages for the most common errors that might happen, such as a mistyped URL or broken link. I like to customize the error pages with helpful information such as a support number the user can call or at least a personalized, company-branded message that provides better information about the error.

Figure 6.5 shows where you can access the default error pages and change these simple .htm files in the text editor of your choice. Before you do that, do the following:

- See if the application has its own custom error messages. Many developers create custom error pages for their applications.
- If the application has custom error messages, open the error pages and redirect the request to those custom error pages.

USING THE IIS MANAGER FOR ERROR PAGES

You can view the current error pages and customize them using the IIS manager, as shown in figure 6.5.

VIEWING THE ERROR PAGES IN POWERSHELL

Can you view the error page configuration and locations in PowerShell? Of course:

```
PS> Get-WebConfiguration -Filter system.webserver/httperrors//. -PSPath iis:\
    | Format-List *
```

If a web application doesn't have its own custom error messages, I like to take the time to make the default ones more personal. If you modify the default error messages they'll apply to all websites and applications for the web server, and normally this is exactly what you want. If you have a situation where each website needs its own custom error messages, you can create a folder with error pages for each site. Open and change the error page configuration for each website to redirect to the correct folder for that site.

You've verified and modified the basic settings for the two bike shop websites. The next step is to install your web application. In the next section you'll see how to prepare for some of the more common applications. I even show you how to easily get everything you need for the rare and bizarre web applications.

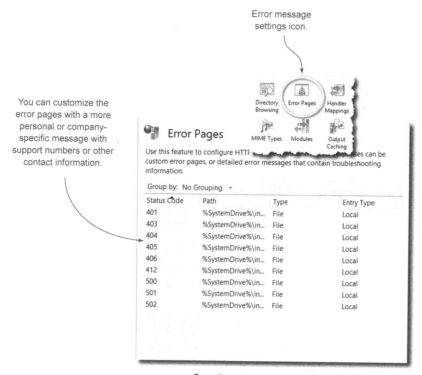

Error message
settings icon.

You can customize the
error pages with a more
personal or company-
specific message with
support numbers or other
contact information.

Copy the custom error pages to each web
server that will host the website or application.

Figure 6.5 Customize your error messages with support and contact information.

6.2 *Supporting common web applications*

There are so many different types of web applications and so many different requirements, it's hard to keep up on the latest and greatest information. Fortunately for you Microsoft has simplified the complexity for both developers and admins.

IIS contains many of the platform components (additional services) to support both old and new web applications, as shown in figure 6.6. These components support many of the web applications you may need to run, though not all of them.

```
[ ] Application Development              Web-App-Dev
    [ ] .NET Extensibility 3.5          Web-Net-Ext
    [ ] .NET Extensibility 4.5          Web-Net-Ext45
    [ ] Application Initialization      Web-AppInit
    [ ] ASP                             Web-ASP
    [ ] ASP.NET 3.5                     Web-Asp-Net
    [ ] ASP.NET 4.5                     Web-Asp-Net45
    [ ] CGI                             Web-CGI
    [ ] ISAPI Extensions                Web-ISAPI-Ext
    [ ] ISAPI Filters                   Web-ISAPI-Filter
    [ ] Server Side Includes            Web-Includes
    [ ] WebSocket Protocol              Web-WebSockets
```

Figure 6.6 Built-in application support

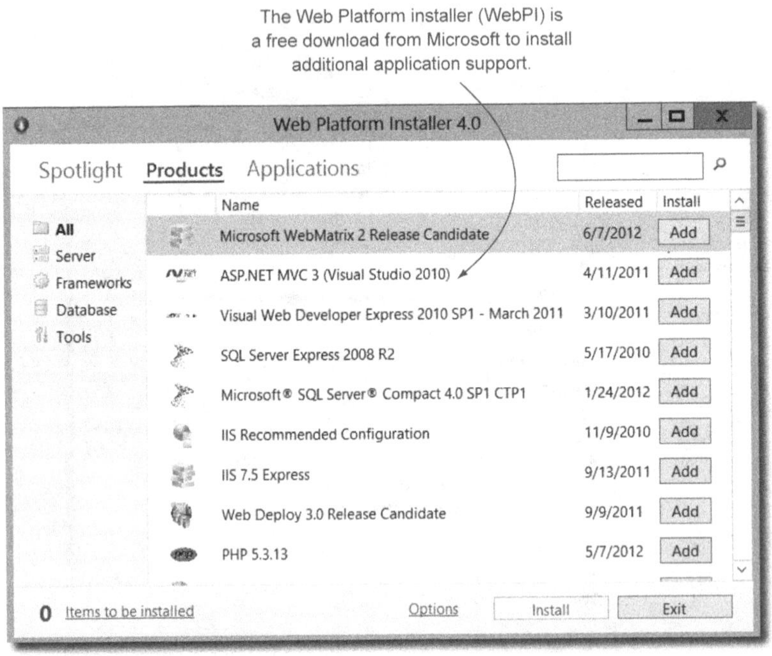

The Web Platform installer (WebPI) is
a free download from Microsoft to install
additional application support.

Figure 6.7   WebPI, one of my favorite tools for installing additional application support

You may have a web application that requires components not shown in figure 6.6. In the past this could make for a long day of research, downloads, and configuration challenges. The situation has been greatly simplified with one of my favorite tools: the Web Platform Installer (WebPI), shown in figure 6.7.

How much is a tool like WebPI worth? How does free sound? You can get it from http://www.iis.net or from Microsoft at http://mng.bz/7HXD.

NOTE You can also run WebPI from the command line using Web-PICmd.exe, which is great for working on Windows Server Core. For more information check out www.iis.net/downloads.

In this section you'll discover which components you need to install, either built in or from WebPI, to support the most common web applications.

Stop! WebPI will install the components you need

I get questions from admins and developers all the time about how to install *x*. Before you open a browser and start searching the internet, open WebPI. Platforms, frameworks, applications, and everything else you're looking for is in WebPI and has been made easy to install. PHP, Azure addons, MVC, WordPress, and Joomla are a few examples. If a developer asks you to install MVC (which they will), open WebPI and install it. Microsoft spent a lot of time making WebPI easier than manually downloading and configuring these components. I only mention the major ones, so check WebPI for your additional needs.

Let's get started with using the built-in support for the most common web applications like ASP and ASP.NET. I also show you how to add platforms using WebPI, such as PHP.

6.2.1 *Supporting applications running with IIS 6 Compatibility Mode*

Not every application you install will be recently developed. Some, such as Microsoft Exchange and SharePoint, may contain older code that requires special support under IIS 7/8. Enter IIS 6 Compatibility Mode, a series of components you can install to support web applications written with this older code or even written entirely for IIS 6 (see figure 6.8).

Those older web applications didn't support the new Integrated Managed Pipeline and application pools (remember chapter 4?). When you install Compatibility Mode, IIS tries to emulate the older environment, Classic Pipeline, and older application pools so that the web application will function.

Websites and applications designed for IIS 7/8 use XML files to store their configuration, but those older applications need something different. In IIS 6 and prior, configuration information was stored in a special location called the Metabase. IIS 6 Compatibility Mode simulates the Metabase so those older applications function.

This all sounds good, and it's worth a try if you want to move the old application to IIS 7/8, but it doesn't always work. Keep in mind that IIS is simulating an old environment and it's not perfect. Some older web applications won't work even with Compatibility Mode.

Above and beyond

A question I'm often asked by students is, "Will I need IIS 6 Compatibility Mode for newer applications?" The strange answer to that question is yes. One example is Microsoft Exchange 2007 and 2010. In fact, Exchange won't install without Compatibility Mode installed first. In the installation instructions for Exchange, IIS 6 Compatibility Mode is one of the required prerequisites. If you manage a Microsoft Exchange server, or any application that's using IIS 6 Compatibility, don't remove this component.

So what do you do if an older application won't run on IIS 7/8 even with Compatibility Mode turned on? Keep running it on Server 2003 and IIS 6. I know that sounds like a stupid answer, but until the day comes when you can update the web application, perhaps with a new version, that's the only solution left.

```
[ ] IIS 6 Management Compatibility          Web-Mgmt-Compat          Available
    [ ] IIS 6 Metabase Compatibility        Web-Metabase             Available
    [ ] IIS 6 Management Console            Web-Lgcy-Mgmt-Console     Available
    [ ] IIS 6 Scripting Tools              Web-Lgcy-Scripting        Available
    [ ] IIS 6 WMI Compatibility            Web-WMI                   Available
```

Figure 6.8 Some applications may require IIS 6 compatibility support.

You can install IIS 6 Compatibility Mode easily with PowerShell or the Server Manager. Here's how to do it with PowerShell and get all the compatibility components:

```
PS> Add-WindowsFeature web-mgmt-compat -IncludeAllSubFeature
```

Next up? Time to prepare your web server with the components for the most common IIS applications: ASP and ASP.NET.

6.2.2 *Supporting ASP and ASP.NET applications*

Web developers use pre-built libraries of functionality to quickly develop web applications. These libraries make development faster because developers don't have to write every single little feature for the web page. Instead they can use one of the library functions.

If you want to run a web application built on a specific platform, the platform needs to be installed on your web server. ASP and ASP.NET are two common platforms for web applications and are easily installed to support those applications.

INSTALLING SUPPORT FOR ASP APPLICATIONS

ASP is an older development platform but still often used. If you have an ASP application, installing support for it is fairly simple. You can install the component with the IIS manager or PowerShell using this example:

```
PS> Add-WindowsFeature -Name Web-ASP
```

ASP has several configuration options listed in figure 6.9, but normally the developer of the application has already made the necessary changes in the application's configuration files. In fact, your job as admin may be as simple as to install the ASP component and copy the web pages into the website folder without making any configuration changes.

For a single application on a single server, the IIS manager is a great tool to make configuration changes. To do this on multiple servers, you'll probably want to use the WebAdministration module with PowerShell. Later in the book you'll create multi-server management scripts, but I want you to use this in the lab at the end of the chapter to check the ASP settings:

```
PS C:\> Get-WebConfiguration -Filter system.webserver/asp -PSPath iis:\ |
    Format-List *
```

TRY IT NOW   Take a quick moment and view the current ASP configuration for your web server. Later, in the lab, you'll make changes to this configuration, but try out the Get-WebConfiguration cmdlet right now.

INSTALLING SUPPORT FOR ASP.NET APPLICATIONS

Similar to ASP, ASP.NET is a web application development platform, but ASP.NET is the current standard for IIS applications and is widely used by developers. This also means that there are several configuration settings (hundreds), specific to the application, that can be adjusted.

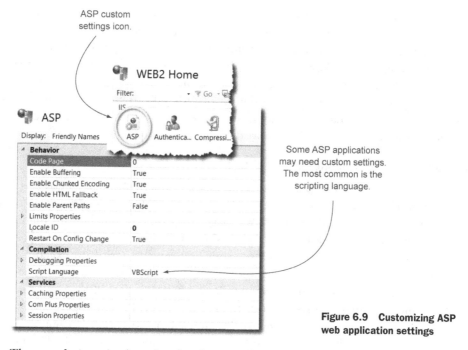

Figure 6.9 Customizing ASP web application settings

The good news is that the developers who created the web application will have defined these configurations in the ASP.NET configuration web.config file. As an administrator you may never need to access the ASP.NET configurations shown in figure 6.10, but you should check the application documentation to see if any changes are expected.

Installing support for ASP.NET is once again simple with PowerShell, and after it's installed, you'll see all the configuration settings in the IIS manager:

```
PS> Add-WindowsFeature -Name Web-ASP-Net
```

Remember at the beginning of the chapter when you needed to configure support for an ASP.NET application? You successfully accomplished that goal. You should review

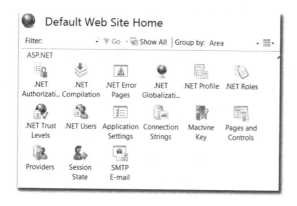

Figure 6.10 ASP.NET settings are configured though the IIS manager, web.config, or PowerShell.

the application documentation to see whether you need to make any configuration changes, but I expect most of that has already been done in the web.config.

ASP and ASP.NET are common components to add to your IIS web server to support typical applications. Most Microsoft products such as Exchange, Lync, and SharePoint require these components as well. The reason is simple: Microsoft created them for developers to make web applications for IIS. What if you have something a little different? Perhaps you have a web application that was created for any web server, not just Microsoft IIS. IIS can easily support those other web applications.

6.2.3   *Supporting CGI applications*

One of the first web application technologies developed to make web apps better was Common Gateway Interface (CGI). Most web applications at the time weren't applications; they were simple, static HTML pages incapable of much more than displaying text and hyperlinks. CGI changed that by creating a standard for web servers that permitted content to be delivered to a web browser and scripts to execute to provide functionality, such as submitting a form of information. CGI web applications are still used today, so you should be happy to know that Microsoft IIS supports them. What I find most useful is that IIS supports the newer platform technologies as well.

The scripting languages used for CGI and the newer FastCGI are probably familiar names to you, such as Python and Perl. Websites built using CGI initially ran on UNIX-based web servers like Apache, but Microsoft IIS can also run them.

You install support for CGI using Server Manager or the following PowerShell command:

```
PS> Add-WindowsFeature -Name Web-CGI
```

Once installed the IIS manager will add a new icon, as shown in figure 6.11, giving you access to basic configuration settings.

Support for CGI in IIS 7/8 is important if you have older CGI-based applications. What about the new stuff? IIS 7/8 supports the new web platform technologies, including one of the most important: PHP.

Figure 6.11   CGI settings in the IIS section

6.2.4   *Supporting PHP applications*

At the beginning of this chapter, I told you that you needed to support two web applications for the bike shop: one ASP.NET and one a Drupal content-management application. You probably use many of the newer applications every day, such as WordPress, Joomla, and Drupal, but never realized the underlying platform.

I'm not a developer so I don't know the specifics of making applications with these technologies, but I do know that one of the requirements is PHP. PHP is a scripting and development language similar to ASP.NET and is common outside of Microsoft-developed web applications.

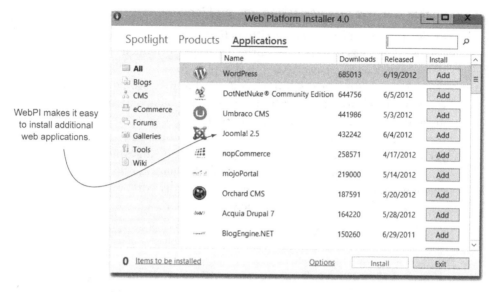

Figure 6.12 The WebPI application list makes installing new applications easy.

Installing PHP used to be a complicated task to perform, along with installing an application on PHP, such as WordPress, into IIS. Today WebPI makes it easy. Open WebPI, install PHP from the Products menu, and choose your application (such as WordPress) from the Applications menu, shown in figure 6.12.

WebPI is the best place to start when you need a platform for IIS, but don't forget to check www.iis.net for more detailed information about the platforms and applications supported in IIS. Keep in mind that WebPI installs components—it doesn't remove them. If you're upgrading one version of PHP to another, this isn't an issue because you normally don't need to perform an uninstall first. If you do need to uninstall something that was installed with WebPI, check http://forums.iis.net for some help.

6.3 *Monitoring your applications*

Before you finish this lunch, there's one more topic to discuss regarding your web applications. As an admin you need to monitor the health and security of the web server and its web applications. The job responsibilities for many admins will end here, with basic monitoring. But I'm hoping you'll hang with me as we build advanced information on this topic throughout the book. This a great time to get started monitoring and logging your web applications, and I also want to share a few tips and tricks up my sleeve that will help you find and fix website problems. You might even be able to get a free lunch from a developer!

The first step is diving into the logs that IIS creates for every client connection. You'll see how to search for information from the logs and improve troubleshooting for yourself and developers by enabling Failed Request Tracing and ASP.NET tracing.

6.3.1   *Search the logs for information and problems*

By default IIS logs every client connection to your web server and web applications. You use these logs to look for security issues, performance and capacity problems, and statistics such as who's using your web application.

As you progress through the book, the log files are going to start to fill up, and you'll use this information to find and solve problems. I want you to get started looking at these now because, even with a single server, you can begin to monitor requests coming to your websites. Without the need for complicated software, you can quickly get an idea of how busy your websites are becoming and who's accessing them.

Figure 6.13 shows the log settings in the IIS manager and when you might need to customize them, but most admins find the defaults work well.

This same information can be viewed in PowerShell:

```
Get-WebConfigurationProperty system.applicationHost/sites/siteDefaults -Name
    logfile
```

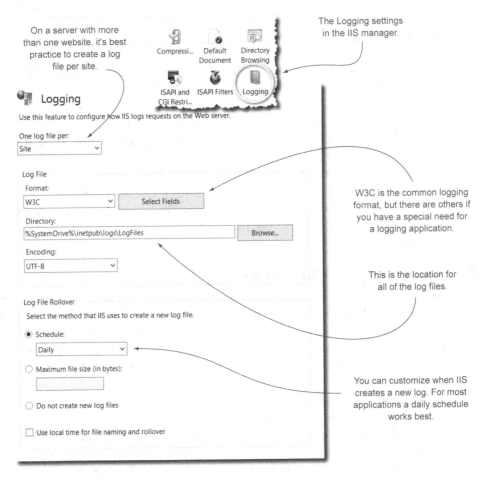

Figure 6.13   Configuring the log settings for your web server

The log files are text files and can be viewed in something as simple as Notepad. The problem with that, though, is you're only viewing a single log file, and it may contain an enormous amount of data you don't need to see. There's a better way, and that's by *searching* (also known as *parsing*) the log files for specific information. PowerShell has a great cmdlet for parsing large amounts of text data called `Select-String`.

Above and beyond

The log parsing program called LogParser is common in the IIS world. You can download it from www.iis.net. Many admins find LogParser harder to use than PowerShell at first, but it's a good tool. It requires a good grasp of SQL—but I have a suggestion to help. David Makovec, one of the reviewers of this book, reminded me of a great tool to help with using LogParser: LogParser Studio, available at http://mng.bz/ M6W7. This tool contains built-in queries to help you become immediately effective with LogParser.

The best part about using PowerShell to parse the log files is that instead of examining one at a time, you can search across all log files for information. Let me give you a couple of examples. To list all log files for every website:

```
PS> Get-ChildItem -Path C:\inetpub\logs -Filter *.log -Recurse
```

To list all HTTP requests that occurred at 9:00 p.m.:

```
PS> Get-ChildItem -Path C:\inetpub\logs -Filter *.log -Recurse |
   Select-String -SimpleMatch "21:00"
```

To list all requests from clients to a particular URL:

```
PS> Get-ChildItem -Path C:\inetpub\logs -Filter *.log -Recurse |
   Select-String -SimpleMatch "MySite/TestPage.asp"
```

To list all requests to/from a particular IP address:

```
PS> Get-ChildItem -Path C:\inetpub\logs -Filter *.log -Recurse |
   Select-String -SimpleMatch "10.211.55.30"
```

`Select-String` is a wonderful cmdlet for parsing, and that's merely the beginning. As you progress through the book, I show you how to improve the search using regular expressions, but for now this is a great way to start examining who's accessing your websites.

6.3.2 *Enable Failed Request Tracing*

Remember earlier when you looked at the error pages? Those error pages, even when personalized, don't provide much information about what's causing a particular problem. Let's fix that right now with a technique that will help you and web developers trace problems. You can turn on better error messages, capture the results, and then turn the feature off.

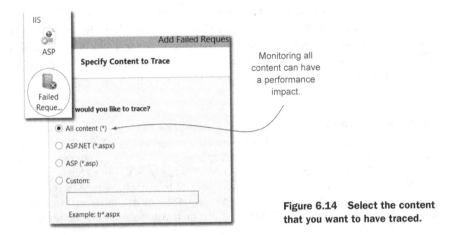

Figure 6.14   Select the content that you want to have traced.

Web applications can be complex, and many developers and admins would like to get better error messages with highly detailed information when something goes wrong. Failed Request Tracing (FRT) is a great solution for that.

Before you can enable and configure FRT, you must first install it:

```
PS C:\> Add-WindowsFeature web-http-tracing
```

To enable and configure FRT, click its icon in the IIS manager and select the content you want to trace. Tracing does require additional processing, so the goal is to only trace the type of application platforms that are necessary. In figure 6.14 the default All Content is selected. I prefer to narrow this down if I can, often only selecting ASP.NET.

You have the option of tracing all possible errors, and if a web application is misbehaving, you may want to start with all of them. If possible try to narrow down the error that users are complaining about. You can even ask them, "What error are you receiving?" If they're receiving 404 errors, then trace for 404 errors only, as shown in figure 6.15. Doing that doesn't impact the server performance as much as tracing for all of them.

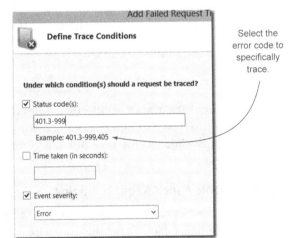

The last configuration screen for FRT is the level of *verbosity* (how much detail) you'd like the trace to produce. It's best to provide the highest detail, which happens to be the default, as shown in figure 6.16.

Figure 6.15   You can trace all errors, but it's better to only trace the specific ones you believe may be the problem.

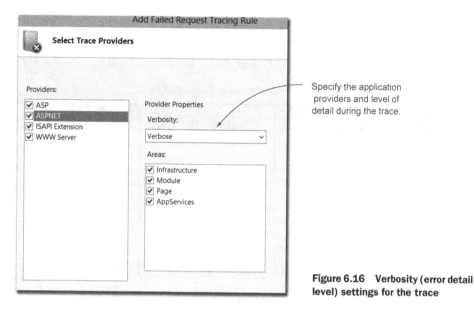

Figure 6.16 **Verbosity (error detail level) settings for the trace**

Let's say you enable FRT for 404 errors, a common error to receive when a web page isn't found. If a browser tries to access a URL that doesn't exist (http://MySite/ oops.htm), you'll receive the typical 404 error page (or the custom one you created). The error is traced and logged to a log file located in C:\inetpub\logs\failedreqlog-files\w3svc1.

To view the trace and receive a much more detailed error report, use your browser to open the .xml file in the folder, and you'll see a page similar to figure 6.17.

This is an excellent source of detailed error information that you can use to troubleshoot a web application or pass along to the developers of the web application.

ENABLING ASP.NET TRACING

If you're monitoring an ASP.NET application and have a development team on site, they most likely will want to enable detail error tracing at a web page level rather than the site level that FRT provides. That allows developers to get closer to the web page that generated the error and diagnose specifics.

To be honest, configuring this requires some coding knowledge and is the responsibility of the developer. The reason I mention it is that I want you to have some links to information about how to configure this in case you have a developer that doesn't know how. Get them to buy you lunch!

Here are some links to enable and use ASP.NET tracing:

- http://mng.bz/DDCJ
- http://mng.bz/ee6X
- http://mng.bz/DI2I

It's time to take the concepts and work you've done in this chapter and put them into practice. Before you return to work, try out the lab.

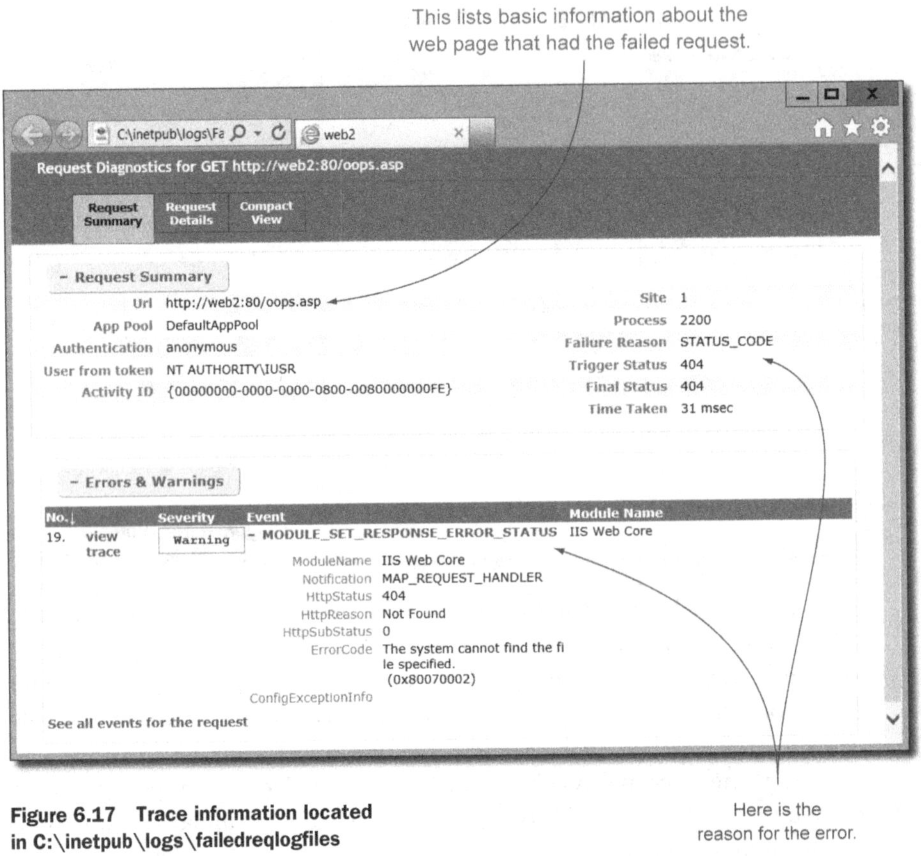

This lists basic information about the
web page that had the failed request.

Figure 6.17   **Trace information located
in C:\inetpub\logs\failedreqlogfiles**

Here is the
reason for the error.

6.4   Lab

The development team is getting ready to hand over the web pages for the three websites you created in your last lunch. In this lab you'll prepare two application websites
and one website for file download testing. Here's how to plan for the three sites:

- WebBikez is the main application site hosting ASP.NET pages.
- WebBikezRepair is the repair application site that will host Joomla CMS for
  video content.
- WebBikezUsedBikes is the download site for used bike photos.

TRY IT NOW

If you didn't get a chance to perform the Try It Now sections, I've repeated them here
for your convenience. Once complete, you can start the lab with task 1.

  1 The bike shop websites will support dynamic compression. I want you to enable
     it for them. First install dynamic compression. Then open the compression set-
     tings for the WebBikez and WebBikezRepair websites and make sure that
     dynamic and static compression are enabled.

2 For the bike shop's two websites, set the Default Document to Launch.htm as the top priority. (Hint: You can adjust the priority in the actions pane.) Create two simple web pages as you did in previous chapters, one called Launch.htm and one called Default.htm. Using your web browser, access the website and notice that the higher-priority web page is the one automatically loaded.

3 Take a quick moment and view the current ASP configuration for your web server. You're about to make changes to this configuration, but try out the Get-WebConfiguration cmdlet right now.

TASK 1

Enable dynamic compression for the application websites WebBikez and WebBikez-Repair. They should have a default start page of Launch.htm. The WebBikezUsed-Bike site shouldn't have a default start page and shouldn't support dynamic compression.

TASK 2

The UsedBike site will hold pictures of bicycles that customers can easily download. The marketing team is taking the photos this week. To prepare the site for the photos, enable Directory Browsing for this site. Copy some photos or simple text files into the site. Using the site URL (www.WebBikezUsedBikes.com), access the site to verify that a list of files is displayed.

TASK 3

The WebBikez site will host an ASP.NET application. The development team needs you to install/enable ASP.NET for your web server.

TASK 4

You've decided to customize an error page for 404 errors (Page Not Found). You want to brand it for the bicycle shop. Create an HTML document for the new error message, named My404.htm, and place it into the WebBikez website root. Inside the file add the following:

```
<p> Page not found, Contact WebBikez support at 555-5555 </p>
```

In the error pages for the WebBikez site, double-click the current 404 message and select Execute a URL on this site. Enter the URL /My404.htm.

Test the new error page by attempting to use a bad URL such as http://www.Web-Bikez.com/oops.htm.

TASK 5

The video website (WebBikezRepair) will host several PHP applications and a Joomla CMS for the videos. In preparation for the video CMS, the developers need you to add PHP to your web server for this site. Using WebPI, add PHP to your web server. If you'd like an added bonus, go ahead and install the Joomla or WordPress applications using WebPI.

6.5   *Ideas to try on your own*

When you have some extra time and want a challenge, I suggest you make your own blog site using WordPress. Create a website in a virtualized environment such as www.<YourName>.loc. Using WebPI add the Wordpress application and complete the process to launch a personal blog. You can enhance your blog site by using WordPress to download additional themes.

You might even decide to launch your own personal blog site to the internet. In that case, use a production web server and build your blog site. If you do launch a blog, send me an email so I can visit!

Securing your sites and web applications

For many web admins this may be the most important chapter and the most confusing. The concept of security makes sense, but the process can be a little complicated. This is a chapter that you'll want to refer back to often when setting security for your websites.

I've run across many websites in IIS where it was clear that the admin didn't understand how to set up proper security and left the defaults in place. IIS is secured by default, but many admins aren't closing all the possible security holes and thus aren't providing a well-secured platform.

Is this important? Yes. Web servers are the primary targets of hackers to gain access into your company. Good security means you probably won't have a problem. Bad or complacent security makes your websites a target.

This chapter focuses on the different authentication methods, controlling who can access your websites, and how best to secure the filesystem permissions for your web pages. I mention some additional services for special cases along the way.

I hope you have a vitamin-enriched lunch prepared for today because you're going to need all your mental power. Let's get started.

7.1   *Controlling who can access your site*

Ask yourself this question: "When I create a website, who should be able to access it?" You might follow that up by asking, "Does it contain confidential company information or is it customer product information?" If you've ever configured security for a file server on your network, these questions will be familiar.

If a website has general, free information for the public, then you don't care who has access to it. But as soon as it contains confidential information, the *who* matters. In our bike shop example, the main site WebBikez is a public site, but when it's time to order products you'll need to know *who*. This section is about configuring who can access your websites and your applications, depending on the type of content those websites hold.

Before we dive into this section, I want you to make some changes to the testpage.asp I had you create in chapter 3. Currently that page gives you information about your web server and website but not about the clients accessing them. I want you to add what you see in the following listing to the bottom of testpage.asp so you can start to see client information.

> **Listing 7.1   Adding client information to your testpage.asp**

```
Client Information<br>
------------------ <br>
Client Name = <%= Request.ServerVariables("REMOTE_HOST") %><br>       <-- Report IP address, port, web request protocol
Client IP = <%= Request.ServerVariables("REMOTE_ADDR") %><br>
Client Port = <%= Request.ServerVariables("REMOTE_PORT") %> <br>
Client Request = <%= Request.ServerVariables("REQUEST_METHOD") %> <br>
*If not anonymous<br>
Client User Type = <%= Request.ServerVariables("AUTH_TYPE") %><br>     <-- Report authentication method and username
Client User Name = <%= Request.ServerVariables("AUTH_USER") %><br>
```

There are several methods of controlling who has access to a website—in fact, in this chapter there are five—but the three most important and frequently needed are covered in this section: anonymous access, Windows authentication, and basic authentication (see table 7.1). The remaining two methods, forms-based and authorization rules, can be integrated at any time and are used for specific cases, so I'm saving those for the end of the chapter.

Table 7.1   Authentication types

Authentication Type	User Location	Access Notes
Anonymous access	External	Best for public websites that don't contain confidential information
Windows authentication	Internal	Best for internal private sites (SharePoint) that require confidential access
Basic authentication	External	Best for websites accessible from the outside that contain confidential information

Each of the three authentication mechanisms is slightly different to configure. In this section you'll work with the main three: anonymous, Windows, and basic. Let's start with the default authentication method: anonymous.

7.1.1 Configuring anonymous access

Imagine if every website you browsed in the world required a username and password. Imagine trying to remember them all! For websites providing general public information, there's no need for security to be that high.

To make accessing public websites easier and less confusing, internet users are considered *anonymous*, much like the guest account in Windows, and don't need to provide a username or password (see figure 7.1). As the web admin you don't know who anonymous truly is, so IIS gives anonymous users limited permissions to access a website—for the most part, they're granted the ability to read the web pages.

Microsoft Windows is a highly secured operating system that requires credentials (username/password) for every user. Anonymous access is mapped to the built-in user account IUSR and the group account IIS_IUSRS. These accounts can further restrict access using filesystem permissions. Microsoft has already done that for you to a large extent by making sure that anonymous users can't harm (delete or deface) your websites.

In most cases the preconfigured settings that Microsoft has implemented for anonymous access for public websites are fine, but if you're hosting more than one public website on a web server, you can tighten up the security even further. I'll show you the default settings, but let me also show you what I prefer to do to control anonymous access. The anonymous authentication settings are located in the IIS manager, as shown in figure 7.2.

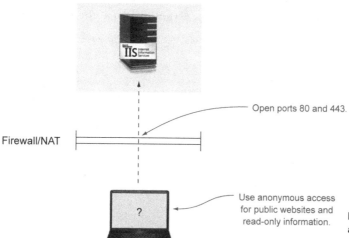

Open ports 80 and 443.

Firewall/NAT

Use anonymous access for public websites and read-only information.

Figure 7.1 Anonymous access is tightly restricted by default.

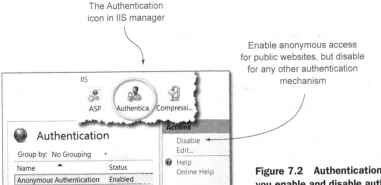

The Authentication icon in IIS manager

Enable anonymous access for public websites, but disable for any other authentication mechanism

Figure 7.2 Authentication settings is where you enable and disable authentication methods.

Authentication settings lists all available authentication methods, and if you've been following along with the book, you've probably only seen anonymous so far. You'll install other methods soon, but notice that you can enable/disable anonymous access. By editing the settings you can control the user account that anonymous runs under (figure 7.3). The default IUSR is sufficient in most cases. You can even create a custom account if you want, but I prefer to change the user account to use the application pool identity.

By using the application pool identity (which is unique for every website), you isolate websites from each other on the same server. This is a better security practice because it prevents the possibility of a hacked website accessing another website and permits easier control of permissions.

In a multiple web server environment, as discussed in chapter 19, you'll automate anonymous configuration settings. For now I want you to see how to use PowerShell for a single website. You'll use PowerShell and WebConfiguration cmdlets to make the changes. The following are some examples. To get a list of authentication mechanisms:

```
PS> Get-WebConfiguration -Filter /system.WebServer/security/authentication |
    Foreach-Object{$_.sections}
```

To get anonymous authentication settings:

```
PS> Get-WebConfigurationProperty -Filter system.WebServer/security/
    authentication/anonymousAuthentication -PSPath IIS:\  -Name enabled |
    Select-Object value
```

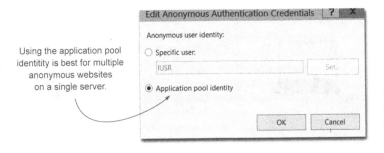

Using the application pool identity is best for multiple anonymous websites on a single server.

Figure 7.3 Using the application pool identity isolates websites from each other.

To enable/disable anonymous authentication for the entire web server (note the example shows how to disable):

```
PS> Set-WebConfigurationProperty -Filter system.WebServer/security/
    ➥authentication/anonymousAuthentication -PSPath IIS:\  -Name enabled -
    ➥Value False
```

To enable/disable anonymous authentication for a website or application (note the example shows how to disable):

```
PS> Get-WebConfigurationProperty -Filter system.WebServer/security/
    ➥authentication/anonymousAuthentication -PSPath IIS:\  -Name enabled -
    ➥Location MySite
```

```
PS> Set-WebConfigurationProperty -Filter system.WebServer/security/
    ➥authentication/anonymousAuthentication -PSPath IIS:\  -Name enabled -
    ➥Value False -Location MySite
```

> **TRY IT NOW** Use one of your existing websites or make a new one for this chapter and change the anonymous authentication user from IUSR to the application pool identity. Make sure to verify that your website works using the special test page you created in an earlier chapter.

Anonymous authentication is designed for public websites, but if you have a website that provides confidential information (such as with SharePoint), you want users to properly authenticate using a Windows account. The next two sections focus on secured access using a username and password.

7.1.2 *Configuring Windows authentication*

Windows authentication is the best method for internal websites that contain confidential or personalized information. Products such as Microsoft SharePoint and Exchange are excellent examples that use Windows authentication for internal users, as illustrated in figure 7.4.

Windows authentication uses the username and password the user logged on to their computer with and passes it to IIS (local accounts or Active Directory) for security access. This means that users don't need to re-type their username and password every time they access the website; it's handled automatically for them.

First let's look at installing Windows authentication, and then I'll show you the advanced configuration settings.

Windows authentication isn't installed or enabled by default. You can use Server Manager or PowerShell to install it. Here's an example using PowerShell:

```
PS> Add-WindowsFeature Web-Windows-Auth
```

After Windows authentication is installed, you need to enable the authentication on the website in the IIS manager. You'll do this shortly to the bike shop, but keep this in mind: you need to disable anonymous authentication when you enable Windows authentication or your internal users will continue to use anonymous. If you don't see the new authentication method you enabled, you may need to refresh or even restart

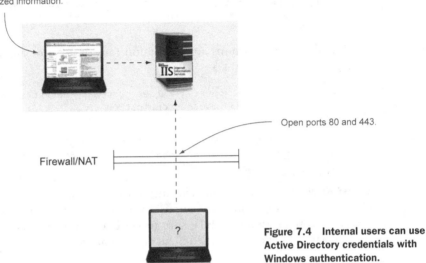

Windows authentication is best for internal users who need access to confidential or personalized information.

Open ports 80 and 443.

Firewall/NAT

Figure 7.4 Internal users can use Active Directory credentials with Windows authentication.

the IIS manager. Remember this throughout this book. Sometimes a refresh or a restart of the GUI manager may be required to find the new component.

Windows authentication includes advanced settings that increase security by preventing authentication relay attacks. The new Extended Protection was introduced in IIS 7.5 and is turned off by default. Clients' computers must be able to communicate with the new protection, so two settings are provided to support new and older clients. The Accept setting (figure 7.5) is the best setting for most environments; for newer clients this setting uses the Extended Protection; for older clients it doesn't. The Required setting enforces Extended Protection, and older clients that can't use this will be rejected.

Use the following examples as guides for configuring Windows authentication with PowerShell. To get information about Windows authentication settings:

```
PS> Get-WebConfiguration -Filter system.WebServer/security/authentication/
    windowsAuthentication | Format-List *

PS> Get-WebConfigurationProperty -Filter system.WebServer/security/
    authentication/windowsAuthentication -Name enabled | Select-Object value
```

To enable/disable Windows authentication (note example demonstrates how to enable):

```
PS> Set-WebConfigurationProperty -Filter system.WebServer/security/
    authentication/windowsAuthentication -Name enabled -Value true
```

To enable/disable Windows authentication per site or application (note example demonstrates enabling):

Add extra security by setting
the Extended Protection
level to Accept.

Kernel-mode authentication
improves authentication
performance in Active
Directory environments and
should not be disabled.

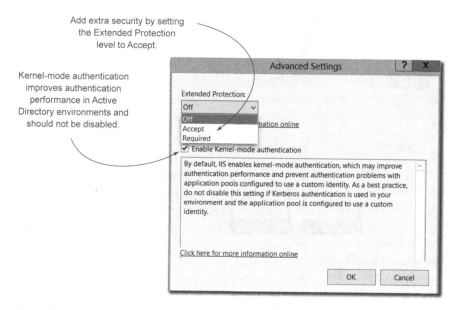

Figure 7.5 Configure Extended Protection to prevent authentication relay attacks.

```
PS> Get-WebConfigurationProperty -Filter system.WebServer/security/
    authentication/windowsAuthentication -Name enabled -Location mysite -
    Value true
```

TRY IT NOW Make sure you have a test page with the client settings discussed at the beginning of the chapter. Install and enable Windows authentication. Be sure to disable anonymous authentication. Access the website (you may have to log on the first time) and notice the client section on the web page. It should display your Windows authentication username, as shown in figure 7.6.

Figure 7.6   Testpage.asp client section displays current user accessing website.

Windows authentication works great for internal users accessing websites that contain confidential data. But sometimes users will travel outside the company and still need access to those websites. The *basic* authentication mechanism, covered in the next section, allows outside users this access.

7.1.3 *Using basic authentication*

Basic authentication allows users from the internet to access private and confidential content by providing a valid username and password. Basic authentication works in all browsers and all firewalls and proxy servers, as illustrated in figure 7.7.

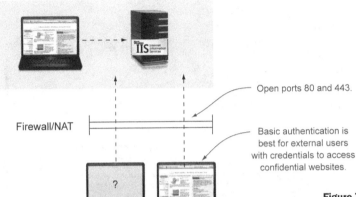

Open ports 80 and 443.

Basic authentication is
best for external users
with credentials to access
confidential websites.

**Figure 7.7 Basic authentication
is for internet-based users.**

The biggest challenge with basic authentication is that it transmits usernames and passwords in clear text. Read that again—yes, I said it transmits usernames and passwords in clear text. Anyone with a protocol analyzer can capture your credentials. Seems stupid to use this authentication right? When you use basic authentication (and you will often), you must make sure that the communication from the client to your web server is secured with certificates and Secured Socket Layer (SSL). You'll apply certificates and get SSL working in chapter 9 for this reason. For now it's okay because your VM's aren't a production environment.

As with the Windows authentication you installed earlier, basic authentication must be installed before it can be enabled. Use PowerShell to install basic authentication:

```
PS> Add-WindowsFeature Web-Basic-Auth
```

As with Windows authentication, after basic is installed you can enable it in the IIS manager, as shown in figure 7.8.

Once basic authentication is enabled (and secured with SSL), users from the outside can use their usernames and passwords to access websites and applications. By default, users must also provide the domain name that contains their credentials, as shown in figure 7.9.

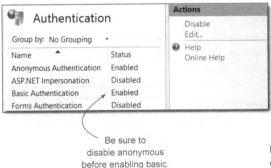

Be sure to
disable anonymous
before enabling basic.

**Figure 7.8 Enable basic authentication
only after securing the website with SSL.**

Normally users must type in their
Active Directory domain and
username. This can be made
easier for the user.

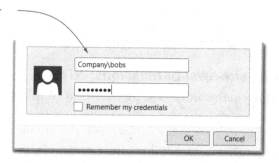

Figure 7.9 Normal login process for users using basic authentication

You can make this easier for users by editing the basic authentication settings and specifying a default domain, as shown in figure 7.10, so they no longer need to type this additional information.

As with the other authentication mechanisms, you can adjust these settings using PowerShell. To get configuration information about basic authentication:

```
PS> Get-WebConfiguration -Filter system.WebServer/security/authentication/
    ➥BasicAuthentication | Format-List *

PS> Get-WebConfigurationProperty -Filter system.WebServer/security/
    ➥authentication/BasicAuthentication -Name enabled | Select-Object value
```

To enable/disable basic authentication:

```
PS> Set-WebConfigurationProperty -Filter system.WebServer/security/
    ➥authentication/BasicAuthentication -Name enabled -Value true
```

To enable/disable basic authentication per site or application:

```
PS> Set-WebConfigurationProperty -Filter system.WebServer/security/
    ➥authentication/BasicAuthentication -Name enabled -Location MySite |
    ➥Select-Object value
```

TRY IT NOW In your virtual lab environment you can enable basic authentication for testing. But don't do this in production until you've completed chapter 9 and have secured this with SSL. If you want to try it out now, disable all other authentication methods and enable basic. Access your website and note that you're prompted for a username and password.

Make it easier for
users to log on by
filling out the default
domain for them.

Figure 7.10 Improve the client experience by setting the default domain.

Now that you can prompt for credentials and control *who* can access your websites, you need to control *what* they can do to them. The next section focuses on using the authentication credentials combined with NTFS security to control what a user can access.

7.2   *Setting site-level permissions: NTFS*

The three authentication credentials you configured in the last section control *who* can access your web server and websites. Those credentials combined with NTFS security permissions will control *what* they can do to the websites. As an example, you don't want anonymous users to have the ability to delete your web pages! The next step in the process of securing a website is to take the authentication credentials and configure them with the proper NTFS filesystem permissions to the web pages.

By default, all authenticated users in your company can access every website and application. This is rarely the type of access you want; I certainly don't want everyone accessing confidential accounting information. I only want an accountant to have access to those web pages. You control access by setting the filesystem permissions.

There are two different ways to configure what websites and pages a user can access: NTFS permissions and URL authorization. The first method, NTFS permissions, is the one I prefer because it works with any type of web application—ASP, ASP.NET, CGI, PHP, and so on. This method is also the most familiar to Windows admins because it's the same process you perform when applying NTFS permissions to a file server.

The second method of controlling access—URL authorization, discussed in the last section of this chapter—is a newer addition to IIS and applies only to ASP.NET web applications.

In this section you'll configure permissions for users and groups and configure permissions for the application pools using the most common method that supports all applications. Let's start with the one most familiar to admins: setting permissions for users and groups.

7.2.1   *Configuring permissions for users and groups*

Configuring permissions for the web pages in your website and application containers is the exact same process as it is for file servers. In fact, you'll use those tools (the Security tab) in this section as you've used them in the past when configuring file servers.

Above and beyond
I'm not using PowerShell in this section. Setting permissions using PowerShell is complicated at best, and for a single server with a few websites, it isn't the best tool. Later in the book I show you a few methods using PowerShell to automate permission assignments across multiple servers when the complexity is outweighed by the management gain.

Open the file
permissions here.

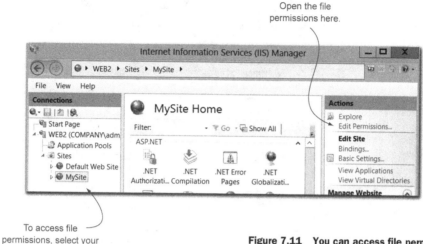

To access file
permissions, select your
website here.

**Figure 7.11   You can access file permissions
using the IIS manager or Windows File Explorer.**

In this section you'll use the Security tab to assign custom permissions for users and groups. You can use File Explorer and navigate to the website folders, but the IIS manager can make it quicker and easier. Take a look a figure 7.11. Select your website or application on the left and then choose Edit Permissions on the right.

The Security tab will open to display the current (default) permissions. Once the Security tab opens, as shown in figure 7.12, you'll notice the default permissions. The local Administrators group should always remain in this list, but the local Users group is the one you want to remove and then replace with your own users and groups for permissions.

The permissions you see in the Security tab are inherited from the parent folder. I'm sure you've run into this many times when setting file server permissions: you won't be able to edit the list of permissions until you block the inherited ones. There are two steps to this process:

1 Blocking inherited permissions
2 Adding users and groups to the permission list

These are the default users and groups that have access to the web application.

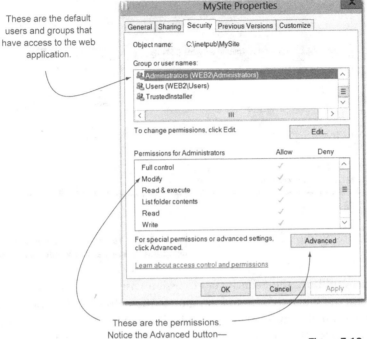

These are the permissions. Notice the Advanced button—you will need to click this to block inheritance.

Figure 7.12   **The default users/ groups and permissions for a website**

STEP 1: BLOCKING INHERITED PERMISSIONS

You probably have done this a hundred times in the past on a regular file server, but just in case, let me show you again. As in figure 7.12, to block the inherited permissions, on the Security tab click the Advanced button.

When the Advanced Security Settings for the website dialog box appears (see figure 7.13), click the Disable inheritance button. You'll be prompted to convert (copy) the parent permissions to this folder or remove all permissions and start with a clean slate.

Normally you want all the default permissions except for a few, so I prefer to convert (copy) the permissions from the parent. This saves time and troubleshooting if I forget a required permission assignment.

STEP 2: ADDING USERS AND GROUPS TO THE PERMISSIONS LIST

In figure 7.14 I added the user Bob Smith and the group Sales to the list of people who can access the website. Notice that I removed the group Users, which was permitting everyone to have access.

In the lower pane you'll set the desired permissions for the users and groups. The default is to give them the most basic or minimum permissions, and this is normally sufficient. Check the web application documentation to see whether it needs a higher permission level. At this point in my example, the only people who can access the website are Administrators, Sales, and the user Bob Smith.

Select the first option to convert
permissions to explicit. You will
now be able to adjust permissions.

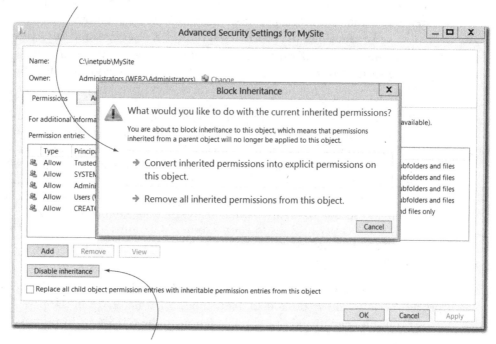

To block inheritance and be
able to manage permissions,
click Disable inheritance.

**Figure 7.13 Block inheritance so
you can change file permissions.**

After removing Users, add in
specific users and groups.

Assign the permission to
web pages that you want
them to have. Remember,
the less, the better.

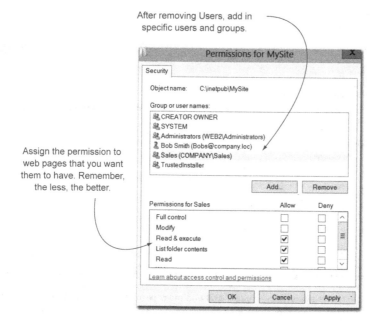

**Figure 7.14 Add users
and groups for custom
site permissions.**

NTFS PERMISSIONS ARE DONE, BUT ONE MORE THING...

Many web administrators make a mistake at this point in the process. If this were a file server, you'd be done setting permissions, but this is a web server, and there's one more "entity" that must have permissions. In fact, if you attempted to access this website now, before finishing the process, you'd receive an error similar to figure 7.15. Before we move into configuring the application pool security, you may be tempted to try setting security settings for one of your websites. I'm good with that, but keep in mind that because it's not finished, you'll receive an error like the one in figure 7.15.

> **TRY IT NOW**   If you want to start practicing with this now, you can, but remember it's not going to work yet. Feel free to wait until after the next section. In your lab environment, create a new Active Directory user you can use for testing permission access. I created one called Bob Smith, but you can pick whatever name you like. And I want you to get a login prompt, so enable basic authentication. Remember: do this only in your lab environment until I show you how to secure basic in chapter 9. Assign Bob Smith (or whatever your user is named) permissions to your website. Make sure to remove the Users group. You can now attempt to log in, but remember you'll get an error similar to the one in figure 7.15.

Assigning permissions for users and groups *feels* like the last step in the permissions process because you've done it so many times on a file server in the past. For a web server you still need to add one special identity to the NTFS security permissions: your application pool.

This is a common mistake that admins make when setting security. You must finish the process by adding permissions for the application pool.

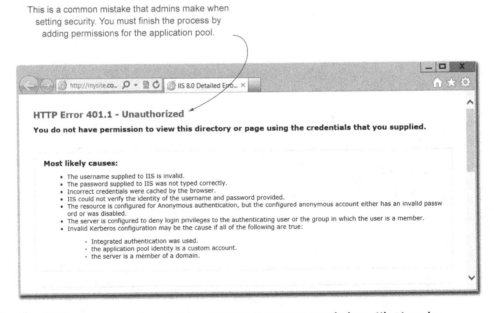

Figure 7.15   Someone made a mistake—there's still one more permission setting to make.

7.2.2 *Configuring application pools permissions*

The most common mistake when setting website and application permissions is to forget about the application pool for the site. Remember that application pools have a worker process that handles client requests and supplies the web pages to the clients. The worker process needs to have access to the web pages.

Before you adjusted the permissions, the application pool gained access to the website using the group Users. That group gets removed so you can customize permissions as you did in the last section. There are two steps to this:

1 Setting the application pool identity
2 Setting the application pool permissions

Before you set the permissions for the application pool to the web pages, let's make sure the application pool is using the best identity for security.

STEP 1: SETTING THE APPLICATION POOL IDENTITY

Application pools have a special security context (identity) that provides the application pool with minimum permissions required to operate. In the Advanced Settings of the application pool, you can see this identity (see figure 7.16), called Application-PoolIdentity.

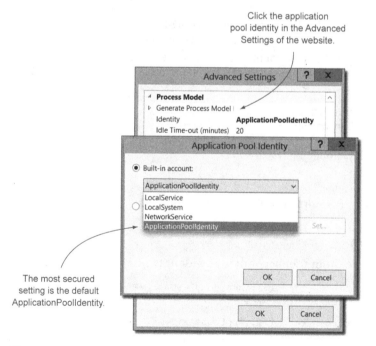

Figure 7.16 **Verify the application pool identity is set to ApplicationPoolIdentity for best security.**

The ApplicationPoolIdentity identity is the best and most secured one to use. The others listed involve backwards-compatibility support for older versions of IIS applications, so don't choose them unless needed by an older application.

> **Above and beyond**
>
> It's possible to create a custom account (known as app pool isolation), but your best bet is to use the default ApplicationPoolIdentity in IIS 7.5 and 8.
>
> App pool isolation is used for web servers that are hosting multiple websites for different customers. The idea is to protect the website and application pool of CustomerA from CustomerB located on the same server. This is a common practice in large hosted environments, but if you're not dealing with that specific concern, stick to the default identity.

You can also set the application pool identity using PowerShell. Here are some examples. Here's how to get the current identity:

```
PS> Get-ItemProperty -Path IIS:\AppPools\MyTest -Name
    ➥ProcessModel.IdentityType
```

> **Application pool identity values for PowerShell**
>
> When using PowerShell to change the app pool identity, you must use a specific number that represents the account. The values are Int32 (integers). I found this on MSDN years ago, but here are the identities and their corresponding numbers:
>
> LocalSystem = 0
> LocalService = 1
> NetworkService = 2
> SpecificUser = 3
> ApplicationPoolIdentity = 4

To set an identity (example for NetworkService):

```
PS> Set-ItemProperty -Path IIS:\AppPools\MyTest -Name
    ➥ProcessModel.IdentityType -Value 2
```

To set your own custom user account as the identity:

```
PS> Set-ItemProperty -Path IIS:\AppPools\MyTest -Name
    ➥processmodel.identityType -Value 3

PS> Set-ItemProperty -Path IIS:\AppPools\MyTest -Name processmodel.username -
    ➥Value Administrator

PS> Set-ItemProperty -Path IIS:\AppPools\MyTest -Name processmodel.password -
    ➥Value P@ssw0rd
```

With the identity configured, the second part of this process is to set the NTFS permissions for the application pool.

Application pool
identities are located on
the web server.

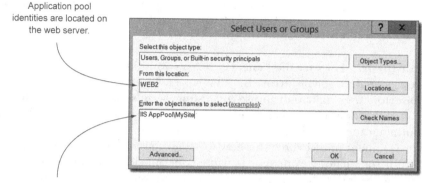

The syntax is unique:
IIS AppPool\<yourappPool>.

Figure 7.17 Configuring permissions for an application pool

STEP 2: SETTING THE APPLICATION POOL PERMISSIONS

To assign permission for the application pool, open the Security tab for your website as you did in the last section. Add a new entry, but instead of typing the name of a user or group, notice the special name shown in figure 7.17.

Using the unique (and required) syntax, enter your application pool into the list. That's it! Now when you attempt to log in to the website using a username that's been granted permission, as in figure 7.18, you'll be successful.

Testing access
by using an account
that has permissions
to the website

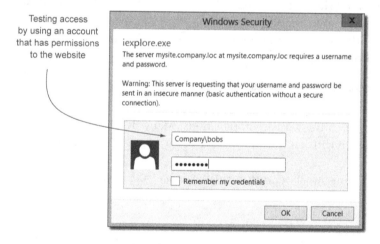

Figure 7.18 Login prompt to test security permissions

Notice in my example that I used the username BobS (Bob Smith) to log in. The client section of the testpage.asp (see figure 7.19) will display his name, confirming that the user was permitted access.

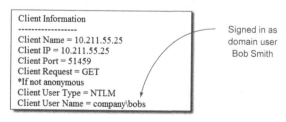

Signed in as
domain user
Bob Smith

Figure 7.19 Successful authentication of a test user account

This is a great time to relax for a moment and try out this process. In the lab you'll perform this process again, but I find a simple example helps to understand the process better.

> **TRY IT NOW**   Let's try the same Try It Now you did earlier, except this time you shouldn't get an error. In your lab environment create a new Active Directory user that you can use for testing permission access. I created one called Bob Smith, but you can pick whatever name you like. Also, enable basic authentication to get a login prompt. Remember, do this only in your lab environment until I show you how to secure basic in chapter 9. Assign Bob Smith (or whatever your user is named) permissions to your website. Make sure to remove the Users group. Assign the website application pool permissions and attempt to log in to the website.

Wow, you've accomplished a lot in this chapter so far and are probably ready for the lab, but hang on—by my count you've only seen three of the five authentication methods. You've also configured NTFS permissions for your user and groups, but I still need to show you a faster way to control permissions for ASP.NET sites.

7.3   *Advanced/Optional access control*

So far you've experienced the heart of setting up security for your websites and applications. In this section I want to briefly describe an additional (optional) way of assigning security to a website or application written in ASP.NET. I also want to show you a few more authentication methods, such as URL, forms-based, and client certificate authentication, that you may find useful someday. Let's start with another way to set security for ASP.NET applications.

7.3.1   *Setting authorization rules for ASP.NET applications*

Authorization rules were introduced in IIS 7 as an easier method to assign permissions for users and groups for ASP.NET applications. Many developers who write ASP.NET applications prefer URL authorization and often configure security directly in the Web.config file.

To use URL authorization you must first install the component. Here's how to install it using PowerShell:

```
PS> Add-Windowsfeature web-url-auth
```

Once it's installed you can open the URL authorization settings for your ASP.NET website or application and configure the users and groups that should be permitted access (see figure 7.20).

You can use Windows identities or Active Directory identities or you can create your own users and groups directly on the website.

If you're interested in going deeper into authorization rules, don't worry. I'll post information on MoreLunches.com. You can also check out this article on Microsoft's TechNet: http://mng.bz/FULn.

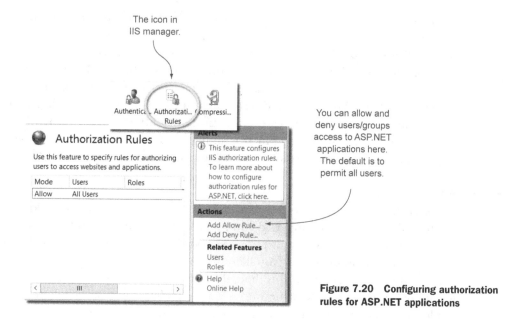

Figure 7.20 Configuring authorization rules for ASP.NET applications

7.3.2 Forms-based authentication

Forms-based authentication is common for products such as Microsoft Exchange and SharePoint. Instead of seeing a login prompt, the client is redirected to a web page where they can enter their credentials.

Forms-based authentication permits the web designer/developer to create a custom-branded web page for login rather than the ugly popup prompt. There isn't much for a web admin to do to configure forms-based authentication. Most of the hard work, such as making the form page, is done by the developer. When you install the component ASP.NET, forms-based authentication will appear in the IIS manager authentication settings and can be enabled if needed.

Forms-based authentication is like basic in that usernames and passwords are transmitted in clear text, so you should have SSL in place before turning this feature on. In chapter 9 you'll set up certificates and SSL to protect this authentication mechanism. For more information see http://mng.bz/tc11.

7.3.3 Client certificate authentication

Client certificate authentication uses certificates rather than usernames and passwords to give clients access to a website or application. The certificate is mapped to a user account on the web server or from Active Directory which has permissions to the website. When the client connects to the website and presents the certificate, they're granted access.

This has the benefit of reducing possible attacks from hackers because clients don't type usernames and passwords (which hackers try to crack); instead they present the certificate. If you don't have the certificate, you don't get access.

To implement this type of authentication, you need a firm understanding of certificates, certificate authorities, and mapping certificates to accounts. That's outside the scope of this book, but you should be aware of the capability. You can find additional information about client certificate authentication at http://mng.bz/Cli9.

Let's move on to the lab and practice setting security on a couple of websites to test the authentication mechanisms and NTFS filesystem security.

7.4   Lab

The security for outside users to access the bike shop websites has been determined, but the bike shop hasn't purchased and implemented certificates yet. Because of this, they don't want to test with outside users because usernames and passwords would cross the internet in plain text (you'll do this in chapter 9).

To test security options at this time, the bike shop would like to perform internal testing using users from their network. You'll establish and test the internal security model and later (in chapter 9) modify the security for outside user access.

This lab is challenging. You'll need to create some users in your VM Active Directory and assign security for them. When you make users, you can name them however you like, but I provided some names to make the lab easier. Assign each user a password (which you'll have to remember). Try your best to complete the tasks without checking the answer key. If you get stuck, don't hesitate to get the step-by-step answer at MoreLunches.com.

TRY IT NOW

In case you didn't get a chance to perform the Try It Now sections, I've repeated them here for your convenience. Once complete, you can start the lab with task 1.

1   Use one of your existing websites or make a new one for this chapter and change the anonymous authentication user from IUSR to the application pool identity. Make sure to verify that your website works using the special test page you created in an earlier chapter.

2   Make sure you have a test page with the client settings discussed at the beginning of the chapter. Install and enable Windows authentication. Be sure to disable anonymous authentication. Access the website (you may have to log on the first time) and notice the client section on the web page. It should display your Windows authentication username, as shown in figure 7.6.

3   In your virtual lab environment you can enable basic authentication for testing. But don't do this in production until you've completed chapter 9 and have secured this with SSL. If you want to try it out now, disable all other authentication methods and enable basic. Access your website and note that you're prompted for a username and password.

4 If you want to start practicing with this now, you can, but remember it's not going to work yet. Feel free to wait until after the next section. In your lab environment, create a new Active Directory user you can use for testing permission access. I created one called Bob Smith, but you can pick whatever name you like. And I want you to get a login prompt, so enable basic authentication. Remember: do this only in your lab environment until I show you how to secure basic in chapter 9. Assign Bob Smith (or whatever your user is named) permissions to your website. Make sure to remove the Users group. You can now attempt to log in, but remember you'll get an error similar to the one in figure 7.15.

TASK 1

First up, you need some users and groups to represent the internal network of the bike shop. In Active Directory make three Organization Units with the following users:

- OU named Sales with two users, Bob Smith and Sally Smith. Create a group called Sales and add the two users to the group.
- OU named Mechanics with two users, Meefy and Millie. Assign them to a group named Mechanics.
- OU named RegUsers with two users, Frank Smith and Jill Smith. Create and assign the users to a group named RegUsers.

TASK 2

In this lab you'll use basic authentication (not Windows authentication) to force a login prompt for testing. If you use Windows authentication, you'll need to log off/ log in to your entire desktop each time, so for the sake of convenience, basic authentication will be used.

Enable basic authentication for all three websites. In your internal testing environment, there's no risk in not having certificates at this time. Make sure to disable anonymous authentication on each site.

TASK 3

Assign security for the three websites using the following security guidelines:

- The Administrator (you) should be able to access all websites.
- The WebBikez site should be accessible by the group RegUsers and Bob Smith.
- The WebBikezRepair site should be accessible by the group RegUsers and Mechanics.
- The WebBikezUsedBike site should only be accessible to Jill Smith. Jill needs *write* ability to copy photos into the site.

TASK 4

Before testing can begin, the application pools need to have permissions set to the websites. Using PowerShell verify that the application pools all have the identity ApplicationPoolIdentity. Assign the application pools' NTFS permissions to their respective websites.

TASK 5

The bike shop wants you to use several test scenarios to validate the security model. In each case you should access the website using your web browser and be prompted with a login. Using the user accounts described, test whether they have access to the site. Here are the scenarios:

- Can you (the Administrator) access all three sites? Why?
- Can Bob Smith access the WebBikez site? Why?
- Can Meefy access the WebBikez site? Why?
- Can Millie access the WebBikezRepair site? Why?
- Can Sally access the WebBikezUsedBike site? Why?

7.5   *Ideas to try on your own*

You can't practice this enough. When you have some time, I want you to add your own users and groups and set additional security. Make up your own scenarios and try them out. The real test is to examine a production web server and see whether the security is up to snuff.

Also, try out URL authorization and add user access to ASP.NET websites with this method. The WebBikez site is a good place to try that out.

Securing the server

Any time you "plug" something into the internet—a web server, mail server, or your phone for the latest sport scores—you've opened up a hole that some malicious person (or bot) can attack. You already know this. Preventing these attacks is a constant battle.

Can you prevent all possible attacks from the internet with 100% certainty? Yes, if you don't attach anything to the internet. That's unreasonable, so the goal is to protect your web server (and therefore your customers) as best you can within the budget you have available.

Internet security is a vast and complicated topic, and I can't cover it all in a single chapter. My goal in this chapter is to show you the types of attacks that may affect you and suggest a common-sense approach with hardware and software firewalls to secure your web server. You'll implement built-in IIS features such as IP/domain restrictions to assist in the effort. I want you to have additional resources if you need to go deeper. You're not alone in this endeavor. From the developers writing the applications, Microsoft updating and patching IIS to prevent security weaknesses, and your overall network security (firewalls), you can provide a reasonably secured environment.

So far in this book you've built and secured the websites for the WebBikez bike shop. Now the focus changes to securing the web server. Let's first look at who and what is attacking you and how to prevent those attacks.

8.1   *Network protection for IIS*

You'll examine several best practices in this chapter that will help you secure your web servers, depending on how many you need to protect and your available budget. It helps to have an understanding of *what* is attacking you. This section starts out by describing the types of attacks commonly faced by your web server today and then dives into firewall and monitoring options to protect your web server from these attacks.

8.1.1   *What are you worried about?*

I find that the more I understand about security and the types of attacks that a web server may face, the better I can help avoid those risks. As the web administrator you can't always control all aspects of securing your web servers with only IIS tools (although you did a great job in the last chapter). You may need other people, or teams of people, to help with network security. Most of the attacks can be mitigated with a good third-party firewall, discussed in the next section.

What kinds of attacks might you face? Mostly *bots*—automated script attacks. But occasionally a human attempting to do harm may be behind an attack. I cover the most common attacks here.

> **Above and beyond**
>
> Want more information? I provide a good starting point for you here, but it's not complete or exhaustive by any means. Many internet resources have a wealth of additional information, but I like checking current attack trend reports, like the WhiteHat Statistics report at www.whitehatsec.com.

CROSS-SITE SCRIPTING

This type of attack is the most common attack today. It typically involves an attack based on a weakness or security hole in the browser (called an *exploit*). A hacker uses the exploit to inject a client-side script into web pages that other users are viewing. The script is executed in the browser on the client, launching embarrassing ads and infecting the client with malware. As an admin, recognizing a cross-site scripting attack and alerting the security team is essential. Preventing this type of attack is done through the web page code; the developer of the application should use good, secured coding practices to help avoid these problems.

INFORMATION LEAKAGE

Information leakage is a generic term describing the possibility of attack from leaking sensitive information or technical details through the normal use of a website. Typical examples are error messages that provide too much detail about web servers and scripting comments that may contain database passwords. Good coding practices generally have the most impact on this. It's difficult for an admin to control this for all applications without the support of a third-party firewall.

CONTENT SPOOFING

This is a similar attack to cross-site scripting, only without the script. Instead the hacker defaces the website, replacing images or adding banners. Content spoofing can be prevented with good coding practices, third-party firewalls, and IIS's request filtering (discussed later in this chapter).

CROSS-SITE REQUEST FORGERY

Commonly abbreviated CSRF, this is an attack using the customer's (user's) existing, trusted connection to another website. A user visits a new website that maliciously attempts to use their stored credentials to access another website that the user frequents, such as Facebook. The malicious site posts spam or other content to Facebook without the user's knowledge. Again, good coding practices, firewalls, and request filtering will help avoid this, as discussed later.

SQL INJECTION ATTACKS

This type of attack is accomplished by including portions of SQL commands in a URL that can exploit the database. You can prevent injection attacks by filtering the URLs so that these commands aren't permitted. IIS and most third-party firewalls have this filtering capability. IIS has a request filter that can be enabled for this purpose.

In fact IIS has components to help protect against all these types of attacks, and you'll learn those in this chapter. Although the components in IIS are helpful, you should consider additional firewall products specifically designed to prevent these attacks. The next section discusses the options available to you when considering additional firewall protection.

8.1.2 *Firewall security*

The best security for your web servers is a firewall to protect them. You have many choices to choose from, including the built-in Windows Firewall and add-on third-party firewalls. Choosing the right firewall for your company is a decision outside the scope of this book, but your decision should employ protection from the type of web attacks already discussed. My goal in this section is to illuminate some of the available options based on size, price, and configuration complexity. You probably already have a firewall in place working to protect your web servers, but if you don't, this is a good place to start gaining firewall knowledge.

There's a longstanding debate about hardware versus software firewalls, and I'm certain that you've heard the arguments or even been part of them. I see advantages to both types. Small web server implementations can save on costs without sacrificing quality using a software firewall. Hardware-based firewalls are more expensive and require more knowledge to configure but can handle much larger implementations and traffic.

Let's talk about both options, starting with software-based firewalls.

SOFTWARE FIREWALLS

Software-based firewalls are generally easier to implement and a little more cost-effective for smaller web server implementations. There are two types:

- Windows Application Firewall (WAF)
- Infrastructure firewall

A WAF is a high-quality firewall that's installed directly on the web server (see Figure 8.1). The built-in Windows Firewall provides only basic port blocking, whereas WAFs provide greater protection against the types of attacks discussed earlier. WAFs also collect and monitor your IIS logs and display critical logging information, such as attacks from bots, easily. This is an enormous benefit because trying to track and block an attack using PowerShell or other simple IIS logging tools isn't practical.

Windows Application Firewalls are practical and affordable for single or small web server implementations. They provide excellent protection and don't require the changes to your infrastructure that a hardware firewall requires. Products such as Port80Software's Server Defender (www.port80software.com) and those at www.white-hatsec.com are great examples of WAF type software.

An infrastructure firewall, although software-based, is similar to a hardware-based firewall, as shown in figure 8.2. It's placed between the web server and the internet. All requests go through the firewall, where the requests can be scanned and filtered, similar to a WAF. But with the firewall in front of the web server, it can protect more web servers.

Software firewalls, including WAFs, have graphical interfaces to make them easier to configure and monitor, and they're generally less expensive than their hardware-based

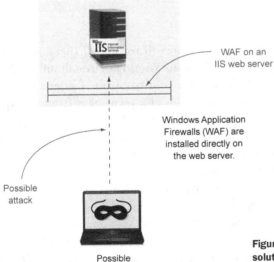

WAF on an
IIS web server

Windows Application
Firewalls (WAF) are
installed directly on
the web server.

Possible
attack

Possible
hacker

Figure 8.1   A WAF is a cost-effective solution for even the smallest web server implementation.

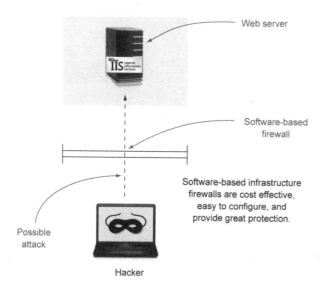

Web server

Software-based
firewall

Software-based infrastructure
firewalls are cost effective,
easy to configure, and
provide great protection.

Possible
attack

Hacker

**Figure 8.2 Software-based firewalls
are less complex than hardware-
based firewalls but still provide good
performance for small and medium
companies.**

cousins. A typical example of a software-based firewall is Microsoft's Threat Management Gateway (TMG), which is a full-featured firewall that can prevent the types of attacks discussed earlier.

Software firewalls have incorrectly gotten a bad reputation for being slower than hardware-based firewalls and not as secure. Although they generally aren't designed to handle as much traffic as a hardware-based firewall, you may not need that level of performance. The security of the firewall, or the ability of a hacker to directly attack a firewall, is a real concern, though not as much as it used to be. Years ago attacks to the operating system the firewall software was installed on could open weaknesses, but that's largely been removed as a concern today.

On the other hand, if performance is high on your list and you have many web servers, you may need to consider a hardware firewall.

HARDWARE FIREWALLS

Cisco Systems and Barracuda Networks are great examples of top-of-the line hardware firewall manufacturers. In fact many infrastructure and security specialists won't consider anything less. Hardware-based firewalls provide a high level of performance for larger web server implementations (see figure 8.3). Choosing the best firewall for your performance needs depends heavily on the amount of traffic (number of users) on your websites and the number of web servers you need to protect. You'll examine how to collect performance data to assist in this decision later in the book, but keep in mind that protecting web servers may in fact be only part of the decision process when purchasing firewalls. The protection of other server types and resources, along with firewall features such as VPN needed for other aspects of the business, will also play an important role.

Hardware firewalls have been traditionally trusted for network security; they're fast and reliable, mainly due to proprietary hardware and software. A hacker has a hard

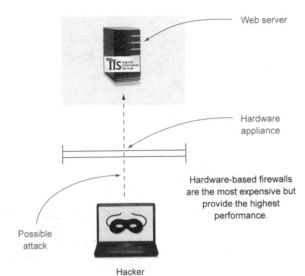

Web server

Hardware
appliance

Hardware-based firewalls
are the most expensive but
provide the highest
performance.

Possible
attack

Hacker

**Figure 8.3   For some security engineers
a hardware-based platform from Cisco or
Barracuda is the only answer.**

time cracking them because of the closely guarded secrets of the proprietary hardware and operating system.

The biggest challenge to implementing hardware-based firewalls is cost, and I don't mean merely the cost of the hardware, which can range from $500 to tens of thousands of dollars, depending on performance and feature demands. Infrastructure and additional purchases of switches and cabling changes will need to be made, not to mention an experienced engineer to configure the firewall. The *total cost of ownership* (TCO) should be planned for to make sure that it meets your company's *return on investment* (ROI). Purchasing and implementing a costly hardware-based solution for a single web server that could have easily been protected with a WAF isn't practical. Don't get me wrong—hardware-based firewalls are considered the best practice by many security engineers. Make sure your firewall design meets your needs.

8.1.3   Using the Windows Firewall

This section on firewalls wouldn't be complete without a brief discussion of the built-in Windows Firewall. I'm sure you have plenty of experience with this firewall; it's turned on by default and lives on every Windows OS client and server.

The Windows Firewall is a basic port-blocking firewall and, when combined with a few of the built-in features of IIS, such as domain blocking and request filtering (discussed shortly), can provide some level of good protection. I do want to point out that Windows Firewall isn't intended to provide the kind of protection you get from a WAF, Microsoft TMG, or other third-party firewall. It wasn't designed for that purpose. That doesn't mean you should go turn it off. Every ounce of protection is helpful, but don't rely on it as your only option. A good WAF or hardware-based solution designed to prevent the multitude of attacks discussed earlier is the best option.

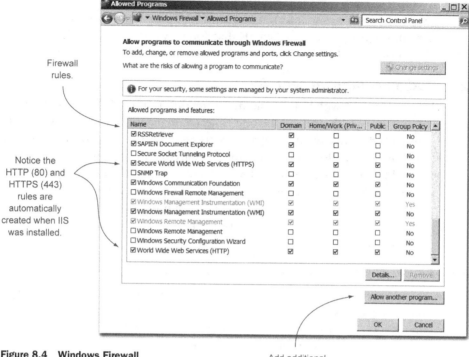

Firewall rules.

Notice the HTTP (80) and HTTPS (443) rules are automatically created when IIS was installed.

Figure 8.4   Windows Firewall rules for HTTP and HTTPS

Add additional ports here.

One thing you do need to do regardless of your firewall solution is set the Windows Firewall on the web server to allow access for the ports you use for your websites. By default when IIS is installed on a server, it opens ports 80 and 443, so those are already configured, as shown in figure 8.4.

You should open Control Panel and check these settings to make sure ports 80 and 443 are open.

TRY IT NOW   This is a good time to check the firewall on your web server to verify that ports 80 and 443 are open. You can access Windows Firewall in Control Panel, in the System and Security category. Select the Firewall option and view the current configuration. The Windows Firewall will list HTTP and HTTPS as being open.

The rule of thumb to follow is to not permit ports that you don't need. For example, later in this book you'll secure several of the bike shop's websites for HTTPS. If there are no public websites that need HTTP (80), then you can close that port.

The most common mistake made when using the Windows Firewall, or any firewall for that matter, is that if you create a website binding that needs a different port than 80 or 443, you need to open that port at the firewall. You'll see an example of that when you configure the web server for remote management.

Once a good quality firewall is in place and configured, you're ready to connect your web server to the internet and allow the public to access your websites. IIS contains more protection components that you may find useful as additions to your overall security plan. Let's take a look at some of those in the next section.

8.2 Adding additional security

In today's world, with bots constantly trying different types of attacks to penetrate web servers, the best choice and the one easiest to manage is a third-party firewall solution, as discussed earlier. Small companies starting out with a new website may not have the initial budget to afford a software- or hardware-based firewall. For those cases, IIS contains additional components that, when combined with Windows Firewall, can provide a good level of security until a better solution can be employed.

This section examines two of the more common protection components in IIS: IP Address and Domain Restrictions, and Request Filtering. First up: blocking unwanted networks and domains.

8.2.1 Blocking by network: IP and domain restrictions

IIS can provide IP address and domain blocking to prevent known hacker-based networks from accessing and attacking your server. You can manually add these addresses to an Allow or Deny list. Normally this is handled by the firewall solutions discussed earlier, but if you're starting out and don't have one of those firewalls yet, IP Address and Domain Restrictions is a good feature to use if you know who's attacking you.

> **Above and beyond**
>
> For IIS 7.5 and IIS 8, a recently released Dynamic IP Address Blocking feature can be added to IIS. This reduces the management time by dynamically building a Deny list. Check www.IIS.Net for more details if you're interested.

The IP Address and Domain Restrictions component isn't installed by default. It's listed under the Security categories, and you can quickly install it using PowerShell:

```
PS> Add-WindowsFeature Web-IP-security
```

Once installed, a new icon will appear in the IIS management section of the IIS manager. As illustrated in figure 8.5, you can click to create Allow and Deny entries for the networks you want to permit or block.

By default you don't have the ability to block by domain names; if you want that feature, you have to turn it on. The reason it's not turned on by default is that it requires the web server to do additional work every time a request is made. To block a domain, the web server has to perform a reverse lookup in DNS, and that impacts performance. To enable IP Address and Domain Restrictions, choose Edit Feature Settings from the Actions menu and select Enable domain name restrictions, as illustrated in figure 8.5.

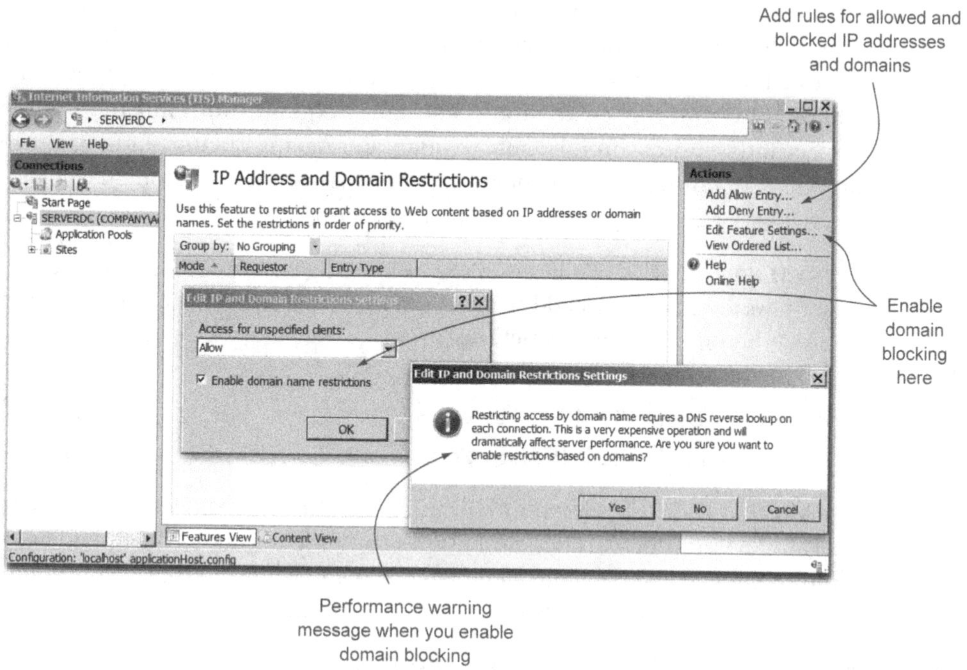

Add rules for allowed and
blocked IP addresses
and domains

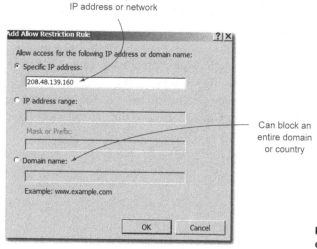

Enable
domain
blocking
here

Performance warning
message when you enable
domain blocking

Figure 8.5   Enabling the domain blocking feature

Also notice the performance-warning message that's displayed when you enable this feature (figure 8.5).

When adding your own rule, you specify the IP address, network range, or domain name to allow or block, as shown in Figure 8.6.

Blocking a specific
IP address or network

Can block an
entire domain
or country

**Figure 8.6   Adding a rule to allow
or deny an IP address or domain**

Rules can be created at the server level, affecting all websites, and at the individual website level for custom restrictions. The IP Address and Domain Restrictions component of IIS is a good tool that's only limited by the time-consuming management of adding and removing restrictions. The time required will limit the number of web servers and websites you'll be able to maintain. Again, a better solution is a third-party firewall that can make this easier. Many of those solutions automatically detect a poison network and notify you to add the restriction.

> **TRY IT NOW** The WebBikez web server is facing a series of attacks. The bicycle shop would like you to add IP and domain restrictions. Install the component and add the following restrictions:
>
> IP address Deny: 208.48.139.160
>
> IP network Deny: 208.48.140.0/24
>
> Domain name Deny: RuffBikes.Com

Blocking networks and domains has limited usefulness; you can't block everything, or no one can visit your websites. Sometimes you have to examine the request that's coming into your web server and determine if it's harmful. IIS has a component named Request Filtering for this need.

8.2.2   *Block common attacks using Request Filtering*

The ability to examine and discard an HTTP request based on something you don't like inside the request is one of the most important tactics to prevent hackers from ruining your websites. IIS's Request Filtering is a powerful tool for web security specialists and developers because it adds a layer of request protection if no third-party solutions are present on the network. Several different types of filters can be configured, from blocking file types to preventing SQL strings (injection attacks).

The challenge with the Request Filtering built into IIS is that you must know what you want to block and then configure it for the server and individual websites. This is similar to IP Address and Domain Restrictions in that you must already know what you need to add. I don't want to sound like a broken record, but this is another example of why a WAF or hardware-based firewall, which already has these configurations and can automatically add detected bad requests, is the best recommendation.

Still, a small shop like our bicycle shop may find use for Request Filtering until the time comes for a third-party solution. Figure 8.7 shows the categories of filters that can be added.

Each tab has an Allow/Deny
for the different filter types.

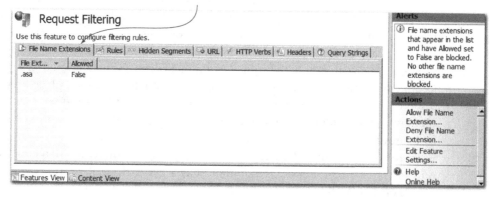

Figure 8.7 Adding Allow/Deny criteria to the different filters

Request Filtering can be configured to handle several types of situations, including the following:

- *File Name Extensions*—List of filename extensions allowed or denied access. By default IIS permits all file types. You may want to block the request of .gif files or code pages such as .js.

- *The Rules tab*—Specific parameters such as headers and filename extensions that will be scanned.

- *Hidden Segments*—A segment is the part of the URL path that lies between the slash (/) marks. The request filter will deny access to hidden segments, which don't display in directory listings.

- *Deny URL Sequences*—Blocks specific URL text from being received such as double dots (..). These double dots can be an indication a hacker is trying to move out of the content area by moving up a level in the directory.

- *HTTP Verbs*—Specifies a list of HTTP verbs that will be allowed or denied access.

- *Headers*—Specifies the headers and their size limits that will be denied access.

- *Query Strings*—Blocks query strings such as those used for SQL injection attacks.

Configuring each selection is a straightforward click of a button. There are detailed steps at http://mng.bz/mO01, but I bet you won't need them. The challenge in adding an Allow or Deny is discovering what needs to be added. Many third-party firewalls can detect attacks and offer to adjust rules. Again, the details of web security are outside the scope of this book, but if you want to become part of the security team at your company, look for a web security hacking book like *Hacking Exposed Web Applications*, 3rd Edition, by Joel Scambray, Vincent Liu, and Caleb Sima (McGraw-Hill, 2010).

In the next section I discuss a couple more tools that may help if you think you're under attack, and then it's time for a short lab before you end your lunch.

8.3 *Monitoring process for hacking*

Security, and web security in particular, is a career all by itself. As the web administrator you should be able to properly secure your websites and servers (as you're doing in this book), but every additional ounce of knowledge about security can be used to assist the security/firewall team and developers along the way.

The tools mentioned here require additional research and study, but if you want to become more involved in the security side of the web, this is a good place to start. Plan to spend some time reading the *Hacking Exposed* series of books. If you dive in deep, you may even consider a certification such as the Certified Information Systems Security Professional (CISSP).

In this section you'll be exposed to a couple of methods for detecting whether your server is under attack. Remember that a good firewall prevents this, but it's always good to check.

8.3.1 *Logging files*

One day in the office you receive a few emails complaining that the website seems slow. After checking into it you notice that the website and the server are reacting slowly without apparent reason, so you inspect the situation further by scanning the log files.

As discussed in chapter 6, you can parse (search) through the IIS log files for information using PowerShell or a free tool such as Log Parser. Using PowerShell you can create scripts to look for specific requests, the number of requests from an IP address, and much more. Later in this book I show you how to make some scripts for performance and capacity planning when monitoring your logs.

When it comes to security monitoring, although it's possible to write scripts to monitor the logs for security events, it isn't practical for two reasons:

- You need to script for every possible security threat that might impact your web server, including injection attacks, content spoofing—all possibilities.
- You need to make decisions when an attack is occurring or has occurred, such as adding an IP address Deny rule.

For experienced web security engineers, that's a normal day, but for most of us inadvertent IIS admins, we need some help. Here's an example: suppose you want to monitor your logs for specific 404 errors that are generated when Request Filter denies an HTTP request. You locate the 404 errors on Microsoft's www.iis.net site (table 8.1).

Table 8.1 HTTP 404 sub-status codes

HTTP Sub-status	Description
404.5	URL sequence denied
404.6	Verb denied
404.7	File extension denied

Table 8.1　HTTP 404 sub-status codes *(continued)*

HTTP Sub-status	Description
404.8	Hidden namespace
404.10	Request header too long
404.11	URL double escaped
404.12	URL has high bit chars
404.13	Content length too large
404.14	URL too long
404.15	Query string too long
404.18	Query string sequence denied
404.19	Denied by filtering rule

You can use PowerShell to look for these errors in your logs. In chapter 6 you searched your logs for basic information, but let me give you a reminder here of an example scanning for a 404.5 error:

```
PS> Get-ChildItem -Path C:\inetpub\logs -Filter *.log -Recurse | Select-
➥ String -SimpleMatch "404.5"
```

You could create a series of these searches and save them as a PowerShell script, but that's a lot of work. This is when I turn to my third-party firewall or WAF tool. Not only do these tools monitor the log files for every request made of the web server, they can also take action if a request looks suspicious. At 2:30 a.m. I'm sleeping, but my firewall is actively blocking the bots attacking my server. Microsoft built IIS with many options to support your security needs, but that assumes you're a security specialist and can manage the security throughout the day.

For security monitoring of your logs, the best practice is to use one of the firewall products discussed earlier and have those tools highlight issues and provide solutions.

8.3.2　*Using Process Explorer for IIS*

As a Windows administrator I'm sure you've heard of Sysinternals, a company originally run by diagnostic tool and security guru Mark Russinovich. Microsoft bought Sysinternals back in 2006, and the diagnostic and troubleshooting tools are still developed and released at http://mng.bz/sC82.

These tools are free to download and cover a wide variety of troubleshooting and diagnostic scenarios, such as locating non-legitimate processes and services and memory-leaking processes. Two tools that many IIS admins (and Windows admins in general) use are Process Explorer and Process Monitor. Think of Process Explorer as an advanced version of the Windows Task Manager. Using Process Explorer you can monitor processes and DLLs, see which files they have open, and find out who "owns" the process. Process Monitor shows real-time process activities, processing access, and registry entries and directories.

For IIS admins Process Explorer and Process Monitor can help monitor application pools and web application DLLs for memory leaks. A security person can use these tools to identify processes and DLLs that have been compromised or that shouldn't be running at all. As an example, if you were monitoring the logs for the bike shop website and noticed a lot of 404.14 errors (URL too long) from the Request Filter, that could indicate a hacker trying to inject or upload a virus. Using IP Address and Domain Restrictions, you block the attack, but then you notice your web server is performing slowly. This could be an indication of a memory leak from the attack. You could use Process Explorer and Process Monitor to identify the memory leak and possibly identify who attacked you before running your virus cleanup. If you think your web server has been attacked or compromised or has a virus, these tools can help identify and possibly trace the attack. For more, check out http://mng.bz/144G.

Armed with all this security information, your lunch is coming to an end. Before you go back to work, try the short lab.

8.4   Lab

This chapter focused on securing your network infrastructure to protect your web servers, which makes for a rather unusual lab. If you didn't do the chapter 8 Try It Now sections, you should, but there's something else I think you should do as well.

TRY IT NOW

In case you didn't get a chance to perform the Try It Now sections, I've repeated them here for your convenience. Once complete, you can do the lab (task 1 is the only task).

- This is a good time to check the firewall on your web server to verify that ports 80 and 443 are open. You can access Windows Firewall in Control Panel, in the System and Security category. Select the Firewall option and view the current configuration. The Windows Firewall will list HTTP and HTTPS as being open.
- The WebBikez web server is facing a series of attacks. The bicycle shop would like you to add IP and domain restrictions. Install the component and add the following restrictions:

  IP address Deny: 208.48.139.160
  IP network Deny: 208.48.140.0/24
  Domain name Deny: RuffBikes.Com

TASK 1

There's only one task for this lab and it gives you a chance to explore more about protecting your server. Your lab VM is perfect for some experimentation. To learn about firewalls and the protections they can provide, take a few minutes to download an evaluation copy of a WAF, such as Port80Software's Server Defender. Although I don't recommend any particular product, by trying out a WAF you can compare the amazing amount of control and monitoring that a third-party tool provides to trying to manage all of it yourself in IIS.

Building experience with a WAF can help you understand the features and benefits of other options, such as hardware-based firewalls. You'll be better equipped with the knowledge of which features to look for regarding web servers.

8.5 *Ideas to try on your own*

I've learned a lot about security from the real-world experience of working with IIS. You can too without the risk of losing a production server or website. Consider trying the following when you get a chance:

- If you have a spare computer around the office, install IIS with an evaluation copy of a WAF, create a couple websites, and place the web server on the internet if it's permissible by your network team. You can also try this at home using your internet connection. If possible, purchase an internet domain and set up a DNS record that points to your website. Experiment and, more importantly, monitor the types of attacks that are coming into your server and see how a good firewall is protecting you. Get comfortable with the log monitor in the tool you choose so you see and experience real attacks without danger. Good virus protection is recommended, and you shouldn't hesitate to format the hard drive after your experimentation just in case.
- Adding a little extra research to your lunch diet will help you be better prepared for the next big wave of attacks. By referencing a book from the *Hacking Revealed* series or another of your choice, you can better help your networking team and developers in their struggle to protect your websites and servers.

Protecting data with certificates

Are you comfortable entering your credit card information into a website? How about one that has no protection or encryption? Protecting sensitive data from prying eyes as it flies from your customer's computer to your website is a top responsibility of the administrator.

Secure Socket Layer (SSL) is an encryption technology created by Netscape to protect data from being stolen by encrypting the communication between the customer and the server. Every time you add https:// to a URL, you're using SSL encryption to protect your confidential data. The web requests are encrypted and (usually) sent through the firewall's default port of 443 to the website, which responds back over the encryption tunnel, as shown in figure 9.1.

To create an SSL encryption tunnel for HTTPS, you install a certificate—often purchased from a Certificate Authority (CA) or self-made. The certificate has an encryption mechanism that protects your customer's data from being stolen. The science behind this is called Public Key Infrastructure (PKI), which is beyond what we can cover here. But correctly obtaining, installing, and configuring certificates for your websites is what you'll do in this chapter.

Along the way you'll learn about the different certificate types and the process of installing an SSL certificate using a simple example on your own test server. Then you'll help WebBikez configure the secured websites for email, shopping, and more.

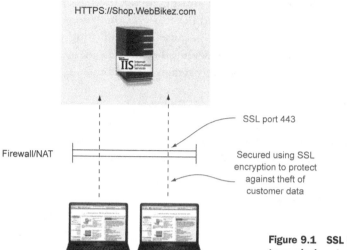

Figure 9.1 SSL (and certificates) encrypt transmissions to protect data from hackers.

Let's get started by examining the different types of certificates available so you can decide which one is right for you.

9.1 Not all certificates are the same

Choosing a certificate for your website is an important step in the process of securing transactions. Your users must feel comfortable supplying credit card and address information to your websites. Not all certificates are the same, and the type of certificate you purchase is important.

This section will help remove the confusion surrounding certificates so you can purchase the correct one for your needs. We'll examine trusted and non-trusted certificates and the primary types of certificates, such as High Assurance and Extended Validation, as well as single and multiple certificates.

Let's start with the differences between trusted and non-trusted certificates.

9.1.1 Trusted and non-trusted certificates

First and foremost, the certificate you install for your secured website will be trusted or non-trusted. *Trusted* means the customer's browser recognizes that the certificate is from a trusted Certificate Authority (CA) and will automatically install and use the certificate without displaying any error messages. To be a trusted certificate, the certificate must be generated from a trusted CA that appears in a list of trusted authorities in the security options of the browser. I'm sure you've heard of one or two of the major CAs, such as VeriSign, Thawte, and GoDaddy. For websites that need HTTPS, getting a certificate from a trusted CA is the best choice.

On the other hand, using a certificate that's not trusted—one that you create yourself (called Self-Signed) or one from a non-trusted authority—will result in a warning message informing the user that the website isn't trusted and could be harmful.

Non-trusted certificates are often used during initial testing of a website because they're free and easy to make. You should never use a non-trusted certificate once the website launches to customers, though, because of the warning messages customers will get. The idea is that the customer, seeing the warning messages, won't continue on to the website because it could possibly steal information from them.

9.1.2 *Types of certificates*

There are three types of certificates available today for web servers. Two of them— Extended Validation (EV) and High Assurance (HA)—are trusted, and one, Self-Signed, isn't. Self-Signed certificates should only be used for testing. Let's look at each of these options.

EXTENDED VALIDATION (EV) CERTIFICATE

The EV certificate, a trusted certificate, helps prevent phishing attacks. This certificate supplies a much higher level of confidence to your customers than the other certificates discussed here, but is also much more expensive, costing around $1,000 as compared to a $50 HA certificate. When you visit a website like www.verisign.com that uses an EV certificate, the address bar in your browser will turn green, as seen in figure 9.2. Obtaining an EV certificate also requires additional background checking and business verification on the part of the CA. This is the main reason why the certificate is so highly regarded.

> ### High Assurance (HA) certificate
>
> Most businesses purchase the High Assurance certificate. To obtain it, you need to validate your business address and that you own the domain (not nearly as extensive a check as for an EV certificate). When you visit a website that uses an HA certificate, the address bar in your browser remains unchanged, as in figure 9.3. You can obtain inexpensive HA certificates, ranging in price from $50 to a few hundred dollars from places such as www.GoDaddy.com.

Extended validation certificates are the best
security and change the browser bar to green.

Figure 9.2 An Extended Validation certificate is the best choice, and the most expensive.

High assurance certificates are the most common.
These certificates leave the address bar clear.

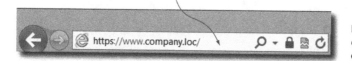

Figure 9.3 **High Assurance
certificates are a good,
economical choice.**

NON-TRUSTED OR SELF-SIGNED CERTIFICATE

As I mentioned earlier, you should only use a non-trusted certificate during testing of the website, not for production. Any certificate that has not been validated by an official Certificate Authority is considered dangerous. When you visit a website that's using a non-trusted certificate, you'll receive a warning message, and the navigation bar will turn red, as in figure 9.4.

A red bar is an indication that the website could be harmful. As you'll see later, a Self-Signed certificate is easy and quick to generate and is often used in the initial configuration of HTTPS for testing purposes. If you use one for testing, don't forget to replace it with a genuine trusted certificate before you move the website into production.

If your websites require SSL and are accessible to the public, you should use a trusted certificate. The price range for a certificate varies based on encryption quality and vendor, so you'll need to do some research to choose the best options for you.

9.1.3 *Single and multiple certificates*

The number of certificates you'll need to purchase is determined by two factors: the number of websites and the virtual IP addresses you use.

WHEN YOU NEED A SINGLE CERTIFICATE

Single certificates are created based on the URL of the website for which you want to use HTTPS. For the URL Shop.WebBikez.com, for example, you'll create a certificate using that URL. If you have additional websites such as Download.WebBikez.com and mail.WebBikez.com, you'll need to purchase an additional certificate for each URL.

If you have several websites, this can start to get expensive. There are two other types of certificates you can purchase to help reduce the cost.

Non-trusted and Self-Signed certificates are
bad (should only be used for testing) and
change the browser bar to red.

Figure 9.4 **Self-Signed certificates should only be generated and used for
testing purposes.**

WHEN YOU NEED MULTIPLE CERTIFICATES FOR THE SAME DOMAIN:
WILDCARD AND SAN CERTIFICATES

Suppose you have three websites on the same domain that all need SSL (HTTPS):

- Shop.WebBikez.com
- Download.WebBikez.com
- Mail.WebBikez.com

To save money, you don't want to purchase individual certificates for each of them. Because the websites are part of the same domain, you have two options: the Wildcard certificate and the Subject Alternate Name (SAN) certificate.

- *Wildcard certificate*—A Wildcard certificate for this example would have the common URL of *.WebBikez.com. With this type of certificate, you could add as many websites for the domain WebBikez.com as you wanted without the need to purchase additional certificates. Choose Wildcard certificates when you need the flexibility to be able to add a lot of sites quickly. Note that there's a possible security risk with Wildcard certificates in that a hacker could use your certificate to bring up a spoof website called HACK.WebBikez.com, and it would appear to be a trusted site. Although this type of hack is unlikely, you can prevent it with a SAN certificate.

- *SAN certificate*—The SAN certificate was originally created to replace the Wildcard because of the possibility of a spoofed website using your certificate. When you register a SAN certificate, you specify the URLs for each website. One certificate is generated for those specific URLs. This provides better security and easier management with one certificate and still reduces the cost because you're only purchasing a single certificate for the sites. Choose the SAN certificate if you're in a more stable environment.

Now that you have an idea of what types of certificates are available and which may be best for you, in the next section you'll start off by installing a single certificate for a single website. After getting that to work, you'll see the benefits of Wildcard and SAN certificates.

9.2   *Implementing certificates on a single IIS server*

Setting up certificates for your websites on IIS 7 and IIS 8 is virtually identical. I'll start by showing you the process of generating and completing a certificate request, and then in the next section you'll add an HTTPS binding and test the results. You'll do this on a simple default website first so you can get the process down. Then you'll look at adding the complexity of installing certificates for the WebBikez shop and face some challenges—and learn some tricks to resolve them.

The process begins in the IIS manager Server Certificates icon, as shown in figure 9.5. The Server Certificates storage is located on each web server, and certificates must be *imported* (copied) to each of the web servers that need them. Certificates are stored on each web server and assigned to a website by adding a new HTTPS binding.

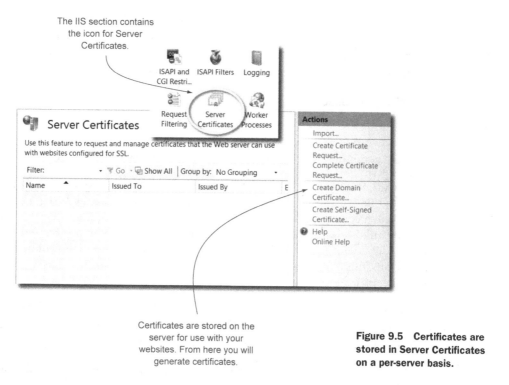

The IIS section contains
the icon for Server
Certificates.

Certificates are stored on the
server for use with your
websites. From here you will
generate certificates.

**Figure 9.5 Certificates are
stored in Server Certificates
on a per-server basis.**

NOTE   IIS 8 has a new feature to store certificates in a single centralized location for all of your web servers. This feature makes the management of certificate revokes and re-issues a snap compared to having them stored on the individual web servers. I discuss this feature in later chapters, when you have multiple web servers.

The server certificates pane is where you generate and complete a certificate request with your Certificate Authority. The actions pane lists four different certificate operations:

1 *Import*—This option imports an existing certificate into the Server Certificates. This is primarily used if you already have an existing certificate.

2 *Create/Complete Request*—These are the options to obtain a new certificate from a Certificate Authority. This process is the one I detail in this section.

3 *Create Domain Certificate*—A simpler version of the Create/Complete Request for networks that have their own online Certificate Authority, such as Microsoft Active Directory Certificate Services.

4 *Create Self-Signed Certificate*—Creates a non-trusted certificate for testing. This certificate shouldn't be used in production and will generate a red bar in a browser. This is a great option for when you're in the testing phase, though, before you purchase a trusted certificate.

The first step in the process is to get a certificate from a trusted source. The IIS manager will help you generate and complete the request from your preferred Certificate Authority. Although you're not going to purchase a real certificate now, let's start by generating the request.

9.2.1 Generating a request

Before a Certificate Authority can give you a certificate, you need to create a certificate request that contains the name (URL) of the website to secure. This is important; certificates are generated for the URL that your customers will type into their browsers.

> **NOTE** Although you won't purchase a certificate as you work through this chapter, I need to show you the process of working with a real CA to generate and install a certificate. In the Try It Now and Lab sections, instead of buying a certificate, I'll have you create a Self-Signed certificate. The Self-Signed certificate will be non-trusted—it will produce a red address bar. This will be fine for the lab, but make sure to refer back to this section when purchasing your trusted certificate.

Some Certificate Authorities can generate and produce the entire certificate on their website and will inform you of that when you buy it, but some don't, so I'll show you the process using the Generate Request option built into the IIS manager.

> **NOTE** Let me show you the process before you try it; wait for the Try It Now section.

Clicking the Create Request option in the server certificates pane will start the process of generating the request for your CA, as shown in figure 9.6.

The Request Certificate form contains two important pieces of information that are used to create and verify your certificate: the Common name and the Organization. The Common name is the URL for the website you want to secure. This must match the URL that your customers will type into their browser (without the https://).

The Organization information, including address, is the legal name and location of your company. During the validation process with your CA (you can expect a series of phone calls), you'll verify this information. Keep in mind that you can't abbreviate the City or State locations.

The next step in the process is to select the cryptographic provider and bit key length, as shown in figure 9.7.

If you're using the CA's website to request your certificate, then the CA determines which cryptographic provider you'll use, based on whichever firms it has chosen to support its certificates. If you're using the IIS manager to request your certificate, you'll usually be okay using the default provider. If your CA wants a specific provider, it'll provide that information on its website.

The key bit length determines the strength of your certificate: the larger the bit length, the stronger the certificate. You'll be tempted to create a bit length as large as

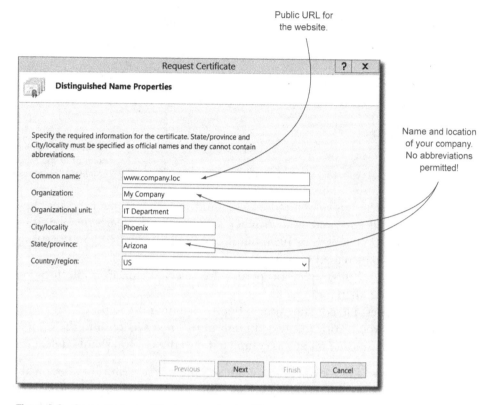

Public URL for the website.

Name and location of your company. No abbreviations permitted!

Figure 9.6 Generating a certificate request using IIS manager

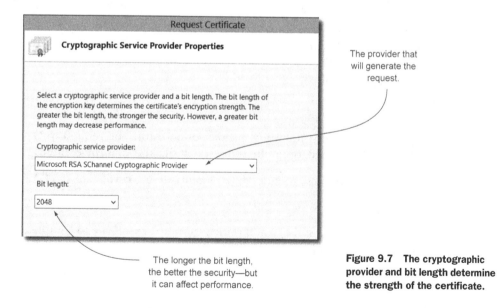

The provider that will generate the request.

The longer the bit length, the better the security—but it can affect performance.

Figure 9.7 The cryptographic provider and bit length determine the strength of the certificate.

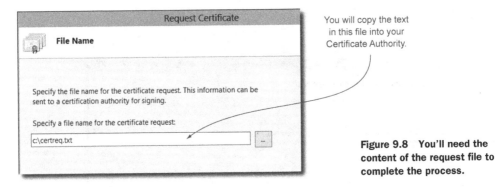

You will copy the text in this file into your Certificate Authority.

Figure 9.8 **You'll need the content of the request file to complete the process.**

the CA supports, but keep two things in mind: one, the stronger the key, the more the certificate will cost; and two, stronger keys can impact performance. It's common today to use a bit length of 1024, but this is gradually changing to the stronger 2048, mainly due to increased security concerns.

After the cryptographic properties are selected, specify a file location for the request, as shown in figure 9.8.

The request file contains your request, including the website URL and your company name. You'll copy this text content in the next section into the CA to complete the request. After the request is completed with the CA, you should delete this file.

> **TRY IT NOW** Even if you aren't ready to purchase a certificate with a real CA, this is a good time to get familiar with the process and create a sample request. Open the IIS manager, double-click the Server Certificates icon, and click Create Certificate Request. You won't be using this certificate, so use my example information to create the request. Enter the following:
>
> *Common Name*—www.TestDomain.com
> *Organization*—My Company
> *Organization Unit*—IT
> *City*—Denver
> *State*—Colorado
> *Country*—US
>
> Choose the default cryptographic properties and store the request to C:\testReq.txt. Using Notepad, open the request text file and view the content.

With the certificate request generated, let's complete the certificate at a CA.

9.2.2 Completing a request

Once you have the request file, you'll return to your CA's website to complete the process. Here are the general steps:

- Copy the request into the website.
- Select the type of certificate you want.

- Pay for it (not detailed—you have a credit card, right?).
- Download the certificate.

I want to demonstrate this process using Active Directory Certificate Services (ADCS). You may not have this available, but the process is similar regardless of whom you purchase your certificate from. Because you may not have ADCS available, I describe the process in detail, so no need to try this yet. Read along as we get started by submitting the request and selecting the certificate type.

SUBMITTING THE REQUEST

In figure 9.9 I'm using Microsoft Active Directory Certificate Services as my CA, so it may be a little different from your CA, but it's the same information.

With your CA, you'll copy the text from the request file into the CA's website. A mistake many administrators make the first time they create a certificate is choosing the wrong Certificate Template. Make sure to choose Web Server as the template. If you miss this, you'll need to contact the CA, delete the certificate, and start over.

COMPLETING AND DOWNLOADING THE REQUEST

In figure 9.10 the real certificate is generated and can be saved to disk or USB drive. Your third-party CA will email you the certificate file (.cer) after they verify that your

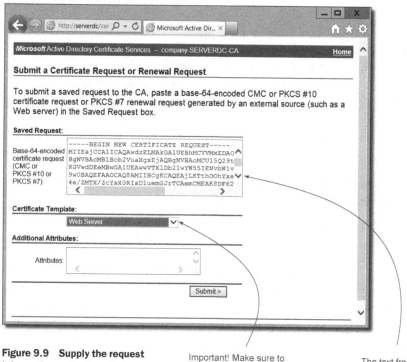

Figure 9.9 Supply the request information and select the Web Server Certificate Template.

Important! Make sure to generate a certificate for a web server!

The text from the certeq.txt file.

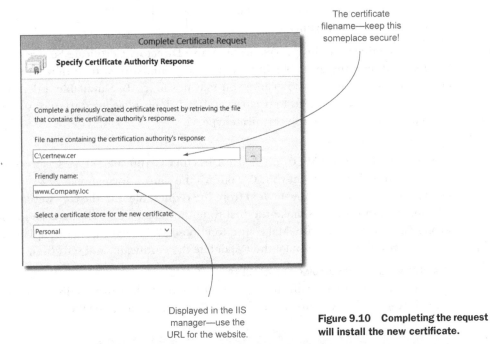

The certificate filename—keep this someplace secure!

Displayed in the IIS manager—use the URL for the website.

Figure 9.10   Completing the request will install the new certificate.

company is a legal entity. Click the Complete Certificate Request option to complete the process and install the certificate, as shown in figure 9.10.

When you complete the process, you'll assign the Friendly name. This name is displayed in the IIS manager and makes it easy to locate the certificate. I prefer to use the URL of the website the certificate is generated for, which makes it easy for me to keep track of.

Before you look at how to assign this certificate to your website, I want to show you how to put your certificate on multiple web servers using the Export/Import options.

9.2.3   *Exporting/Importing a certificate for backup and additional web servers*

If your web server should fail, and you don't have a backup of the certificate, you'll end up purchasing another one. Using a simple export process, you can make sure you have a copy of the certificate just in case. Later in this book you'll scale out IIS to handle additional performance load and reliability using load balancing. In these cases you'll have the same website across multiple servers. You'll need to have the certificate for the website located on each server as well. You can't copy the certificate from one server to another; you have to follow an export/import process.

Let's start by exporting a certificate that will act as a backup and that can also be imported to other servers.

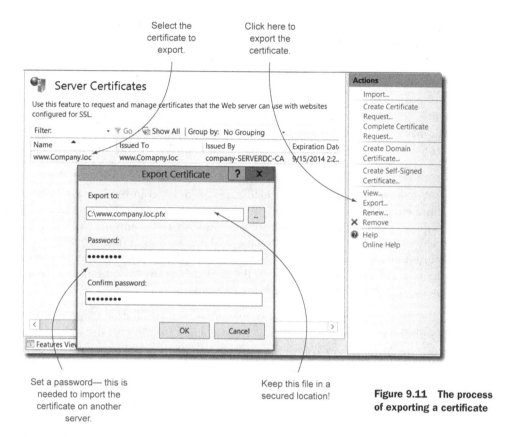

Figure 9.11   The process of exporting a certificate

EXPORTING A CERTIFICATE

On the server that currently holds the certificate, double-click the Server Certificates icon, select the certificate, and choose the Export option, as shown in figure 9.11.

Save the certificate as a .pfx file (an encrypted version of the certificate) and assign the file a password (figure 9.11). In the future, to import this file into a different server or restore the certificate to the same server, you'll need to supply the password.

> **TRY IT NOW** In the Server Certificates icon, create a Self-Signed certificate. You can make the Friendly name anything you like; this is only for an experiment. Once the certificate is created, note that it's listed in the IIS manager. Select the certificate and choose the Export option. Export the certificate to your C:\ drive. Once completed, delete (remove) the certificate in the IIS manager. Yup, go ahead and delete it as if a problem with the server occurred and you lost the certificate. In the next Try It Now, I'll have you import the certificate back into the Server Certificates.

Copy this file to a USB drive or someplace safe—don't leave the file on the server because it could be stolen. With a backup of your certificate, let's see how to restore a lost certificate or add the certificate to another server.

IMPORTING A CERTIFICATE

To import a certificate to another server, or back to the original server if the current certificate was deleted, use the Import option in the Server Certificates icon, as shown in figure 9.12.

Once the certificate has been imported, you'll see the certificate listed in the Server Certificates icon in the IIS manager.

> **TRY IT NOW** Bring back that certificate you deleted in the last Try It Now by importing the .pfx file. When you're finished, create a new certificate (Self-Signed is fine) for the default website on your test computer. You'll use this new certificate in the next section. Make sure that the Common name (Friendly name if using Self-Signed) matches the URL you type in the browser to test the website. As an example, if you have www.Company.loc in DNS, make sure the common name is www.Company.loc.

With a certificate safely installed on our web server, you'll now assign the certificate to the website. In the next section you'll create a new binding for the website and test the certificate. You'll also explore and solve some of the challenges you might run into with host-name–based bindings.

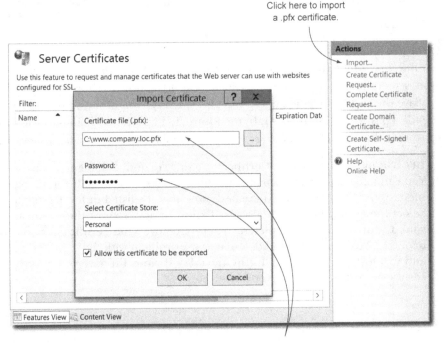

Click here to import a .pfx certificate.

Provide the path to the certificate and password.

Figure 9.12 The process of importing a certificate

9.3 Securing your websites

Once certificates have been installed and stored on the web server, you need to assign those certificates to the correct websites. You assign a certificate to a website by adding a new binding. (We looked at bindings in chapter 5—go head and review that chapter if needed.)

If you've been following along in this chapter, you'll have a certificate (Self-Signed is fine) on your web server created for the default website. The URL I'm using in this example for the default website is www.Company.loc.

In this section you'll create a binding for the default site and test to make sure HTTPS is working. Then you'll create the certificates and binding for a more challenging set of websites for the WebBikez shop, using host names in the binding.

Let's start by adding a simple binding to the default website.

9.3.1 Binding certificates

Certificates stored on the web server are assigned to their respective websites using a binding. As an example, in the IIS manager I'm adding a binding to the default website. When adding the binding, change the protocol type of the binding to https, as shown in figure 9.13. When you do that a new dropdown is added for the certificate. Choose the correct certificate (the one that matches the URL) and click OK to accept the new binding.

At this point you can test the secured website by opening a browser and using https://www.Company.loc as the URL. If you're using a non-trusted, Self-Signed certificate, you'll get a warning message and a red address bar, but your website should still appear. You've successfully secured the default website.

TRY IT NOW Try this with your default website: create a new binding for HTTPS and select your certificate. Open your browser and test the HTTPS connection to your site.

Select https and use the dropdown to choose the correct certificate for the website.

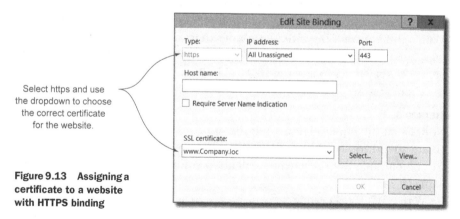

Figure 9.13 Assigning a certificate to a website with HTTPS binding

As simple as this example has been—and most of your websites will be as easy—there are two additional points to consider:

1   *Should I delete the HTTP binding?*—If you want your website to only respond to HTTPS, then you should delete the HTTP binding. A word of caution: some admins want customers to be able to use http in the URL rather than have them redirected to https. This is common for email access—as an example, http://mail.company.loc is redirected to https://mail.company.loc. If this is the case, leave the HTTP binding for the redirection.

2   *Should I require SSL settings?*—Another way to require SSL (HTTPS) is to change the website settings. In the IIS manager the icon SSL Settings has an option to require SSL regardless of what additional bindings you may have for the website.

If you have a single server with one or two websites that need SSL, you now have the solution to correctly applying certificates. If you're like me and have several websites (such as with the WebBikez shop) that use host names in the binding, it becomes a little more complicated. In the last section of this chapter, you'll see how to handle that situation.

9.3.2   *Securing host name (header) sites with SSL*

You may run into a problem if you use host names in your bindings instead of using virtual IP addresses for each website. A single IP address can only have one certificate. If you use host name bindings that share a single IP address, you can only have a single certificate that will apply to all those websites.

Consider two websites and URLs for the WebBikez shop (you'll try this later in the lab):

- Shop.WebBikez.com
- Mail.WebBikez.com

Adding a certificate to these sites follows the procedure you learned in this chapter. Create two certificates with the common names of Shop.WebBikez.com and one with Mail.WebBikez.com. But if these websites share an IP address and use host name bindings, that won't work. In fact in IIS 7 the Host Name field will be greyed out completely when you try to add the HTTPS binding.

There are two methods (secret tricks) around this issue.

METHOD 1

Notice that the top-level domain is the same for each website (WebBikes.com). If you create a Wildcard certificate *.WebBikez.com and select that certificate when you create the binding, the IIS manager will allow you to type in the host name, as shown in Figure 9.14.

With a Wildcard certificate you can assign as many websites as you want, as long as the top-level domain matches. The one drawback is that all the websites use the same certificate. This is fine if the sites are for the same company, as is the case with the

Enter the host name
for the website.

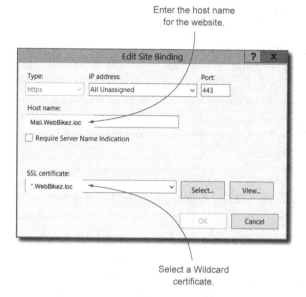

Select a Wildcard
certificate.

**Figure 9.14   Using a Wildcard
certificate for host name bindings**

WebBikez shop. But if you're hosting different company websites, this is a bad practice, and you'll want a different certificate for each website. Take a look at method 2.

METHOD 2

Notice back in figure 9.14 the option to require Server Name Indication (SNI). This is a new feature in IIS 8 and isn't supported in IIS 7. This feature permits you to install different certificates for websites that use host name bindings. Select the checkbox and you can apply URL-specific certificates. I explore this feature in more detail later when we start to scale IIS to multiple servers.

Certificates can also be installed and HTTPS binding configured using PowerShell. Before you try the lab, take a look at how to assign certificates using PowerShell.

9.3.3   *Assigning certificates with PowerShell*

Certificates can be installed and configured using PowerShell along with the Windows native command-line utility CertUtil.exe. This capability becomes important when working with Server Core, which has no GUI, or when deploying certificates to multiple servers at once (discussed later in the book).

With all the information you learned in this chapter, adding the PowerShell piece is pretty simple. It's the same as the GUI, only with commands. I'll use a generic example website (Shop.Company.com), but in the lab you'll perform this for one of the sites for the bike shop. Here's the process:

- Copy the certificate (.pfx) to the destination web server.
- Install the certificate.
- Add an HTTPS binding for the website.
- Bind the certificate to the website binding.

Let me start by copying and importing the certificate, and then I'll be able to add an HTTPS binding and add the certificate to that binding.

COPYING AND INSTALLING A CERTIFICATE

Start the process by copying an exported certificate (.pfx) to the destination web server that contains the websites you want to secure with HTTPS. You can connect (map) a network drive or walk the certificate to the server on a USB stick.

To install the certificate onto the server, use the Windows native command-line utility CertUtil.exe, as in the following example. You must specify the password for the certificate and the location of the .pfx file:

```
PS> certutil -p P@ssw0rd -importpfx c:\shop.Company.com.pfx
```

Make sure to delete the certificate .pfx file from the server after you successfully install the certificate.

> ### Above and beyond
> When you use CertUtil.exe, you need to specify the password for the .pfx file. If you're going to build a script, I recommend replacing the passwords with a variable that gets the password from a prompt, such as the following:
>
> ```
> PS> $Password = (Get-Credential).GetNetworkCredential().password
> ```

With the certificate installed on the server, the next step is to create an HTTPS binding for the website you want secured.

ADDING AN HTTPS BINDING

Using the New-WebBinding cmdlet from the WebAdministration module makes this a snap. The parameters for the cmdlet specify the site name, protocol, port, and IP address for the site. The SSLFlags determines where the certificate is located, which will be used for the binding. The certificate you installed is in Windows certificate storage, but here are all the options:

- *0*—Regular certificate in Windows certificate storage
- *1*—SNI certificate
- *2*—Central certificate store
- *3*—SNI certificate in central certificate store

Here's an example of how to do this:

```
PS> Import-Module WebAdministration

PS> New-WebBinding -Name shop -Protocol https -Port 443 -IPAddress
    ➥192.168.3.201 -SslFlags 0
```

The process isn't complete yet; there's one more step before the website is usable for HTTPS.

BINDING THE CERTIFICATE TO A WEBSITE

One last step remains, and it's often overlooked and forgotten: linking the certificates to the new website bindings. The graphical IIS manager hides this part of the process from you and performs it in the background. You'll have to remember to perform it with commands if you want your sites to work with SSL. This is a two-phase process beginning with getting the thumbprint (unique identifier) of the certificate and then creating the binding. Here's an example of storing the thumbprint of the Shop.Company.com certificate into a variable called `$cert`:

```
PS> $Cert = Get-ChildItem -Path Cert:\LocalMachine\My |
Where-Object {$_.subject -like "*shop*"} |
Select-Object -ExpandProperty Thumbprint
```

Using the thumbprint you can grab the entire certificate and assign it as an SSL binding for the website in one line. The next command uses `Get-Item` to grab the certificate and then `New-Item` to create the SSL binding. SSL bindings are created in the IIS: drive IIS:\SSLBindings along with the binding information.

In IIS binding information is normally displayed as IPAddress:Port:Hostname (*:80:*). But PowerShell interprets the colon (:) as a path indicator. When using PowerShell to set binding information, use the exclamation point (!) instead:

```
PS> Get-Item -Path "cert:\localmachine\my\$cert" |
New-Item -Path IIS:\SslBindings\192.168.3.201!443
```

The bindings are now complete, and the websites can be reached using HTTPS. Now it's time for you to try building several secure sites for the bike shop and applying certificates to each one. Take a few moments to complete the lab and help secure the WebBikez shop.

9.3.4 *Checking for certificate expiration*

Once you add certificates for SSL, you need to check for when they expire. Checking each certificate for a website using the IIS manager takes considerable time, and failing to locate an expiring certificate means the website will become unusable until the certificate is replaced.

Add to that the time it takes to get or renew a certificate, and you could lose access to a website for a couple of days. That's unacceptable, so you need to check the certificates for their expiration dates. PowerShell makes this task simple and easy:

```
PS> Get-ChildItem -Path Cert:\LocalMachine\My |
Select-Object -Property PSComputerName, Subject, @{
n='ExpireInDays';e={($_.notafter - (Get-Date)).Days}} |
Where-Object {$_.ExpireInDays -lt 90}}
```

Notice the `Where-Object`. This line checks for certificates that will expire in less than 90 days. You can change the number to whatever you need, as long as you give yourself plenty of time to renew and replace the certificate.

Later in the book you'll use the preceding command to check for expiring certificates on multiple web servers simultaneously. In large web environments certificate management becomes increasingly harder. In chapter 18 you'll learn about a new feature in IIS 8 called the Central Certificate Store that completely removes the challenge of managing certificates. If you're not using IIS 8 yet, then the preceding command will help.

9.4   Lab

Before you go back to work, I want you to secure some websites for the WebBikez shop. The company has added a few websites for customer shopping and downloads, plus a website for employee email, and needs your assistance in getting them secured. You can perform this lab using the IIS manager or PowerShell, whichever you prefer.

When you create certificates for this lab, you can create a simple Self-Signed certificate. I'm also including tasks that are more realistic and require a CA such as ADCS. In case you'd like to use ADCS on your VM, I've posted instructions for a quick installation on MoreLunches.com.

TRY IT NOW

In case you didn't get a chance to perform the Try It Now sections, I've repeated them here for your convenience. Once complete, you can start the lab with task 1.

1   Even if you aren't ready to purchase a certificate with a real CA, this is a good time to get familiar with the process and create a sample request. Open the IIS manager, double-click the Server Certificates icon, and click Create Certificate Request. You won't be using this certificate, so use my example information to create the request. Enter the following:

   Common Name—www.TestDomain.com
   Organization—My Company
   Organization Unit—IT
   City—Denver
   State—Colorado
   Country—US

2   Choose the default cryptographic properties and store the request to C:\testReq.txt. Using Notepad, open the request text file and view the content.

3   In the Server Certificates icon, create a Self-Signed certificate. You can make the Friendly name anything you like; this is only for an experiment. Once the certificate is created, note that it's listed in the IIS manager. Select the certificate and choose the Export option. Export the certificate to your C:\ drive. Once completed, delete (remove) the certificate in the IIS manager. Yup, go ahead and delete it as if a problem with the server occurred and you lost the certificate.

4   Bring back that certificate you deleted in the last Try It Now by importing the .pfx file. When you're finished, create a new certificate (Self-Signed is fine) for the default website on your test computer. You'll use this new certificate in the next section. Make sure that the Common name (Friendly name if using

Self-Signed) matches the URL you type in the browser to test the website. As an example, if you have www.Company.loc in DNS, make sure the common name is www.Company.loc.

5 Create a new binding for HTTPS and select your certificate. Open your browser and test the HTTPS connection to your site.

TASK 1

Start by creating the following websites if they don't already exist from a previous lab. When you create the websites, uniquely identify their HTTP bindings using a host name or virtual IP address. And make sure to add the DNS records and a sample page on each website:

- Shop.WebBikez.com
- Download.WebBikez.com
- Mail.WebBikez.com

Test each website URL to verify that the sites are functioning normally before continuing to the next task.

TASK 2

Using the Server Certificates in the IIS manager, create a Self-Signed certificate with a Friendly name of SelfSigned.

TASK 3

Create an HTTPS binding for Shop.WebBikez.com and assign the Self-Signed certificate. Access the website using https://shop.WebBikez.com. You should be rewarded with a secured connection, although you'll be warned that this isn't a trusted certificate, and your address bar will turn red.

TASK 4

You still have HTTP access to the Shop.WebBikez.com website. Prevent this by either removing the binding or setting the Require SSL option in the IIS manager.

TASK 5

The other websites—download and mail—need to be secured as well. You can use the same Self-Signed certificate, but if you have ADCS installed on your VM, create a Wildcard certificate—*.WebBikez.com—and apply that certificate to all three websites. Test to make sure that HTTPS is working for each.

TASK 6

Remove the Wildcard certificate from the websites you set up in task 5 and replace it with unique certificates for the complete URL. As an example, create a certificate with a common name Shop.WebBikez.com, and then Download.WebBikez.com, and so on. Assign the certificates to their respective websites. You'll receive an error on IIS 7 unless you created the websites with a unique virtual IP. If you're using IIS 8, select the SNI option to accomplish the task.

Task 7

Back up your certificates by exporting them to a .pfx file. Delete a certificate and see if you can recover it again by re-importing it.

Task 8

Before you leave this lab, make sure all three websites work correctly using HTTPS. If you didn't have a chance to try ADCS to make a better certificate, consider coming back to this lab later.

9.5   *Ideas to try on your own*

Working with certificates can be a daunting task at first, and continuing to experiment beyond the lab in this book is something you should consider. Creating your own websites in your VM that match your work environment and adding certificates is good practice for the future.

You should locate the websites that are using certificates in your own work environment. A common administrative task is to check to see when those certificates are going to expire. You can do this by viewing the installed certificates and examining the expiration dates. You should record this information and plan to renew these certificates before they expire.

FTP and SMTP with IIS

The internet and the technologies that make it useful have improved quickly in the last 20 years. Along the way some technologies have slowly dropped off as they were replaced by newer and better inventions. Demands for improvements in user experience, security, performance, and other web-related features have turned what once were common, well-established internet services into fading memory. That's not to say that all the old services don't still provide value—you'll see that in this chapter. But when was the last time you used Gopher to find something on the internet? (If you haven't heard of Gopher, that's kind of my point.)

Microsoft IIS supports two services you may still run across or need in your career as a webmaster: the venerable File Transfer Protocol (FTP) and an email relay service that uses Simple Mail Transfer Protocol (SMTP). In this chapter you'll help the WebBikez shop establish an FTP site for customers to download bicycle manuals and a secured FTP site for the development team to upload new web applications. You'll also get a chance to examine the Windows built-in SMTP relay service sometimes used for transferring email.

Open your lunch sack and get ready to help WebBikez shop with the first focus of this chapter: FTP.

10.1 File transfers

You've downloaded files, books, PDFs, and other interesting things from a variety of websites. In almost every case you click a link in your browser, and a file download starts. Today, websites and applications transfer files over the HTTP/HTTPS protocol;

it's fast and secure, but more importantly it's easy for any user to understand—click it, and it downloads.

That wasn't always the case. The standard method of downloading/uploading files was to use a TCP/IP protocol, specifically designed for file transfers, called FTP. The drawback to FTP is that it requires an additional client to perform the file transfers. This confuses and frustrates most internet users and is the primary reason FTP sites are gradually being replaced by web applications. That's not to say FTP is dead. In fact FTP is heavily used by IT pros to transfer files over the internet because of its reliability and simplicity. IT pros don't mind using an additional FTP client, and uploading/downloading files over the internet doesn't require building a website and application.

The WebBikez shop wants to use FTP for two goals: to provide a secured place for the developers to upload new web applications and a general public download site for bike manuals. Eventually the bike manuals FTP site will be replaced with a standard web application using HTTP for the file transfers, but until then a simple FTP site will work.

Before you start building the new FTP sites, let's take a look at how FTP works and the network configuration needed to handle it.

10.1.1 *Preparing for FTP*

FTP works by using client software to contact an FTP server and download/upload files. To support it you'll need to do the following:

- Open the required FTP ports on your firewalls
- Support active/passive FTP

To support FTP your network firewall needs to open two additional ports:

- Port 20 for the file transfer
- Port 21, the control port, for the initial connection from the client

FTP serves files to the client in one of two methods: active FTP and passive FTP. In active FTP the FTP server tries to initiate sending the files; in passive FTP the client initiates the transfer. The client software—FTP commands, third-party, or browser—determines the method that FTP will use by telling the server when the client makes the initial request over the control port (21). In the case of active FTP, the client makes a request (such as to download a file), and the FTP server then initiates a new connection to the client to begin the download, as shown in figure 10.1.

Most firewalls on the client side are designed to prevent new connections from outside services initiating requests. This prevents hackers and viruses from downloading files to users' computers without their knowledge. But the client can request the FTP server to respond using passive FTP. The client software initiates both the initial request over the control port 21 and the download request over port 20, as shown in figure 10.1.

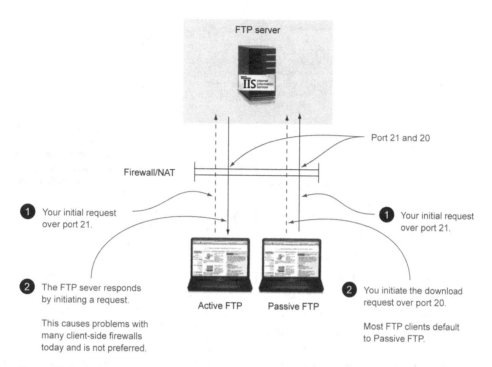

Figure 10.1   Active FTP can be difficult to use because client firewalls today prefer passive FTP.

Although some FTP servers may force active connections, that's generally no longer the case. In fact most FTP client software defaults to using passive FTP, but it's something to check in the software configuration if you're having connection issues.

In Microsoft IIS the FTP site (also known as FTP Server) is configured similarly to a normal website. You can add FTP to an existing website or create a brand new site for file transfers. Let's start with a common, public-access FTP site for WebBikez.

10.1.2   Public-access FTP for anonymous users

Public FTP sites contain files that anyone on the internet can download using FTP client software. Anonymous FTP doesn't require special authentication and is simple for an IT pro to configure without the overhead of a web application to perform the file transfers.

WebBikez shop would like to have a public FTP site for its bicycle manuals. As mentioned earlier, this FTP site will be replaced by a user-friendly web application later, but for now it will serve as a simple way for customers to get the manuals. I'll show you the process, and you can either follow along and build the FTP site now or wait until the lab. Microsoft supports a robust FTP implementation, and the process is similar to creating a website except that the GUI is different. The process can be somewhat confusing your first time through.

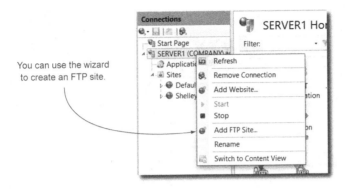

You can use the wizard to create an FTP site.

Figure 10.2   The Add FTP Site menu command launches a wizard that walks you through the complete configuration.

The FTP Server is a component of IIS you can install using the Server Manager or PowerShell:

```
PS> Add-WindowsFeature –Name Web-FTP-Server –IncludeAllSubFeatures
```

Once the feature has been installed, new FTP options will appear in the IIS manager to support the configuration of FTP sites. One such feature is Add FTP Site, as shown in Figure 10.2 This menu command launches a wizard that guides you through the entire process of configuring an FTP site.

Instead of using the wizard, though, I'll take you through the manual process of creating an FTP site. I want you to see the steps involved so that if you have problems you can troubleshoot them better. After you're comfortable with the options discussed in this chapter, use the wizard anytime you need an FTP site as a fast configuration method.

To create an FTP site manually, start by creating an ordinary website as you've done in the previous chapters. You should add a DNS record that points to the server and website and test the site to make sure everything is working normally. In my example I created a website named BikeManuals and added a DNS record Manuals.WebBikez.com.

TRY IT NOW   Create a new website for FTP. You can use the naming convention I'm using or you can create your own.

The root of the website (its physical path) is the location that users will connect to using FTP for downloading files. In the case of the WebBikez shop, the physical path of the site is where the bike manuals will be copied.

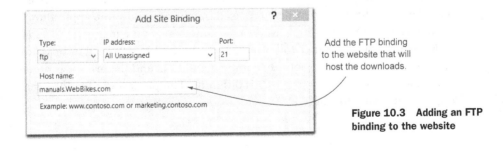

Add the FTP binding to the website that will host the downloads.

Figure 10.3   Adding an FTP binding to the website

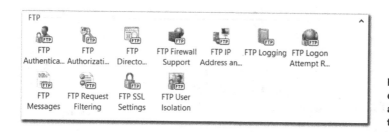

Figure 10.4 The FTP configuration icons appear after you create the FTP binding.

Once the website is created, you won't see any FTP configuration icons until you add a new binding to the website. Figure 10.3 shows a new FTP binding being created using the host name Manuals.WebBikez.com

The only binding you'll need for this site is the FTP binding. You can remove the HTTP binding that was initially created when you made the website.

TRY IT NOW Create a binding using the FTP protocol for the website. I'm using a host name, but if you created the website using a virtual IP, then no additional host name is needed.

Note that a whole new section of icons appears in the IIS manager when you apply the FTP binding, as shown in figure 10.4.

The additional FTP icons are similar to their website brethren. You can configure file type, domain, and IP address restrictions and even create a nice message that pops up when an FTP client connects. You'll have a chance to explore those in the lab.

The process from this point is similar to the process of configuring an ordinary website, so I think you'll find this fairly straightforward. The next step is to select the authentication for the FTP site. In the case of this public FTP site for WebBikez, you'll want to choose and enable Anonymous Authentication, as shown in figure 10.5.

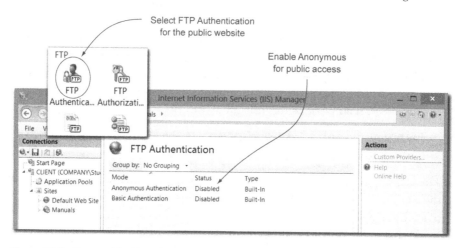

Figure 10.5 For a public FTP site, choose Anonymous Authentication.

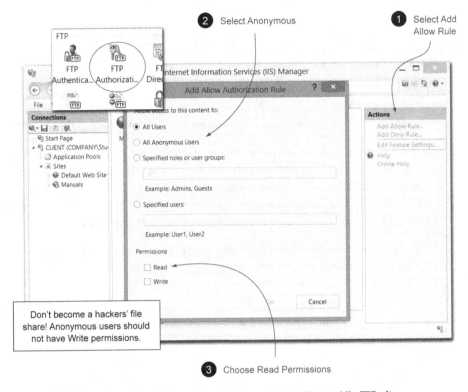

Figure 10.6   Create an authorization rule and set permissions for a public FTP site.

Before the site can be accessed, you need to create an authorization rule for *who* is allowed to access the FTP site. In the case of the public site for the bike shop, we want anyone to be able to download a bike manual, so you'll create a rule like that shown in figure 10.6.

Be careful when setting permissions for a public FTP site. You only want anonymous users to be able to read (download) files from the site. If you mistakenly give anonymous users write access, a malicious user (or any user) can upload harmful files such as viruses to your FTP site. This is a mistake you can't afford to make, so be sure to only assign read permissions for public FTP sites.

TRY IT NOW   Enable anonymous access and create a rule that assigns read permissions to the new FTP site.

The last step for this basic configuration for the bike shop is to set the SSL settings for the FTP site. For a public FTP site using anonymous access, change the SSL setting to permit non-SSL FTP, as shown in figure 10.7.

At this point your FTP site is ready for users to start downloading files. It's best to place some files in the web root and test the FTP site for download. You'll need an FTP client. Any one of them you find on the internet will do: I prefer a free one called FileZilla.

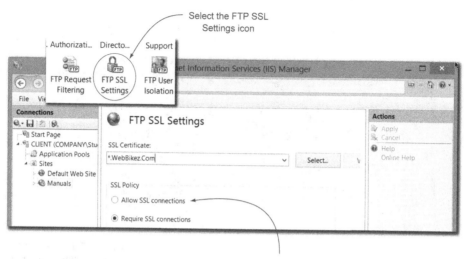

Select the FTP SSL
Settings icon

To support standard FTP for
public access select Allow
SSL Connections

**Figure 10.7   Making SSL not
required for a public FTP site**

Open the FTP client of your choice and enter the FTP site host name and the user-name *anonymous*, as shown in figure 10.8. You should be able to connect and download files.

You can also test your FTP site using the Windows command-line built-in FTP client, as shown in figure 10.9. It's harder to use, but is great for testing.

The current public FTP site serves the needs of the WebBikez shop for downloading manuals. In the next section you'll create a secured FTP site for developers to upload new web applications.

10.1.3   *Isolating users with FTP and SSL*

The WebBikez shop needs a secured place for developers to upload new web applications and code updates. A public website for anonymous users wouldn't be the correct choice. Remember, we don't want just anyone uploading files to our server. Instead, WebBikez wants a secured FTP site where each developer has his or her own private storage location. Microsoft FTP can easily deliver this using SSL FTP user isolation.

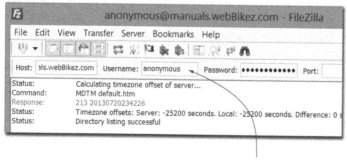

**Figure 10.8   You need an
FTP client to download
from the new FTP site. Get
one from the internet.**

Testing FTP

FTP command and username
anonymous for access

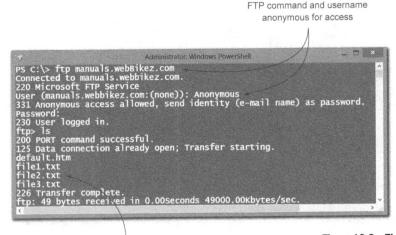

```
Administrator: Windows PowerShell                                _  □  ×

PS C:\> ftp manuals.webBikez.com
Connected to manuals.webbikez.com.
220 Microsoft FTP Service
User (manuals.webbikez.com:(none)): Anonymous
331 Anonymous access allowed, send identity (e-mail name) as password.
Password:
230 User logged in.
ftp> ls
200 PORT command successful.
125 Data connection already open; Transfer starting.
default.htm
file1.txt
file2.txt
file3.txt
226 Transfer complete.
ftp: 49 bytes received in 0.00Seconds 49000.00Kbytes/sec.
```

File list from FTP folder

Figure 10.9 The Windows built-in command-line FTP client

FTP user isolation has many levels of configuration, but you're going to help Web-Bikez by configuring the strictest level of isolation. What this means is that users will authenticate by using an Active Directory account (or an IIS manager account) and be placed into a folder that only they have access to. No one else gets permissions to the folder; it's a private location exclusively for them to store files.

Once again, I won't use the wizard. I want you to see how to do this manually. I'll start with a brand new website called WebBikezDevelopment, with a DNS record that resolves to the new site using Dev.WebBikez.com.

> **TRY IT NOW**   This process is similar to the last section. Start by creating an FTP binding as in the preceding section. You can remove the HTTP binding if desired.

Start by selecting the authentication type for FTP, but this time you don't want Anonymous. You'll need to use a real credential from Active Directory or IIS manager users, so Basic Authentication is the right choice, as shown in figure 10.10.

Remember from previous chapters that Basic Authentication passes usernames and passwords over the internet in clear text, which means you need to enforce SSL. You'll do that soon, but first you'll need to configure FTP for the users and permissions that will be allowed to use the new FTP site. In this case WebBikez wants all users to be able to use the FTP site, and they need permissions to upload (write) files, as shown in figure 10.11.

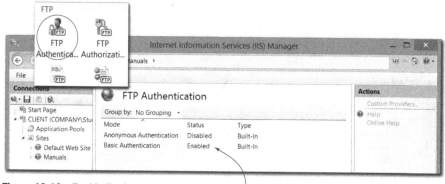

Figure 10.10 Enable Basic Authentication so users can authenticate with credentials.

Enable Basic Authentication to support unique user authentication

Unlike a public FTP site, in this case you can let logged-in users have write access to upload files. Because you're requiring authentication, anonymous users can't access the FTP site and upload bad files and viruses.

TRY IT NOW Select Basic Authentication for your FTP site and create a rule that permits all users to read and write files.

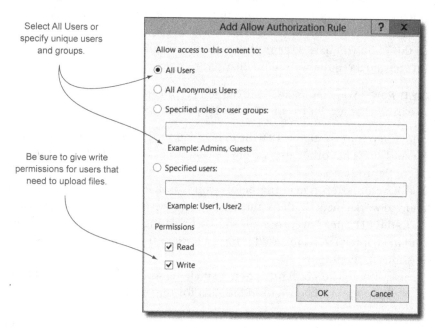

Select All Users or specify unique users and groups.

Be sure to give write permissions for users that need to upload files.

Figure 10.11 Specify users and permissions for the new FTP site.

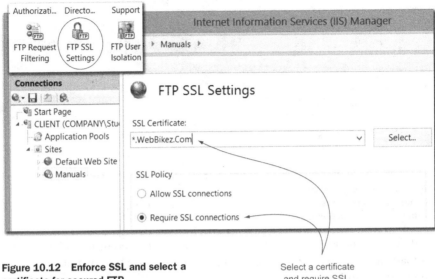

Figure 10.12   Enforce SSL and select a certificate for secured FTP.

Select a certificate and require SSL.

Now it's time to enforce SSL for the FTP site. You'll need a certificate for the site as you would for any other website using SSL. To assign a certificate, in the FTP SSL Settings icon choose Require SSL connections and select the certificate, as shown in figure 10.12.

At this point you have a secured FTP site that requires a user to authenticate, much as you secured a regular website in chapter 9.

TRY IT NOW   You can make a Self-Signed certificate or use a Wildcard certificate from chapter 9 for your FTP site. Require SSL and assign the certificate.

The next step is to configure FTP for user isolation. This places the users in their own folder and prevents other users from having access to them. Select the isolation as shown in figure 10.13.

You have one step remaining before you can open up the new FTP site. For user isolation to work correctly, there must be folders or virtual directories for each user to log in to the FTP site. This process is similar to setting permissions on websites, which you did in chapter 7. Create a folder for each user off the web root and assign the user permissions to the folder.

Users will need to configure their FTP client software to use SSL/TLS. Each FTP client is different, but I configured FileZilla for one of the WebBikez developers (figure 10.14).

When the user connects to the FTP site, they have their own private folder to upload/download files.

TRY IT NOW   Assign user isolation to the FTP site and create a folder for one or two users in your Active Directory on your VM.

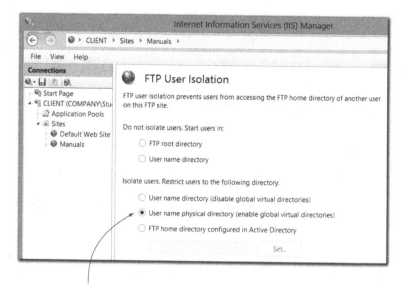

Figure 10.13   Configure user isolation.

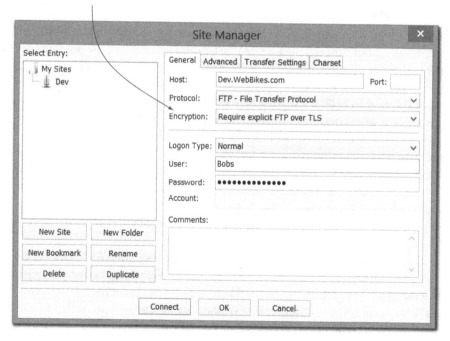

Figure 10.14   Configuring an FTP client for SSL/TLS

As I mentioned at the beginning of this chapter, because FTP sites are more complicated to use for file transfers than a website link using HTTP, FTP sites are gradually becoming a thing of the past for regular users. FTP is still useful when you need to set up a quick file transfer, so IT pros use it often. Microsoft IIS FTP is versatile and can be configured for whatever situation you need.

Before you start the lab and try building a couple FTP sites, I want to discuss one more service.

10.2   SMTP for email

This book is focused on IIS, but I feel I need to also mention a service that touches IIS. It's not truly an IIS service, it isn't a component of IIS, and it has nothing to do with IIS, but it should be mentioned because it's managed through an older version of the IIS manager.

IT pros who work with email systems are familiar with the concept of an email relay using SMTP. A relay takes email coming from the internet and relays it across your firewalls to the email servers inside your protected network. Windows servers and clients have always supported running an SMTP relay service as an inexpensive solution, although today a better choice is Microsoft TMG or a hardware-based solution that can perform virus scanning and spam filtering.

This short section takes a look at what an SMTP relay does and the simple SMTP service that's managed using the IIS manager.

10.2.1   SMTP relays

The old IIS 6 manager included configuration support for SMTP relays, and you can still use that old functionality today. SMTP relays receive and send email to the internet, as shown in figure 10.15. If the relay is receiving email, it then sends (relays) the email to a mail server on the protected network. This configuration prevents a hacker from directly accessing a mail server from the internet. Instead, the hacker hits the relay and is prevented from hurting the mail server.

This is still a common security strategy for email systems, but without using the built-in SMTP components provided by Windows. Today's IT pros working on email systems will implement a smarter SMTP relay (gateway) that can prevent spam, scan for viruses, and drop emails for users that don't exist. Microsoft Exchange has a smart relay called an Edge server, and Microsoft also has Threat Management Gateway to perform this task. Several third-party smart mail relays are available from companies like Symantec and Barracuda.

The built-in Windows SMTP relay isn't the correct choice today, and I mention it only because you'll still see it used. A smart relay is always a better choice. The reason I've taken your time in mentioning this is in case you run across an old Windows-based SMTP relay and are wondering where the management screens are located. Let me briefly show you the installation and configuration for this in case you see it in real life.

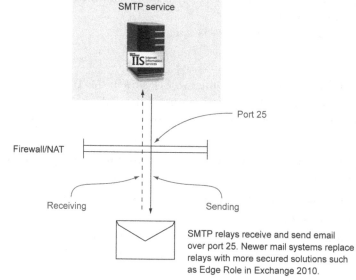

Figure 10.15 An email relay sends and receives email to and from the internet.

SMTP relays receive and send email over port 25. Newer mail systems replace relays with more secured solutions such as Edge Role in Exchange 2010.

10.2.2 Installing and configuring SMTP

To install an SMTP relay using the built-in Windows components is simple. You can use Server Manager or PowerShell, but don't go looking in the IIS sections for SMTP. Here's an example of installing SMTP:

```
PS> Get-WindowsFeature *smtp* | Add-WindowsFeature
```

SMTP has nothing to do with IIS other than its configuration using the old IIS 6.0 manager. When you install the Remote Server Administration Tools (RSAT) for SMTP, you'll see SMTP listed in the old console, as shown in figure 10.16.

If you truly need to use the Windows SMTP service, consider yourself an email engineer and go ahead and create a mail domain. You can configure the rest of your mail settings in the properties of the mail domain. I won't dive into that part because it

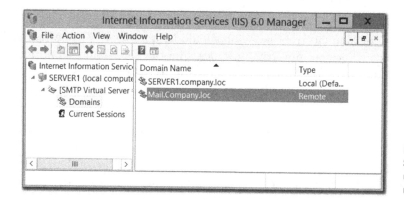

Figure 10.16 SMTP is configured using the old IIS 6.0 manager.

applies to email systems, but if you're more of an IIS pro than I thought, you should know about this last forgotten service.

Now, let's get to the lab and make an FTP site.

10.3   Lab

You worked hard during this lunch building two FTP sites in the Try It Now sections. If you didn't have a chance to build those as you read through the chapter, now is the time. I also want you to try the easy-to-use wizard now that you know all the details.

TRY IT NOW

Here are the Try It Now sections repeated for your convenience. Once complete, you can start the lab with task 1.

1   Create a new website for FTP. You can use the naming convention I'm using or you can create your own.

2   Create a binding using the FTP protocol for the website. I'm using a host name, but if you created the website using a virtual IP then no additional host name is needed.

3   Enable anonymous access and create a rule that assigns read permissions to the new FTP site.

4   Create an FTP binding. You can remove the HTTP binding if desired.

5   Select Basic Authentication for your FTP site and create a rule that permits all users to read and write files.

6   You can make a Self-Signed certificate or use a Wildcard certificate from chapter 9 for your FTP site. Require SSL and assign the certificate.

7   Assign user isolation to the FTP site and create a folder for one or two users in your Active Directory on your VM.

TASK 1

If you didn't perform the Try It Now sections, create two FTP sites for WebBikez, one for public access and one secured with user isolation:

- Manuals.WebBikez.com
- Dev.WebBikez.com

The FTP site for Manuals.WebBikez.com should be a public FTP site where users can read (download) files but not write new files. The Dev site should support user isolation and require users to authenticate. Make sure the site contains an SSL certificate and permits users to upload (write) files.

TASK 2

To understand how FTP works, you created two sites—Manuals and Dev—from scratch. Now it's time to create a couple sites using the FTP wizard. Right-click the Sites container in the IIS manager and choose Add FTP Site to launch the wizard. Using the wizard, create two more sites, one for public access and the other for user isolation.

- *Public site*—FTP.WebBikez.com
- *Secured site*—Uploads.WebBikez.com

10.4   *Ideas to try on your own*

Do you have FTP running in your organization? If it's not accomplishing your needs, why not take a look at using Microsoft FTP? It may solve the problem.

Sharing administrative responsibilities through remote management

As your web environment grows, managing all the tasks involved becomes a monumental job. You have to upload newly developed applications from the developers, modify site settings, check the logs for problems, and keep the web server running smoothly. More often than not I work with a team of people responsible for different aspects of the web environment. In these situations delegating (assigning) permissions and responsibilities to other administrators lightens the load on a single administrator.

To be able to delegate, you have to enable the IIS web server to allow remote administration support. This is beneficial even if you're the sole administrator for the environment. You'll be able to access and manage the web server from any location, not only from the IIS manager on the server. Once remote access has been established, you can assign permissions for other administrators (and developers if needed), being careful to assign only the permissions they need to manage without giving them enough to cause trouble.

In this chapter you'll expand the management of the bike shop by providing remote management capabilities to the server with a GUI and then my favorite: Server Core. You'll also delegate and manage permissions for other administrators.

As the primary IIS administrator, you automatically receive permissions to manage the entire server and all the websites through the administrative login you provide when authenticating to the server. Via a local Administrator account or an Active Directory Domain Admin, you have permissions over the entire server and its websites.

From time to time you'll want other admins and developers to have management access to specific parts of the web server, perhaps for a specific site or application. Maybe another admin only needs to manage one or two of the websites on your server. If you don't want them to have complete access to the entire server, you can delegate only the permissions they need to do their job.

To delegate other admins and developers with permissions to specific websites and applications, you must grant them access using their login accounts, either from the local machine, Active Directory, or a collection of users you can create in the IIS manager. Once permissions are granted, they'll be able to open a local copy of the IIS manager on their own computer and access the sites and applications you granted them.

There are two common scenarios for when you should consider delegating permissions:

- You aren't the person responsible for the website content.
- You aren't the person responsible for a specific website and its administration.

Delegating access for others to administer websites and applications lightens your administrative load and gives those admins responsible for a site or its content the control they need to perform their job.

The task of setting up other admins with permissions is simple, but you have to do something first. By default IIS servers don't permit remote administration. Only the server administrator can access the IIS manager on the physical web server. The first task is to enable remote management for IIS. That's what you'll do in the next section.

11.1 Implementing IIS remote management

Remote administration isn't enabled by default to prevent accidental administration mistakes by other administrators on the network not familiar with IIS and to prevent outside hackers from causing mischief. This situation forces you to visit the physical server every time you want to make changes using the IIS manager. There's a better way!

Remote management of IIS is enabled first by installing the Management Service component and then by configuring its security. In this section you'll enable remote management and connect to IIS, using the graphical IIS manager, and then do the same thing using PowerShell on a Server Core server. In the lab you'll set up the Web-Bikez shop to cement the process. Let's get started with enabling remote management using the IIS manager.

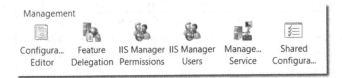

Figure 11.1   New icons to manage remote access and delegate permissions

11.1.1   *Installing remote management using the IIS manager*

To enable remote management of an IIS server using the graphical IIS manager, you must be physically at the server or using Remote Desktop. The remote management tools in the IIS manager only appear on the local computer.

Does that mean there isn't a remote method of enabling remote management? No, there is, as I will show you later in this section using Server Core as an example. But for your first time through the process, using the IIS manager makes it easier to understand.

First you must install the Remote Management Service. This is a component you install using the graphical Server Manager or PowerShell. Here's an example:

```
PS> Add-WindowsFeature Web-Mgmt-Service
```

Once the component is installed, a new series of icons appears at the bottom of the IIS manager under a new Management section, as shown in figure 11.1.

Here are the four main features (icons) that enable remote management and assign permissions:

- Feature Delegation
- IIS Manager Permissions
- IIS Manager Users
- Management Service

I discuss these features throughout the rest of this chapter, but first let's make sure you have everything installed.

> **TRY IT NOW**   You can perform this on your single VM, but it would be best to have an additional server VM with IIS installed, as described in chapter 1. On the VM install the Management Service and open the IIS manager. Select the Server icon in the navigation pane and make sure you see the Management section and the four features.

With the Management Service installed, the next step is to configure and enable it.

11.1.2   *Configuring remote management*

The Remote Management Service requires additional information before you can connect to a remote server. Double-clicking the Management Service icon brings up a new window with many options.

Let's go through the process, starting with configuring the remote management options.

ENABLING REMOTE CONNECTIONS: IDENTITY CREDENTIALS

As tempting as it might be to check the Enable remote connections box and move on to other tasks, you need to be aware of some important configuration settings that affect who can use remote management and the security involved.

The configuration form has three sections, and although the default settings will work to get remote management functioning, they aren't the most secured or best for your environment. Let's go down the list, starting with the first section, Identity Credentials.

The default option for accessing an IIS server remotely is Windows credentials only, which means you can use local Windows accounts or Active Directory accounts, as shown in figure 11.2.

This option works well in the following two cases:

- The IIS server is a member of the Active Directory domain, and you want to assign domain credentials for remote access to the server.
- The server isn't a member of the domain, and you want to create local Windows accounts for each admin and developer.

Most of your publically accessible web servers won't be members of an Active Directory domain for security reasons, and in that case creating local Windows accounts for administration is the normal course of action.

IIS enables creation of user accounts specifically for management of the IIS server and sites. In many cases I find IIS manager credentials to be a much better option than creating local Windows accounts. It's easier, and these accounts only apply to IIS and no other applications that might be on the server, which improves security. Later you'll see how useful this feature can be, so my preference is to change the default to the option that supports IIS manager credentials.

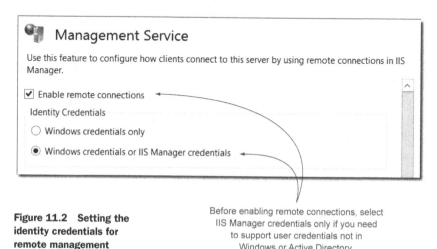

Figure 11.2 Setting the identity credentials for remote management

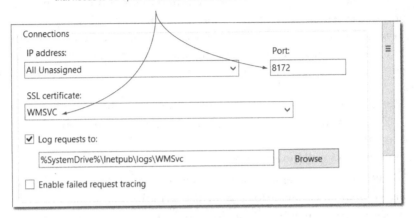

Select a certificate to secure the remote connects
and note the port of remote connections
that needs to be open for access across a firewall.

Figure 11.3   Setting the IP address and certificate for remote management

ENABLING REMOTE CONNECTIONS: CONNECTIONS

As with a new website, you can specify the IP address that the remote management service will respond to when an admin attempts to connect, as shown in figure 11.3. In most cases All Unassigned works fine, but if you're like me and want to create a unique DNS record for remote management (as you've done for other websites), then setting a specific IP address in the dropdown is the way to go.

Note that the Remote Management Service uses port 8172. If you're going to attempt to access the IIS server across a firewall (and many times this is the case), then you need to make sure the firewall has this port open.

You need to select a certificate to encrypt the remote management over SSL. The default certificate WMSVC is a non-trusted temporary certificate that should be replaced. (Refer back to chapter 9 on how to create and assign a new certificate.)

When an admin connects to the Remote Management Service, the connections are logged. Remote management uses a specific set of logs under the WMSVC directory so you can easily locate and view logs specific to remote connections. It's good practice to check these logs for unexpected or unknown client IP addresses that are attempting to connect to your servers. These could indicate someone unknown from the outside attempting to manage your servers.

ENABLING REMOTE CONNECTIONS: IP ADDRESS RESTRICTIONS

As with websites you can configure additional security by setting IP Address Restrictions. The default is to allow all clients, but I prefer to isolate this by denying access for all clients except those that I specify, as shown in figure 11.4.

You can allow or deny access based on a specific IP address or an entire network range, similar to the IP restrictions for websites discussed in chapter 8. To prevent unauthorized users from attempting access, setting these restrictions is a best practice,

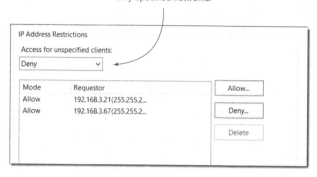

Figure 11.4 **Restricting administrators by IP address or network**

but remember to check this setting when you add additional administrators. A common mistake is to add an administrator and forget to allow their IP address, causing a few moments of confusion and troubleshooting.

ENABLING REMOTE MANAGEMENT

I prefer to make sure my configuration is complete and correct before clicking the Enable setting at the top of the form. It's my mental note that reminds me to verify the list, but you can click the setting before you start configuring if you wish.

When you're finished, click the Apply button in the actions pane to save your configuration. At this point the remote management service is still not ready for you to attempt a remote connection. I often see this after applying the changes: an administrator will attempt to connect, only to receive an error message. That's because the WMSVC service must be started with the new configuration changes before remote management will work. Let's look at starting the service.

STARTING THE REMOTE MANAGEMENT SERVICE

The final step in configuring your server to support remote management is to start the service. The actions pane is where you apply your configuration settings and start the service. When the service starts, the configuration screen becomes greyed out, meaning you can't make any changes to the configuration.

The most common mistake configuring the remote management service is failing to start the service. Make sure to start the service before you leave the configuration page. If you need to make configuration changes in the future, stop the service, make the changes, and then start the service again.

TRY IT NOW On your server VM, configure the Remote Management Service to prepare for the next task.

Once configured with the service running, you can connect to the web server remotely from an IIS manager on your client computer. Let's look at that process next.

11.1.3 *Connecting to a remote web server*

From your client computer or any other server that has the IIS manager, you can connect to a web server that has the Remote Management Service enabled. If you're the server manager (Domain Admin or local Administrator), there's no other configuration to perform.

From the IIS manager on your local computer, select Start Page in the navigation pane and choose Connect to a server, as shown in figure 11.5.

After specifying the server name and supplying your credentials, you'll have a new connection established. From there you can manage the server and its websites.

> **NOTE**   When you install the IIS manager on Windows 7 or Windows 8 through Control Panel, you won't see the Start Page option at the top of the navigation pane. You need to install an additional component that's not available by default on your client computer. Open the Web Platform Installer and install the IIS Manager for Remote Administration component from Microsoft.

This is a good time to take a minute or two and make sure you can access your remote server.

> **TRY IT NOW**   Open the IIS manager on a different computer in your VM environment and connect to the remote server.

You're ready to assign other administrators access to the remote server and delegate access. But first I want to show you how you can implement remote management using PowerShell. If you have multiple servers you need configured for remote management or are working with Windows Server Core, the section after the next one (section 11.3)

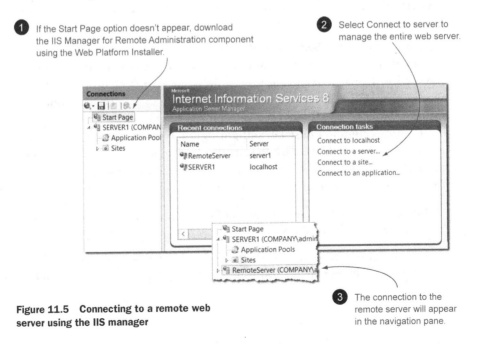

① If the Start Page option doesn't appear, download the IIS Manager for Remote Administration component using the Web Platform Installer.

② Select Connect to server to manage the entire web server.

③ The connection to the remote server will appear in the navigation pane.

Figure 11.5   Connecting to a remote web server using the IIS manager

is the best way available to accomplish the task of enabling remote management. Let's see how to configure remote management with PowerShell on Server Core.

11.2 Implementing IIS Remote Management Service on Server Core

Configuring the Remote Management Service on Server Core is slightly complicated. Server Core doesn't have a graphical interface, and therefore no IIS manager, to perform the configuration. Physically standing at the server or using Remote Desktop doesn't help.

But that's not the only issue. To be honest, I can't physically always be at the server when I want to configure it. In fact I don't want to have to be in some cold data center to configure remote management. The other issue I have is that I need to configure many IIS servers. It doesn't make sense to run around configuring each server one at a time.

The solution is to use PowerShell and PowerShell Remoting to configure the remote servers for remote management. The overall process is the same, but you use PowerShell as the tool instead of the IIS manager.

If you want to use PowerShell to manage IIS, you must have PowerShell Remoting enabled on the IIS servers. There's no avoiding it. There are tricks around this for some tasks, but to fully manage an IIS server you must have PowerShell Remoting. If you haven't enabled PowerShell Remoting, you need to do so now. This isn't a PowerShell book, but let me help you. Go get the free ebook *Secrets of PowerShell Remoting* from http://mng.bz/GeHI. If you need help learning PowerShell, see Don Jones's book *Learn PowerShell 3 in a Month of Lunches* (Manning Publications, 2012).

I've saved the Try It Now sections for the lab in this case. I want you to see the entire process before you try it out. The process begins with connecting to the remote servers and installing the Management Service.

11.2.1 Installing the Management Service

Installing the Management Service on remote servers is fairly simple using PowerShell Remoting. The `Invoke-Command` cmdlet can send the installation commands to the remote servers.

The following example establishes two Remoting sessions to two servers named Web1 and Web2. Keep in mind that this remote session will be used throughout the entire process:

```
PS> $Sessions=New-PSSession -ComputerName web1,web2
```

By using that session with the `Invoke-Command` cmdlet, you can install the Management Service (`Web-Mgmt-Service`), as in this example:

```
PS> Invoke-Command -Session $Sessions -ScriptBlock {Add-WindowsFeature Web-
    Mgmt-Service}
```

At this point the Management Service is installed, but you need to enable and configure it.

11.2.2 *Enabling the Remote Management Service*

There are no PowerShell `WebAdministration` cmdlets that will help in enabling the Remote Management Service. Not to worry, though. You can enable the remote management of IIS by changing a Registry setting on the remote server. If you remember back to the graphical method, this involves clicking the Enable Remote connections check box. When the service is enabled, it has the default settings discussed earlier. You can modify these using PowerShell as well. In this case, I'll use Windows-only credentials, so no additional changes need to occur.

In the following example the `Set-ItemProperty` cmdlet changes the Registry key under HKLM:\SOFTWARE\Microsoft\WebManagement\Server\EnableRemoteManagement to enable the service:

```
PS> Invoke-command -Session $Sessions -ScriptBlock{Set-ItemProperty -Path
    HKLM:\SOFTWARE\Microsoft\WebManagement\Server -Name
    EnableRemoteManagement -Value 1}
```

Keep in mind that the default port number for the remote service is 817. You need to enable that port on any firewalls between you and the remote server.

One thing that you should always change is the default temporary certificate to a trusted certificate. Let's change the certificate in the next section.

11.2.3 *Assign a trusted certificate*

You should always change the certificate for remote management from the temporary non-trusted certificate to a trusted one. This could be a third-party certificate that you purchase or one that's generated and trusted by your own certificate service, such as Microsoft's Active Directory Certificate Services.

I also want to point out that you can change the certificate using the IIS manager by remotely connecting to the server and opening the Management Service settings and making the change. I'll show you how to change the certificate using PowerShell. (For reminders about using PowerShell and deploying certificates, refer to chapter 9.)

The next example stores the trusted certificate installed on the remote server into the variable `$Cert`. The variable will be used to change the certificate binding from the temporary certificate to the trusted certificate in a later step:

```
PS> Invoke-Command -Session $sessions {$cert = Get-ChildItem -Path
    Cert:\LocalMachine\My | where {$_.subject -like "*company*"} | Select-
    Object -ExpandProperty Thumbprint}
```

If you remember the certificate bindings from chapter 9, the next step is to remove the old binding for port 8172 and add a new one. This will change the temporary certificate to the new trusted certificate:

```
PS> Invoke-Command -Session $sessions {Import-Module WebAdministration}

PS> Invoke-Command -Session $sessions {Remove-Item -Path 0.0.0.0!8172}

PS> Invoke-Command -Session $sessions {Get-Item -Path
    "cert:\localmachine\my\$cert" | New-Item -path
    IIS:\SslBindings\0.0.0.0!8172}
```

With the Management Service configured, the last step is to start it. In the next section you'll see how to start the service and configure it for automatic starting if the server should reboot.

11.2.4 Starting the Management Service

This is an easy task, but many administrators forget to configure the service to automatically start if the server reboots. Imagine the server rebooting, and you unable to remotely manage it? The following example changes the WMSVC service startup type from Manual to Automatic:

```
PS> Invoke-Command -Session $Sessions -ScriptBlock {Set-Service -Name WMSVC -
    StartupType Automatic}
```

And finally, here's how to start the service:

```
PS> Invoke-Command -Session $Sessions -ScriptBlock {Start-Service WMSVC}
```

Now you can open the IIS manager on your client computer and connect to the remote servers as the server administrator. What if you have site administrators and developers that need access to only parts of the web server? That answer is in the next section.

11.3 Delegating access to other administrators and developers

By default IIS is completely locked down, preventing other users from managing the web server. Only members of the local Administrators group and the Active Directory Domain Admins group have access.

As I point out at the beginning of this chapter, there will be many times when you want to delegate some web management responsibilities. After making the server remotely accessible, as described in the previous sections, the process is as simple as assigning administrators and developers to the websites and applications you want them to manage. They'll be able to open the IIS manager, connect to the remote website, and perform their tasks without having more permissions than they need and without being assigned administrative privileges over the entire web server.

The steps for this section are simple: you'll assign the users permissions and then decide which management features you want them to have access to. Let's get started.

11.3.1 Configuring permissions for websites and applications

You assign permissions for other admins using the IIS Manager Permissions icon in the Management section. Start by selecting the website for which you want to assign permissions. In figure 11.6 I selected the main website for the WebBikez bike shop. I want a developer (Laura Bartlett) to be able to make changes to the main site.

Once at the website, open the IIS Manager Permissions and add the user credentials from Active Directory, the local Windows accounts, or IIS Manager Users (discussed shortly).

Select the site or application that
the user needs to manage.

Click Allow User to open
the Allow User dialog box.

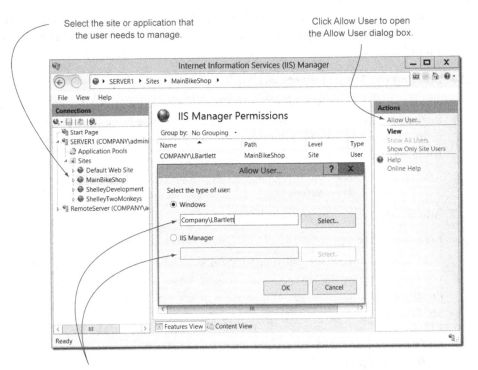

Enter the name of the user. The user
can be from the local Windows accounts,
Active Directory accounts, or
IIS manager-created accounts.

**Figure 11.6 Assigning admins permissions to
remotely manage websites and applications**

In this case Laura will need access to the website files to make content changes.

> **NOTE** If you have admins or developers who need access to the web pages
> themselves, make sure to add them to the NTFS security permissions for the
> website. For a reminder of this, see chapter 7.

At this point Laura can open her local copy of the IIS manager and connect to the
website, as shown in figure 11.7.

Before you go to the lab and try this out for yourself, I want to show you two additional features you can use to improve security.

USING IIS MANAGER USERS FOR REMOTE ACCESS

IIS Manager Users is one of my favorite features of remote management for website
admins or developers. Rather than using their Active Directory credentials or local
Windows credentials, which could give the users too many privileges, IIS Manager
Users are a set of credentials that only allow for IIS management. No other applications on the server are affected.

To create accounts for admins, open the IIS Manager Users icon and add an
account and password for each website admin or developer, as shown in figure 11.8.

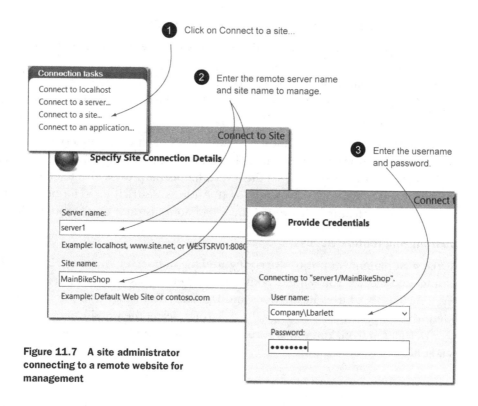

Figure 11.7 A site administrator connecting to a remote website for management

Figure 11.8 Adding IIS Manager Users to manage websites and applications

There are a couple of drawbacks to using IIS Manager Users:

- If you have multiple servers, the accounts will need to be created for each web server.
- Passwords must be managed and changed manually.
- The account names may be different from the user's normal Active Directory account.

These drawbacks are minor in most cases and necessary if your web server isn't a member of the Active Directory domain. Although not a major deal, I wanted you to know.

In some cases you won't want a site-level administrator to be able to change certain features, such as Directory Browsing or IP Address Restrictions. The next section is about restricting features that you as the server administrator don't want modified.

11.3.2 *Customizing feature access*

As the server administrator you've configured the web server and the websites with the settings and security you wanted. Some of those settings can be changed at the website level, such as IP Address Restrictions and Directory Browsing. If you don't want a site administrator to be able to change these settings, select the website and open the Feature Delegation icon. You can control whether each feature can be modified or set to read-only, as shown in figure 11.9.

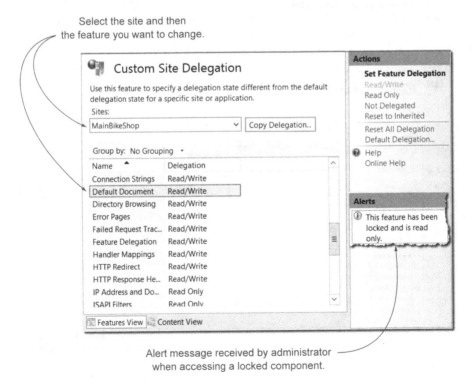

Figure 11.9 **Allowing site administrators access to only the features you want**

Now it's time for you to try this out by helping the WebBikez shop enable remote management and delegate access for a couple of developers to the growing web environment. I hope you enjoyed your lunch. Now wash up and try the lab!

11.4 Lab

If you're working with the complete lab environment described in chapter 1 (three virtual machines) I want you to focus on only one of them for this lab. In the next section, "Ideas to Try on Your Own," I suggest you configure the other servers using PowerShell Remoting.

In this lab I want you to get remote management working on your primary server and configure delegated access for one of your websites. If you followed along in the Try It Now sections, you can skip to task 1.

TRY IT NOW

In case you didn't get a chance to complete the Try It Now sections, I repeat them here for your convenience. Once complete, you can start the lab with task 1.

1 You can perform this on your single VM, but it would be best to have an additional server VM with IIS installed, as described in chapter 1. On the VM install the Management Service and open the IIS manager. Select the Server icon in the navigation pane and make sure you see the Management section and the four features.

2 On your server VM, configure the Remote Management Service to prepare for the next task.

3 Open the IIS manager on a different computer in your VM environment and connect to the remote server.

TASK 1

On your first VM, install and configure the Remote Management Service. I want you to support IIS Manager User identities and apply a new certificate. Make sure to apply the new configuration and start the WMSVC service.

TASK 2

Using the IIS manager, test connecting to the server remotely to verify that the Management Service is working and configured correctly.

TASK 3

Choose one of your websites for delegated access. I used the main WebBikez website in my examples in the chapter. Configure custom site delegation in the Feature Delegation icon and set the Default Document to read-only for your selected website.

TASK 4

Using the IIS Manager Permissions, assign an Active Directory user to manage the website. Create a new user named Michelle if you like.

TASK 5

Create a new IIS Manager User named Bob and assign him a password. Using the IIS Manager Permissions, assign Bob access to the site.

TASK 6

Using the IIS manager, create two connections to the remote website: one for Michelle and one for Bob.

TASK 7

To confirm that the custom site delegation permissions are effective, attempt to change the Default Documents using both Michelle and Bob. Note the information message in the actions pane alerting you that the settings are read-only.

Congratulations! You've enabled remote management of IIS servers, delegated access to other admins to manage the server/websites, and restricted the permissions for the admins.

11.5   *Ideas to try on your own*

The lab in this chapter focuses on remote management for a single server. Now that you have an understanding of the complete process from beginning to end, you should try to configure remote management with multiple servers.

If you have the two additional VMs in your lab environment, see if you can configure the servers using PowerShell as described in the chapter.

Optimizing sites for users and search engines

One value of placing a business on the web is the opportunity to reach more customers. Our WebBikez bike shop is one example of a company providing a unique product and service that many people around the world are seeking. The goal of many developers and web marketers is to reach those users *organically* (without purchasing direct advertising) by optimizing the websites and pages for search engines like Google and Bing. Search engines crawl through websites looking for keywords and phrases that describe the website. When a user types a search term into the search engine that matches one of these keywords or phrases, the website appears in the list of returned search items. The better the keywords and phrases, the better the search match for the user. Optimizing a website to provide the most relevant information to the search engines (to get the best matches) is called search engine optimization (SEO).

As the administrator of a website, you can also help improve SEO by checking for problems that will hinder SEO and repairing and redirecting websites to further improve SEO. In this chapter you'll search for problems such as broken links and you'll correct URLs that are too long. You'll set up automatic redirects to help customers find a website that's moved and even help internal users quickly get to the correct website URL.

There's a lot to accomplish in today's lunch, so let's get started by finding problems on your website that could negatively affect SEO.

12.1 *Search Engine Optimization Toolkit*

Websites get larger over time—new pages are added for new products, and new features are added to better serve customers, all of which grows the size and complexity of the website. This growth introduces problems that affect the SEO of the site. These problems often include broken links and non-relevant content—such as application program files—that affect search results. Developers and web marketers have tools to help them locate problems and optimize search results, and so do you.

In this section you'll use the free IIS add-on Search Engine Optimization (SEO) Toolkit to find and repair the two most common problems with SEO: broken links and hiding non-relevant content from the search engines.

Let's get started by installing the Search Engine Optimization Toolkit.

12.1.1 *Installing and using the Search Engine Optimization Toolkit*

The SEO Toolkit isn't part of the default IIS installation options. Rather it's an additional free feature you can download and install from www.iis.net. You can browse to the tool on the iis.net website or use the Web Platform Installer discussed earlier. I prefer the WebPI because finding the SEO Toolkit with it is faster.

Figure 12.1   The SEO icon after installing the SEO Toolkit

When the SEO Toolkit is installed on your web server, a new icon appears in the Management section of the IIS manager, as shown in figure 12.1.

Before going any further, take a moment to install the SEO Toolkit on your web server so you can follow along.

> **TRY IT NOW** Install the SEO Toolkit on your lab VM using the iis.net website or the WebPI tool. Click the web server in the navigation pane of the IIS manager and verify that the SEO Toolkit is installed in the Management section.

When you launch the tool, the three primary tasks it can perform—Site Analysis, Sitemaps and Sitemap Indexes, and Robots Exclusion—will appear, as shown in figure 12.2.

Site Analysis will crawl your website looking for problems that might affect SEO, such as broken links. The Sitemaps tool creates a map of your website to help search engines navigate the site looking for search terms. Robots Exclusion is a tool that prevents a search engine from crawling non-relevant parts of your site that could confuse the search results.

Developers and web marketers use the toolkit (or something similar) in depth to work on SEO. Not everything the toolkit finds as an issue is truly a problem, and many issues require the developers to repair them. But as an admin you can use this advanced tool to help improve SEO. Let's start with Site Analysis and look for broken links.

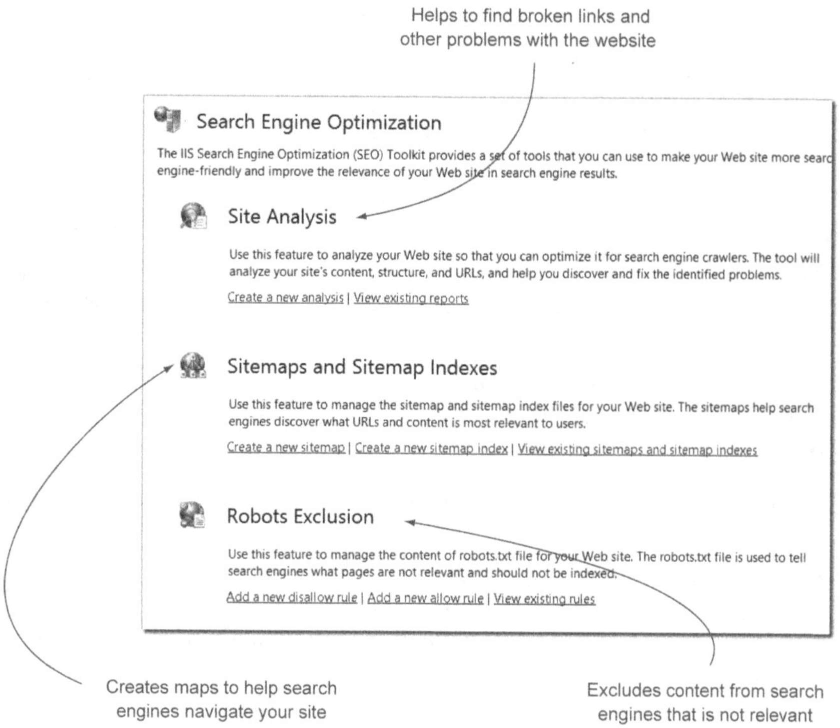

Helps to find broken links and
other problems with the website

Search Engine Optimization

The IIS Search Engine Optimization (SEO) Toolkit provides a set of tools that you can use to make your Web site more search engine-friendly and improve the relevance of your Web site in search engine results.

Site Analysis

Use this feature to analyze your Web site so that you can optimize it for search engine crawlers. The tool will analyze your site's content, structure, and URLs, and help you discover and fix the identified problems.

Create a new analysis | View existing reports

Sitemaps and Sitemap Indexes

Use this feature to manage the sitemap and sitemap index files for your Web site. The sitemaps help search engines discover what URLs and content is most relevant to users.

Create a new sitemap | Create a new sitemap index | View existing sitemaps and sitemap indexes

Robots Exclusion

Use this feature to manage the content of robots.txt file for your Web site. The robots.txt file is used to tell search engines what pages are not relevant and should not be indexed.

Add a new disallow rule | Add a new allow rule | View existing rules

Creates maps to help search
engines navigate your site

Excludes content from search
engines that is not relevant

Figure 12.2 The three primary SEO tools in the toolkit

12.1.2 *Locating broken site links*

Nothing is more frustrating to a customer browsing a website than finding the perfect product or solution to a problem only to click the link and get a "404 page not found" error. It's the curse of the broken link.

Search engines don't like broken links either, and it means your page doesn't get crawled for keywords. Although you as the admin may not be able to fix the broken links (or certain other SEO issues), you can certainly help find them and alert the developers. The Site Analysis tool scans your websites looking for issues that might affect these broken link issues. When you start a new scan, the SEO tool needs two basic options to run: a name for the scan and the URL of the website, as shown in figure 12.3.

The scan's advanced settings give you greater control over the scan, as shown in figure 12.4. Typically I'm not the developer who will be fixing the issues, so I prefer not to store local copies of the web pages. On a large or complex site, that can take a lot of disk space.

Notice that default authentication for the website is Anonymous. This setting doesn't normally need to be changed for a public site, but if you're scanning a secured site, such as a product-ordering application, you'll want to scan the site as an authenticated user.

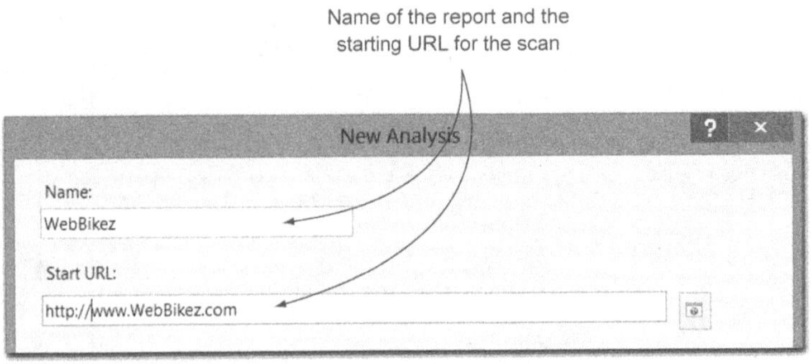

Name of the report and the
starting URL for the scan

**Figure 12.3
Performing a Site
Analysis scan to locate
problems for SEO**

TRY IT NOW Open the Site Analysis tool and scan one of the websites you've created throughout this book. You can also scan a real website such as your company's or even someone else's.

When the scan is complete, a Site Analysis Report is created to display information discovered during the scan, as shown in figure 12.5.

The report provides a great amount of detail to developers and web marketers. As the admin you want to look at the Violations section. Violations lists all the issues discovered by the scan and provides detailed information about the problems and some possible resolutions.

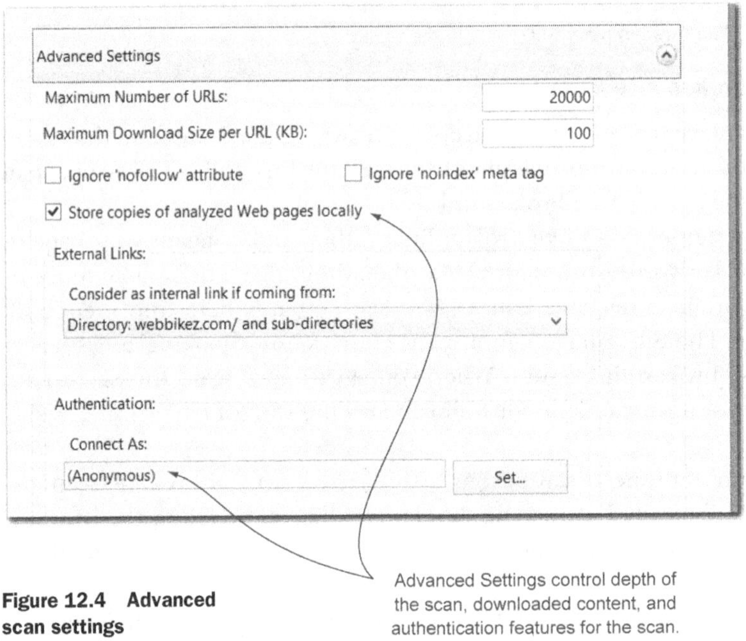

**Figure 12.4 Advanced
scan settings**

Advanced Settings control depth of
the scan, downloaded content, and
authentication features for the scan.

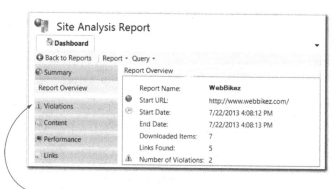

Figure 12.5 Using the Site Analysis Report to discover problems affecting SEO

As the admin, your primary focus is on the section Violations.

For my first scan I scanned a simple website. Notice the error that was discovered under the Violations section in figure 12.6. Not only did it display detailed error information that the URL is broken, but also suggested some possible solutions to fix the problem.

In the case of figure 12.6, the broken URL is due to a DNS error. The IP address for the URL is listed in the error as 192.168.50.100. That's not the correct address for the site, so I easily fixed this issue.

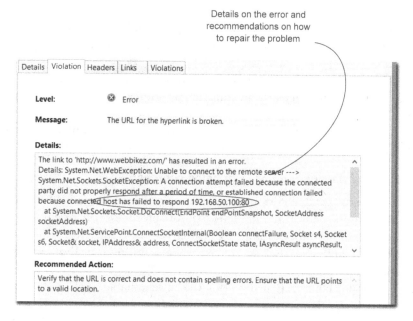

Figure 12.6 Examining and correcting errors using the SEO Toolkit

A report from an active website
showing several warnings and errors
that affect overall SEO

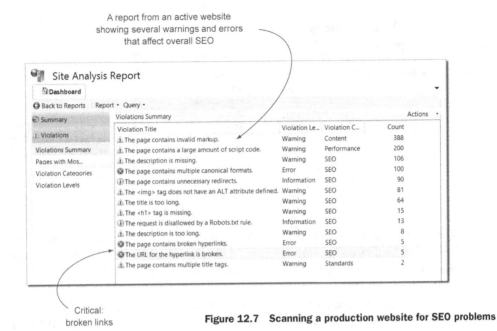

Critical:
broken links

Figure 12.7   Scanning a production website for SEO problems

In figure 12.7 I ran the scan against one of my corporate websites. Note how many possible issues the tool located.

The warning and error messages discovered are mainly problems that I can't fix, so I'll send them to our web team developers, including the most critical problems: the broken links.

The Site Analysis tool provides a wealth of information to help improve the SEO of a website. As the admin you can scan your sites as often as needed and pass that information to the developers.

Another useful tool in the SEO Toolkit can prevent a search engine from crawling certain non-relevant parts of your website to prevent bad searches. That's up next.

12.1.3 *Preventing non-relevant content from being searched*

Websites contain pages that customers want, such as products, manuals, help forums, and company contact information. This type of information is exactly what search engines are looking for, too, to improve search results. But there's also content that could make the search engines less effective when scanning your site, such as the supporting code pages that make the site operate or off-topic content that might be in a forum. There's also content that should never be searchable, such as shopping transactions, invoices, or other corporate confidential data.

One technique of preventing search engines from scanning non-relevant content is to place a file on the site that informs crawling robots to not scan certain folders or parts of the site. Often developers handle this, but if you're adding content and applications to the site, you may want to control it as well. You'll notice when you use the

This particular site has sections
that should not be searched.

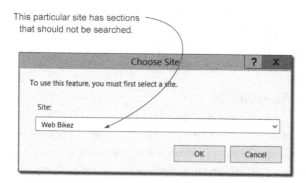

**Figure 12.8 Choosing to block
content from the search engines**

Site Analysis tool that it will report when robots have been blocked so that you can verify that only correct content is being crawled for SEO.

You can block an entire site or selected applications and folders. Choose Robots Exclusion from the SEO Toolkit and select the website you want to add the exclusion file to, as shown in figure 12.8.

The tool lets you select the portions of your site that you want the search engines to avoid when crawling the site, as shown in figure 12.9. Make sure to not mark content you want customers to find.

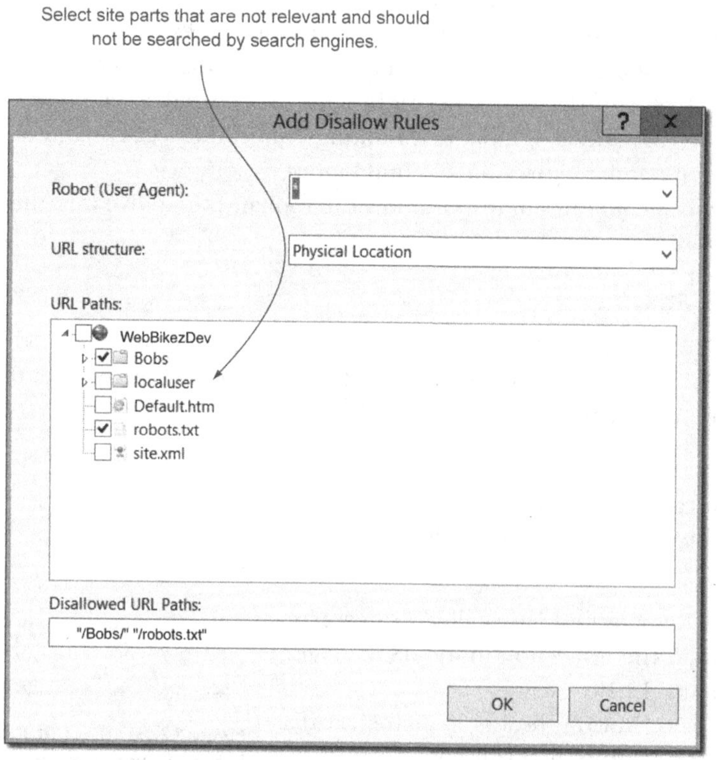

Select site parts that are not relevant and should
not be searched by search engines.

Add Disallow Rules

Robot (User Agent): `*`

URL structure: Physical Location

URL Paths:

- ◢ ☐🌐 WebBikezDev
  - ▹ ☑🗀 Bobs
  - ▹ ☐🗀 localuser
  - ☐ Default.htm
  - ☑ robots.txt
  - ☐ site.xml

Disallowed URL Paths:

`"/Bobs/" "/robots.txt"`

OK   Cancel

**Figure 12.9 Selecting
specific non-relevant
site parts**

When you complete the process, a robots.txt file is placed in the website. The search engines read this file and avoid crawling the non-relevant content, improving your SEO.

A few more techniques regarding URLs can improve your SEO and help every admin managing websites. Let's get started with the basics of URL Rewrite.

12.2   *Improving SEO with URL Rewrite*

URL Rewrite is a powerful, free tool for web administrators and developers to create URLs that are easy for customers to remember and for search engines to find for crawling. Using *rules* you can transform complex URLs into simple ones. When moving sites you can redirect one URL to another and redirect users from non-secured HTTP to secured HTTPS automatically. These are only a few of the tasks you can do with URL Rewrite, but they're the major ones you'll do as web admin when you start using the tool.

I'm not going to beat around the bush: this is a complex tool that requires a great amount of testing and experience. It also requires that you, the web admin, become familiar with a text-parsing language known as regular expressions. *Regular expressions* (regex) parses strings of text data for matches. This is useful when scanning IIS logs for URLs or when using the URL Rewrite tool to transform URLs. Regex has many uses outside of IIS and web administration; any need to scan files for matching text is a good reason to know regular expressions.

I'll show you how to solve two of the most common issues with URL Rewrite—to go deeper you'll need a more complete and advanced knowledge of regular expressions. Don't worry, I'll get you started on the right path. But consider reading Don Jones's *Learn PowerShell 3 in a Month of Lunches* (Manning Publications, 2012) and other books specifically about regular expressions to build more experience.

First you'll locate and install the URL Rewrite tool and then dive into this complex but powerful tool.

12.2.1   *Installing URL Rewrite*

Like the SEO Toolkit in the last section, the URL Rewrite tool is a free tool available from www.iis.net. You can download and install it from the website or with the built-in WebPI tool in the IIS manager.

> **TRY IT NOW** Install the URL Rewrite tool now so you can follow along. Use the Web Platform Installer and search for *URL Rewrite*.

After the URL Rewrite tool is installed, a new icon will appear under the IIS section in the IIS manager, as shown in figure 12.10.

When the URL Rewrite tool is launched, it displays a list of currently applied rules. You won't have

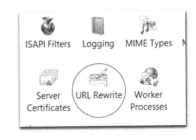

Figure 12.10   The URL Rewrite tool in the IIS section of the IIS manager

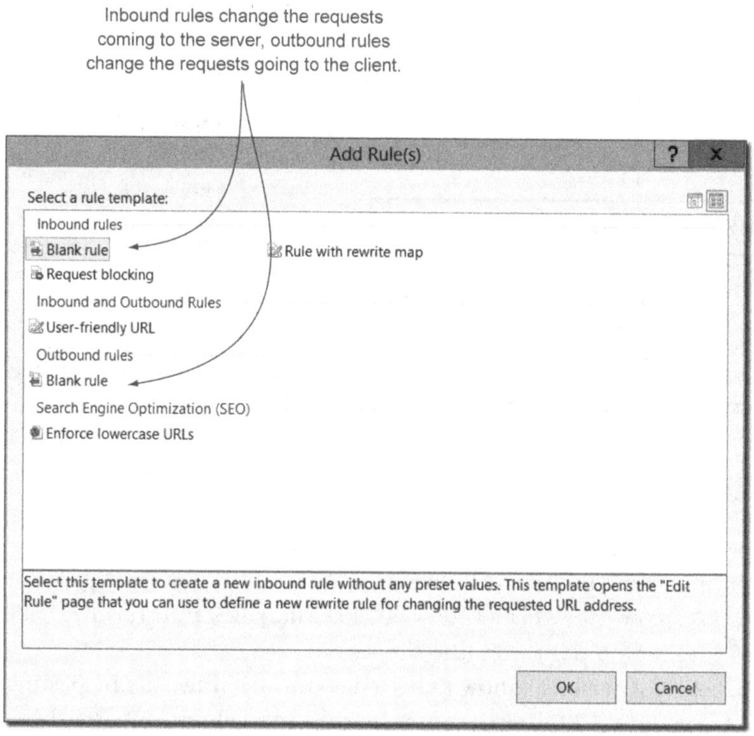

Inbound rules change the requests
coming to the server, outbound rules
change the requests going to the client.

Figure 12.11 Adding new rules to the URL Rewrite tool

any rules yet, so look to the actions pane for the Add Rule link. The Add Rule wizard lets you transform URLs: inbound requests to the web server and outbound requests leaving the server. Most of the time you'll control the inbound and outbound rules by starting with a blank rule. Launching the Add Rule wizard produces the screen shown in figure 12.11.

Most of the time you start with a blank rule template because it provides the most options. In our case, we're going to solve a typical real-world problem of transforming long URLs to short URLs using the User-friendly URL wizard. This wizard doesn't require any knowledge of regex and is a good place to start.

12.2.2 Shortening long URLs for better SEO

Websites that produce dynamically created web pages create long URLs with query strings in them. These URLs are difficult for search engines to crawl through and are a nightmare for a customer to remember. You can create shortened URLs with URL Rewrite to improve SEO and make it easier for customers to remember the web page.

Figure 12.12 lists the entire web address, or URL. Note that I broke it into three sections: the protocol (*http* or *https*), the host name, and the specific part of the address that's the URL. In URL Rewrite, the URL is everything past the slash (/). The URL contains many parts as well, but this is good enough for now.

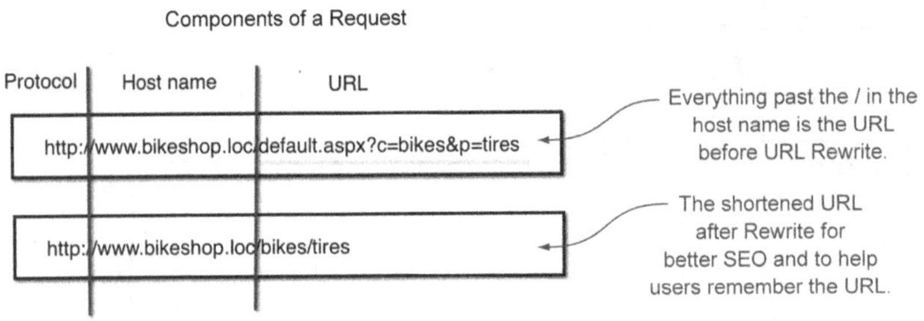

Components of a Request

Figure 12.12 **Making long URLs shorter**

The web URL in figure 12.12 is for our sample bike shop and will display bicycle tires. The long URL is dynamically generated by ASP.NET, the language the developers used to create the site. Such long and ugly URLs are a common issue with websites and products such as SharePoint that use dynamically generated content.

We want to make the URL something easier for customers to remember and type into their browsers when they're searching for tires. We also want to make it easier for search engines to crawl the site and thus improve SEO. In a nutshell, what happens is that when a user types the short URL, URL Rewrite rules transform it back into the long URL to get the web page from the site.

In figure 12.13, you can see how I created a User-friendly rule by pasting the long URL into the first box. URL Rewrite then listed several short URLs to choose from. I chose www.bikeshop.loc/bikes/tires/.

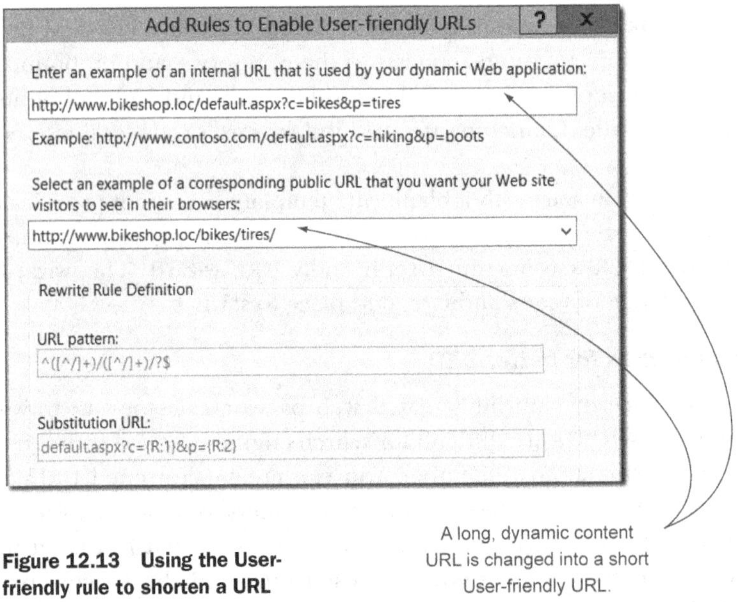

Figure 12.13 Using the User-friendly rule to shorten a URL

A long, dynamic content URL is changed into a short User-friendly URL.

This is a great solution for web pages that customers commonly want but which have long, complex URLs.

URL Rewrite can do more, including solving two other common issues: email and domain name redirects. We'll get to those later. First you need to learn about regular expressions.

12.3 Using regular expressions to improve URL Rewrite

Regular expressions (regex) is a topic that most web administrators avoid. The expression syntax can seem deep and complicated when you're getting started. It's like an onion: every layer takes you to a deeper layer. But to solve the common website redirection problems discussed in this section, you don't need to go that deep.

A good way to think about regex patterns is as a filter. Only the data that passes the filter (regex pattern) will be handled by a rule. You may also find that you start to use regex for things other than those described in this chapter, such as searching IIS logs and other text files. PowerShell has a powerful regex implementation for that reason. Who knows? You may start to enjoy the game (yes, game) of creating better and faster regex patterns to use for searching.

For our purposes, you'll use regex to create basic pattern matching to use with the URL Rewrite tool. The tool even includes a way to test your regex patterns to make sure they work. You'll use that tool shortly to learn about regex. Let's get started with learning some regex basics.

12.3.1 Basic regular expressions every admin should know

This is a topic that's better learned by seeing and doing than having everything explained up front. Let's dive in and start playing with regex. I want you to treat this entire section as a Try It Now. It's important to follow along on your VM and examine the results so you can understand the process. After getting familiar with the regex language and how matches are determined, you'll solve a couple of real-world website redirection problems using your new knowledge.

> **Above and beyond**
>
> You can use PowerShell and the –match comparison operator to test pattern matching, but IIS has a built-in tool to do this. If you're using regex for other purposes beyond IIS, you should try out the PowerShell –match and the Select-String cmdlet.

Launching the URL Rewrite tool for pattern matching

Launch the URL Rewrite tool and add a new blank rule. You'll see several different sections, which I explain later. For now open the Conditions section. Click to add a new condition. In the Condition input box, enter *{HTTP_HOST}*, as shown in figure 12.14.

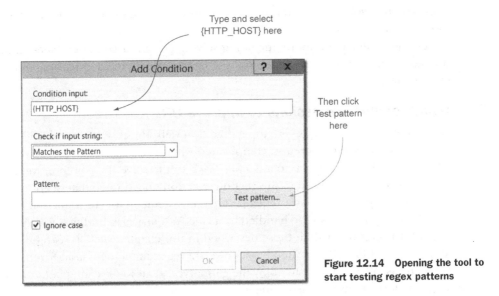

Figure 12.14 **Opening the tool to start testing regex patterns**

The Condition input is for server variables (discussed in chapter 3). In this demonstration you're going to try building regex patterns to test matches on the host name (www.BikeShop.com) of an HTTP address.

Click Test Pattern, and you'll see a screen similar to figure 12.15. The top part of the form is where you enter the test data and regex pattern (filter) for testing. When you click the Test button, your results are displayed if there's a match. You'll run several tests, but I'll only show the graphic once, in figure 12.15.

Note that the top box is where you type the data to be tested. The middle box is where you enter the regex pattern. Let's try a simple example. In the Pattern box, type *www.BikeShop.com.* In the Input data to test box, enter *www.bikeshop.com* and click the Test button. You should have a successful test. If you mistype the input data or the regex pattern, you'll notice no matches displayed.

Using the test tool, I'll show you some common regex patterns and language syntax. Try these out as you go along to get a feel for how the patterns work.

USING REGEX TO FIND A MATCH

Regex looks for a pattern match in a string of data—for example, an HTTP request the user types into a browser or a log file—and displays hits, or matches. The pattern match works as a filter, and in the case of IIS you can build rules to control what happens next if a match is found. Simple regex patterns (filters) can produce unexpected results. As an example, the test pattern of *www.BikeShop.com* will match several test data results. You can try these in the test data, and they'll all work:

- www.bikeshop.com
- wwww.bikeshop.com
- www.bikeshop.commmm
- ThisIsCoolwww.bikeshop.comAndFun

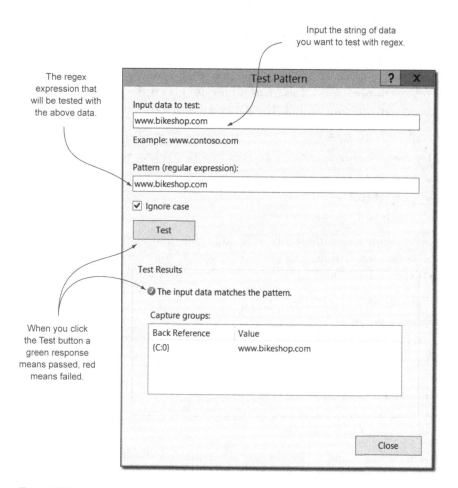

Input the string of data
you want to test with regex.

The regex
expression that
will be tested with
the above data.

When you click
the Test button a
green response
means passed, red
means failed.

Figure 12.15 Testing regex patterns

They work even though they aren't exact matches because our regex pattern doesn't limit the beginning or ending of the string. To make the match *not* permit the leading or trailing characters, you use two special regex characters that signal to the pattern the beginning and the end of the string. In this case begin the pattern with a ^ and end the string with a $. Type this regex pattern: *^www.bikeshop.com$*. Now try the preceding bullets again. This time the beginning and trailing characters don't match, and only the first bullet (www.bikeshop.com) works.

One additional note: the periods need to be read by regex as characters you want tested, so a backslash \ is placed before them. This \ is an escape character that means *check for the next character.* For the best match so far, the pattern should look like this:

```
^www\.bikeshop\.com$
```

CHECKING FOR THIS OR THAT

Regex also has a special character that represents logic's OR. For example, if a customer sends an HTTP request that contains either *www.bikeshop.com* or *www.bikeshop.net* in the URL, you want to redirect them to www.BikeShop.org. The pipe character | is the regex OR operator. I'll use parentheses to group the top-level domain and set a regex pattern for .com or .net. The pattern would look like this:

```
^www\.bikeshop\.(com|net)$
```

Try the following as test data and see how the pattern works:

- www.bikeshop.com
- www.bikeshop.net
- www.bikeshop.org

If you've been trying these out with me, note that *www.bikeshop.org* failed the test because the *.org* portion wasn't in our pattern. If you wanted *.org* to also pass the test, here's what it would look like:

```
^www\.bikeshop\.(com|net|org)$
```

EXTENDING A MATCH

Regex has two characters that permit patterns that extend further than what you define. As an example, suppose I want a pattern that would be successful if a customer typed one of the following:

- www.BikeShop.com
- www.BikeShopRepair.com
- www.BikeShopSales.com

The characters .* and .+ are similar. The .* means *allow anything to follow* (like the * wildcard you use at the command line), and the .+ means *something must follow*. Notice the distinction between the two. With .* anything *can* follow; with .+ something *must* follow. Use the following pattern and try the preceding three bullets as test data. Here's the regex pattern:

```
^www\.BikeShop.*\.com$
```

All three worked. Now try with this pattern:

```
^www\.BikeShop.+\.com$
```

In this case the first bullet failed because the .+ requires that there be characters following *BikeShop*.

MAKING PARTS OPTIONAL WITH REGEX

Sometimes you'll want to apply a rule on an HTTP request whether the customer typed the entire URL or not. You want to make parts of the URL optional in the filter. Customers may type a URL without the *www*—instead of typing *www.BikeShop.Com*, they type *BikeShop.com*. The character ? is the optional character in regex. Here's an example of making the *www* part of the address optional:

```
^(www\.)?BikeShop\.com$
```

You can test this in the tool. You'll see that the user could type either *www.bikeshop.com* or *bikeshop.com*. One last regex trick and then we'll solve some real-world problems with your new knowledge.

CHECK FOR ANY CHARACTERS WITH REGEX

Regex also allows you to check for specific characters and approve them or not. The [] define a character class you want to check for. In my example I want to create a regex pattern that will allow the customer to type the following URLs into their browser:

- www.BikeShop.com
- www.BikeRepair.com
- www.MyShop123.com

For the domain portion of the address, I use [] and specify characters that are permitted, such as:

```
[a-zA-Z0-9_]
```

That example would permit upper- and lowercase alphanumeric characters and the underscore. To make the rule accept multiple characters, I need to include a .+ symbol like this:

```
[a-zA-Z0-9_].+
```

To check for a web address using any characters in the domain, I could create a pattern similar to the following:

```
^www\.[a-zA-Z0-9_].+\.com$
```

Try the bullet items and see that they all pass the test.

GOING DEEPER WITH REGEX

Earlier I said that I'd show you how to solve two common problems using the URL Rewrite tool and regex. That's coming up next. But I want you to know that there are many ways to accomplish the same goal using regex. This has only been an introduction to some of the characters and symbols that regex uses.

Now let's solve two real-world problems.

12.3.2 *Using URL Rewrite to redirect website domains and improve SEO*

Let's get right to the problem. Have you noticed in your web browsing that sometimes you can type the *www* and sometimes you don't have to? As an example *www.Bike-Shop.com* and *BikeShop.com* both work. The reason *BikeShop.com* works is because an A record entry in DNS points to the entire domain to your web server. This helpful

Enter the name of
the rule here.

Edit Inbound Rule
Name:

BikeShop.loc

Match URL

Requested URL: Using:

Matches the Pattern   Regular Expressions

Pattern:

.*   Test pattern...

☑ Ignore case

Enter .* here to accept all URLs
that come from a user request.

**Figure 12.16   Creating the rule
name for website redirection**

feature is automatically set up in many DNS zones, and most websites respond this
way—but it can reduce your SEO and confuse customers.

You shouldn't disable/remove this feature, but to improve SEO, you want the website, regardless of what was typed, to always redirect the browser to the proper address
and URL that has the *www.* To accomplish this, do the following:

1   Open the URL Rewrite tool and create a new inbound blank rule.

2   Enter the rule name and .* pattern for the URL (remember, the URL is everything after the host name), as shown in figure 12.16.

3   Below the URL match is a section named Conditions (not
displayed). This is where you
practiced regex patterns in the
preceding section. Add a new
condition that will analyze
only the host name of the
address. This is the
{HTTP_HOST} parameter, as
shown in figure 12.17.

4   The regex pattern is testing
the address that the user or
search engine used to get to
the website. You want a pattern that tests for the site without the *www,* such as
^BikeShop\.loc$.

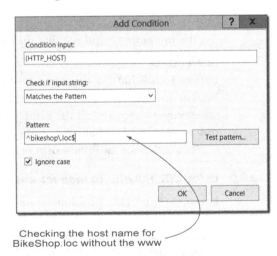

Add Condition   ?   X

Condition input:

{HTTP_HOST}

Check if input string:

Matches the Pattern

Pattern:

^bikeshop\.loc$ Test pattern...

☑ Ignore case

OK   Cancel

Checking the host name for
BikeShop.loc without the www

**Figure 12.17   Entering the pattern without the *www*
for the redirect**

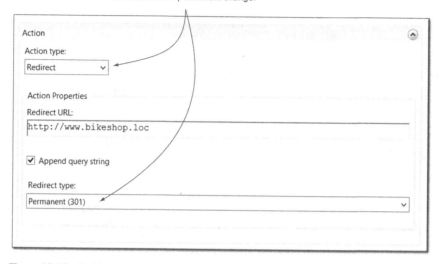

Figure 12.18   Redirecting to the correct address

5 In the Action section at the bottom, select Redirect in the Action type drop-down and supply the correct and proper address with the *www*, as shown in figure 12.18.

6 Set the rule to make this redirect permanent so search engines keep the new address.

Now whenever a customer or search engine browses to your website using *BikeShop.loc* in the navigation bar, the address is automatically changed to *www.BikeShop.loc*. With this one rule you've redirected customers to the correct website and improved SEO.

12.3.3   Redirecting customers to a secured website

The last common problem we'll solve together using URL Rewrite and regular expressions is so common it affects not only web admins but mail engineers with Microsoft Exchange and SharePoint admins. Customers are so used to typing *http://* for the protocol they forget to change this to *https://* for secured websites. As the web admin, you can do that for them automatically and make their lives easier.

Consider that our bike shop has the following two secured websites for customers and employees: one to purchase products from and one for employees to check their email (notice the email site also includes an additional URL folder):

- https://shop.BikeShop.loc
- https://mail.BikeShop.loc/owa

Customers and employees use the HTTP protocol instead of HTTPS when they type the address. That throws an error to the customer and isn't nice. We want to automat-

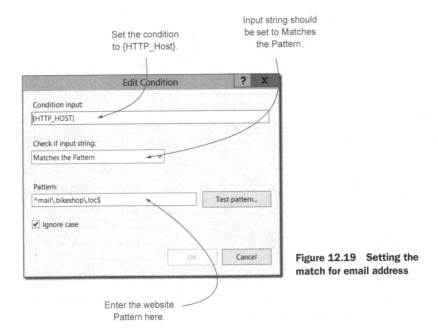

Figure 12.19   Setting the match for email address

ically redirect them to the correct site without their even knowing there was an issue. You can solve this by setting up a redirect with URL Rewrite. Because the solution is the same for both sites, I'll focus on the email site. Employees often type *http://mail.BikeShop.loc* to get to the email site. I'll redirect them to the correct address and URL and also change the protocol to HTTPS with one rule.

Create the rule and add a condition to match the pattern for *mail.BikeShop.loc*, as shown in figure 12.19.

Add an additional condition to check that HTTPS isn't being used, as shown in figure 12.20.

Set the redirection to the correct address and URL, as shown in figure 12.21. With this solution, whenever an employee types *http://mail.bikeshop.loc* into the navigation bar of their browser, they're automatically redirected to https://mail.bikeshop.loc/owa/.

Wow, that was a lot of information for today's lunch. If you've been following along, you should be getting a handle on how to improve the SEO of your websites. Before you stop for the day, let's try a lab.

Input	Type	Pattern
{HTTP_HOST}	Matches the Pattern	^mail\.bikeshop\.loc$
{HTTPS}	Matches the Pattern	^OFF$

Figure 12.20   Checking for HTTP by setting condition HTTPS to OFF

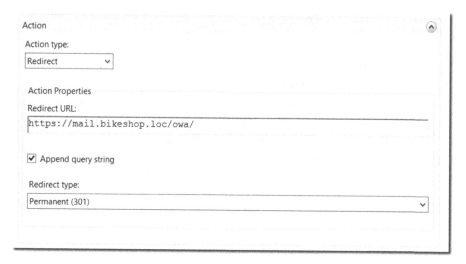

Figure 12.21 Setting the correct address and URL for email

12.4 Lab

Most of this chapter has been a giant lab for you to test and try things out as you learned them, so I won't overwhelm you with a lot more. I do want you to take a look at the WebBikez websites and make some SEO corrections.

TRY IT NOW

If you didn't get a chance to perform the Try It Now sections, I have repeated them here for your convenience. Once complete, you can start the lab with task 1.

1 Install the SEO Toolkit on your lab VM using the iis.net website or the WebPI tool. Click the web server in the navigation pane of the IIS manager and verify that the SEO Toolkit is installed in the Management section.

2 Open the Site Analysis tool and scan one of the websites you've created throughout this book. You can also scan a real website, such as your company's or even someone else's.

3 Install the URL Rewrite tool. Use the Web Platform Installer and search for *URL Rewrite.*

TASK 1

Using the SEO Toolkit analyze all the websites you've built for the WebBikez shop. Although you won't find much, this will help you get comfortable using the toolkit. Try blocking part of a website from being searched by applying a robots.txt file.

TASK 2

Create a redirection so that if a customer types *WebBikez.loc* (without the *www*) into a browser, they're redirected to www.WebBikez.com.

TASK 3

Using the following regex pattern, write out an explanation of what this filter will match, and include some examples that will match this filter and some that won't:

```
^((http|https)://)?(www\.)?[a-zA-Z0-9_].+\.(com|net|org)$
```

12.5   *Ideas to try on your own*

The Search Engine Optimization Toolkit is a handy tool for developers and administrators alike. You've seen in this chapter that it can provide useful information regarding SEO. Try using the SEO Toolkit for your own websites and see if you can detect and possibly repair any issues discovered.

Building a web farm with Microsoft Network Load Balancing

Does your company rely on its websites for sales and customer support? At some point all businesses learn that their web presence is critical to continued sales and support, and losing that presence (through web server failure) can be financially painful. Add to this the fact that many companies experience growth and an increased demand for their web services. More and more customers regularly use company websites, increasing the load on them and slowing them down. You can fix these problems by adding additional web servers to a load balance. A *load balance*, known as a *web farm* in IIS, is a process of adding high availability to help prevent the failures of your websites and increase overall performance.

The concept of a load balance is simple: you place copies of your websites on other web servers so that if one server fails, another server will pick up the load. It's similar to having an online backup ready to take over the work if something goes wrong.

In this chapter you'll help the WebBikez shop protect its websites from failure and increase the performance of this ever-growing company's websites. To do that you'll deploy the built-in Microsoft Network Load Balancing software (NLB) to create a new web farm and then deploy a website to the new farm. NLB is a great way to learn and experience the confusing topic of load balancing, and that's the reason I wrote this chapter. It's a good product and learning it is a good way to understand the more complex solutions discussed in chapter 14.

If you haven't worked with a load balance or cluster before, the concepts can be a little confusing at first. Let's start by removing the mystery of load balancing.

13.1   Introduction to the load balancing web farm

As a web administrator I have this fear of losing a web server and the websites hosted on it. As soon as a website goes live for production, my stomach turns if I have no protection from failure. A backup isn't good enough—think how much time it would take to build a new server and restore those websites and configurations. That's why, as soon as I create a website that the business relies upon, I create a web farm (load balance) to protect it.

A simple web farm for IIS consists of two or more IIS servers, each with an exact copy of the same websites (I discuss other configurations in later chapters). What makes the web farm work is that customers access the web servers using an IP address that connects to the load balance hardware/software, known as a *cluster* IP address. The load balance then connects the users to the web servers and sites for any server that's online, as shown in figure 13.1.

Should a web server fail, the load balance sends new requests to another server that's online. Simple load balancers direct users to the first server that responds. Therefore if a server is gradually getting slow due to having too many users, another server will respond faster, balancing the load. With a web farm you get the safety of having another server in case one fails and an increase in performance for growing websites.

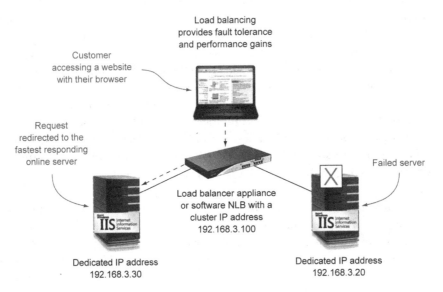

Figure 13.1   How a load balance works

In this section you'll discover the advantages of using Microsoft NLB and some of the drawbacks. NLB is built in to your server's operating system and is simple to get running. First I look at how NLB works differently from a hardware load balancer.

13.1.1 *Using Microsoft Network Load Balancing*

The Microsoft NLB works a little differently from many other hardware/software load balancers. There's no appliance in front of the servers to act as the load balancer or traffic cop, so each of the servers in the Microsoft NLB must be aware of the online status of the other servers. To do that each server has a local configuration containing a list of all the servers in the load balance. Each server then uses a heartbeat (similar to ping) packet to check the status of the other servers. If a server goes offline, all the servers in the NLB detect it and update their local configuration so that no new traffic is sent to the offline server, as illustrated in figure 13.2.

This simple process of having the load balance software on each server provides *fault tolerance* (the ability to handle a failure) and increased performance—without the need for major networking changes to switches and cabling or for purchasing additional appliances to perform the job of load balancing.

Let's look at some more advantages and a few of the disadvantages before you configure NLB.

13.1.2 *Benefits and issues with Microsoft NLB*

The primary benefit to using Microsoft NLB is that you already own the software. It performs well and provides great protection if a server fails.

NLB also provides an increase in performance because each server can respond to customer requests. Here are some of the overall benefits of Microsoft NLB:

- Built-in to the server operating system
- Easier to configure than many hardware-based load balancers
- Requires no or minimal network changes
- Can grow up to 32 servers in a single load balance as your performance demands grow

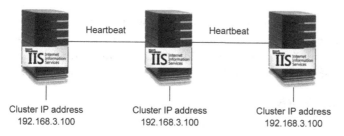

Each server is configured to respond to the cluster IP address 192.168.3.100.

Figure 13.2 Microsoft NLB uses a heartbeat to detect server failures.

Microsoft NLB's limitations are as important as its benefits. Microsoft NLB isn't perfect for every situation. Let's look at some of the issues involved with using Microsoft NLB.

UNDERSTANDING THE ISSUES OF NLB

Microsoft NLB is a good product for small businesses on a tight budget to achieve a better level of fault tolerance and performance. There are some issues with NLB that may not make it the right product for you. Note that I still want you to do the lab even if it's not—the concepts you learn in this chapter are important for the following chapters as you examine other options.

What's wrong with NLB? Well, nothing. It's designed as a simple, no frills load balance that works well in the right situations. Let's look at some of the situations where it doesn't work well.

NLB DETECTS SERVER FAILURES, NOT WEBSITE FAILURES

Microsoft NLB detects when a server, not an application, fails in the load balance. NLB is a Layer 3 load balancer (Layer 3 in the OSI model), meaning that it only has enough intelligence to detect whether a server's network interface card is no longer responding to heartbeats. The entire server has crashed, the cable has been removed, or some other network issue has occurred.

If you have multiple websites running in your web farm, the Microsoft NLB can't detect a failure for an application such as a website. If a website stops functioning due to a problem such as an application pool crash, NLB doesn't switch to another server. Customers therefore may still be redirected to the dead website because NLB has detected no problem.

The resolution to this issue is to use a load balancer that has more intelligence in the application layer. I discuss one such load balancer in chapter 14.

ISSUES WITH SSL

Microsoft NLB is best used for web servers that host public websites, not ones that use SSL. In Microsoft NLB, customers are connected directly to the server that has the website they're accessing. If a failure occurs, or if the customer needs to be moved to another server to balance the load, the SSL connection is destroyed. That forces the customer to create a new SSL tunnel, which usually means they have to log in to your site again.

A hardware/software appliance load balancer that sits in front of the web servers doesn't have this issue. The SSL connection is between the customer and the load balancer. On the back end, if a server fails and the load balancer switches to a different server, the SSL connection is unaffected. The customer never knows there was a failure.

13.1.3 *When to use Microsoft NLB*

Knowing all that, when should you use it? Here's a quick summary list of the best cases for using NLB:

- When protecting public websites that don't require SSL
- When you can't afford the additional cost and complexity of a separate load balancing device

- When detecting a server failure as opposed to an application failure is "good enough" protection
- When you want an increase in performance without additional cost

I like Microsoft NLB—particularly for small companies—as long as the disadvantages are clearly understood. Also NLB is a great way to learn and experience the confusing topic of load balancing, which is one of the reasons I wrote this chapter. It's a good product and a good way to understand more complex solutions.

Let's dive into creating a Microsoft NLB so you can see exactly how it works.

13.2 Deploying a web farm using Microsoft NLB

Installing and configuring Microsoft NLB is fairly easy with the graphic utilities:

- Server Manager installs the NLB feature
- NLB Manager finishes the configuration

If this is the route you want to go, there are plenty of Google and Bing resources available, but this is one of those times when PowerShell is the best answer.

You'll install the NLB feature on your web servers and configure NLB on each server. PowerShell Remoting makes that fast and simple. Also if you're using Server Core (as I am) for your web servers, this is the best solution. Rather than bore you with countless graphic screens, let's do this the easy way.

In this section you'll create a load balance for the WebBikez shop by performing the following tasks:

- Creating the PowerShell Remoting connections to the web servers
- Installing the NLB feature
- Creating and configuring the load balance with Microsoft NLB

You can follow along on your own VMs during the Try It Now sections or wait until the lab. Either way you should take the time to do this yourself—as I've said, the experience will be useful in future chapters.

The first step is to create a PowerShell Remoting connection to the web servers. After this connection is made, you'll be able to install the required NLB feature to build the load balance. Let's start by creating the remote connections.

13.2.1 Creating the remote connections

The first step is to create PowerShell Remoting connections to the servers that will be part of the load balance. To start you'll need the two additional servers mentioned in chapter 1. These will become part of the new load balance. The two web servers I'm using for the WebBikez shop are named Web1 and Web2. They have PowerShell Remoting enabled and haven't had IIS or the NLB feature installed.

You should perform all the PowerShell commands from your client computer (in the lab you can pretend your domain controller is a client). In the real world most admins don't have direct access to the servers, and this is why PowerShell makes this so easy. (Data centers are cold places anyway.)

The first step is to create the remote sessions to the web servers using PowerShell Remoting. I store the sessions into a variable called $Sessions as in this example:

```
PS> $Sessions = New-PSSession –ComputerName Web1, Web2
```

That connects you to the remote computers so that commands can be sent using the Invoke-Command cmdlet.

> **TRY IT NOW**   Make a PowerShell Remoting connection to your two other VMs, as in the example just given. Windows Server 2012 has PowerShell Remoting enabled by default, so it should work. But if you're using Windows Server 2008 R2, you may need to run the Enable-PSRemoting cmdlet on the remote server first.

Now it's time to install the features and roles needed for a web server and NLB.

13.2.2 Installing the NLB feature

The next step is to install the NLB feature on each of the servers that are to be a part of the load balance. The name of the feature is NLB, and you can use the Install-WindowsFeature cmdlet to perform the install.

> **Above and beyond**
>
> In PowerShell v2 the cmdlet that adds roles and features to a server is called Add-WindowsFeature. In PowerShell v3 this has been changed to Install-WindowsFeature. If you're using PowerShell v3, you can still use the Add-WindowsFeature name because it's now an alias to the Install-WindowsFeature cmdlet. I wanted to give you examples that worked for both versions of PowerShell, so I'm using the Add-WindowsFeature cmdlet instead of the v3 only cmdlet Install-WindowsFeature.

Your servers don't have the Web Server (IIS) role installed, so you're going to install both the Web Server (IIS) role and the NLB feature. You can use Get-WindowsFeature to get the PowerShell names for the components, which are Web Server and NLB respectively. I'll show you how to install multiple features at the same time. I want to make sure that the module for NLB is installed as well, so I include Remote Server Administration Tools (RSAT-NLB).

To install both the Web Server (IIS) role and the NLB feature, do this:

```
PS> Invoke-Command –Session $Sessions {Add-WindowsFeature Web-server, NLB,
    ➥RSAT-NLB}
```

When the installation completes you'll receive a success message in the PowerShell console. Remember that you can install additional web features such as ASP.NET using that command.

> **TRY IT NOW**   Install the NLB feature and Web Server (IIS) role on your additional web servers.

With both servers equipped with the necessary software, it's time to create and configure the load balance.

13.2.3 *Creating and configuring the load balance with Microsoft NLB*

The Microsoft NLB feature includes a module of cmdlets called `NetworkLoad-BalancingClusters`. These cmdlets can make the creation and configuration of a Microsoft NLB quick and easy. If you're using a client such as Windows 7 or Windows 8, you'll need these cmdlets. To get them, install the RSAT for your client. An example of creating the load balance using the `New-NlbCluster` cmdlet is shown in figure 13.3. The PowerShell command in figure 13.3 configures the first server for the new load balance. You add servers to the existing load balance like this:

```
PS> Get-NlbCluster -HostName Web1 | Add-NlbClusterNode -NewNodeName Web2 -
    ➥NewNodeInterface Ethernet
```

When the additional server (node) is added to the load balance, you'll receive a success message in the PowerShell console.

> **TRY IT NOW** Create your own load balance on your two additional VMs. This process may take around 5 minutes to complete.

Once all the servers are added to the load balance, you'll want to add a DNS record that points to the cluster IP address of the load balance. You can do that through the graphical DNS management utility or with PowerShell if you have Server 2012 or using the RSAT tools in Windows 8, as shown in this example:

```
PS> Add-DnsServerResourceRecordA -Name www -ZoneName company.loc -IPv4Address
    ➥192.168.3.200 -ComputerName DC.company.loc
```

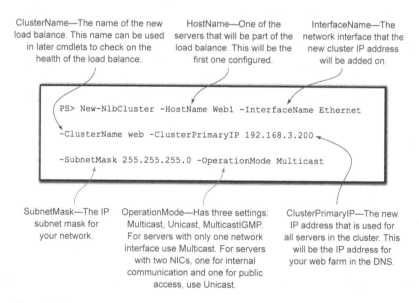

ClusterName—The name of the new load balance. This name can be used in later cmdlets to check on the health of the load balance.

HostName—One of the servers that will be part of the load balance. This will be the first one configured.

InterfaceName—The network interface that the new cluster IP address will be added on.

```
PS> New-NlbCluster -HostName Web1 -InterfaceName Ethernet

-ClusterName web -ClusterPrimaryIP 192.168.3.200

-SubnetMask 255.255.255.0 -OperationMode Multicast
```

SubnetMask—The IP subnet mask for your network.

OperationMode—Has three settings: Multicast, Unicast, MulticastIGMP. For servers with only one network interface use Multicast. For servers with two NICs, one for internal communication and one for public access, use Unicast.

ClusterPrimaryIP—The new IP address that is used for all servers in the cluster. This will be the IP address for your web farm in the DNS.

Figure 13.3　Understanding the parameters with New-NlbCluster

In that example I install two new web servers and join them to a Microsoft NLB. I haven't added the WebBikez websites yet, but I still want to test to make sure everything works. Here's where the default website that's installed automatically comes in handy. Launch a web browser and connect to the default website:

```
PS> Start-Process -Name iexplore http://www.company.loc
```

Later in the chapter you'll test the load balance to make sure it's working properly by failing a server, but let's finish the deployment of the websites first.

13.3   Deploying websites to a web farm using PowerShell

There are several methods to deploy (or make available) your websites to web servers in a load balance, including from a shared location. You'll explore several of those methods in later chapters, but for now let's use the simplest and most direct method of deploying web pages to the web servers and creating new websites in IIS to host them. I think you'll find that this simple, direct method works well for small environments with simple websites.

In the next several chapters you'll explore different methods of deploying websites to a load balance using Microsoft Application Request Routing and Web Deploy. In this section you'll deploy the files for a single website, create the website using the WebAdministration cmdlets, and then test the website.

You'll deploy your own websites in the lab, but I'll demonstrate the process, starting with copying the files to the web servers.

13.3.1   Deploying website files to remote servers

You can copy website files to your remote servers in several simple ways. You could walk around to each server and copy the files from a USB stick or manually map network drives using File Explorer and copy the files to each server one at a time. Both of those methods are valid, so use whichever you prefer.

But if you've been brushing up on your PowerShell skills, there's a much simpler method that will deploy the files to all servers at once. I prefer this method and will teach it to you because you may have 10, 20, or 30 servers in a load balance, not 2.

Create a variable that contains the names of the web servers:

```
PS> $Servers= 'Web1', 'Web2'
```

I like to keep the files for each of my websites on my client under C:\sites. I may have the following structure:

- C:\sites\Bikeshop
- C:\sites\Shopping
- C:\sites\Products

These are the folders for three different sites including the web pages. The following example copies all three of them to the remote servers, keeping the same folder structure:

```
PS> $Servers | foreach{Copy-Item -Path c:\sites\* -Destination \\$_\c$\sites
  ➡-Recurse -Force}
```

That's all there is to it! Each server now has its own C:\sites folder with the files for each website. The next task is to create an IIS website that uses those files.

13.3.2 Creating a website for IIS

Chapters 3–5 demonstrate using PowerShell to create websites and application pools. This is a great chance to pull all the information together and create the websites on multiple remote servers using PowerShell Remoting.

For more details on each command, check the previous chapters, but I hope you'll remember most of this. There are three steps to the process (wait for the lab to try these):

- Create a remote session to the web servers
- Create a new application pool to hold the website
- Create the website

Here are the PowerShell commands to perform those steps:

```
PS> $Sessions = New-PSSession -ComputerName Web1, Web2
```

```
PS> Invoke-Command -Session $Sessions {New-WebAppPool -Name BikeShop-pool}
```

```
PS> Invoke-Command -Session $Sessions {New-Website -Name BikeShop -HostHeader
    ➡www.BikeShop.loc -PhysicalPath C:\sites\BikeShop -ApplicationPool
    ➡BikeShop-pool}
```

Remember to add a DNS record for the new website using the NLB cluster IP address, and you've completed your deployment to a web farm!

13.4 Health and verification for NLB

Once the load balance is built, and you have your websites established, it's good practice to verify that the load balance is healthy and working before you put it into production. In this brief section you'll do that.

Let's start with the health check!

13.4.1 Checking the health of the load balance

When the load balance is created, all servers in the load balance must *converge* their configuration files and check that each server is online. The load balance continues to verify that each server is responding and healthy by sending a *heartbeat*. If the heartbeat is successful with all servers, the load balance is converged. If a server stops functioning due to a failure, the heartbeat fails and convergence is lost.

You can check on the current status of the load balance using the graphical Network Load Balancing Manager or the NLB cmdlet `Get-NlbClusterNode`, as shown in figure 13.4.

In the graphical tool, the servers (nodes) appear in green if they're converged and everything is functioning normally. The nodes appear in red if something's wrong,

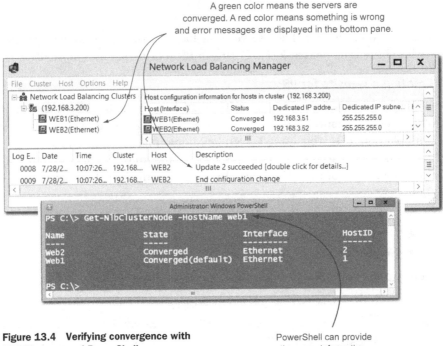

A green color means the servers are converged. A red color means something is wrong and error messages are displayed in the bottom pane.

Figure 13.4   Verifying convergence with NLB Manager and PowerShell

PowerShell can provide the same information.

such as a server failure or a configuration problem that's caused the nodes to lose convergence.

TRY IT NOW   If you built your NLB earlier in the chapter, check the status of the load balance and verify that it's converged. You can use the graphical Network Load Balancing Manager or PowerShell.

You should check for convergence after you initially configure the load balance to make sure no configuration issues occurred. If an issue has occurred, the bottom of the graphical tool will display an error message that will help direct your troubleshooting.

I also check the convergence during testing and verify the operation of the load balance. Let's do that next, and then you can try the lab.

13.4.2 *Verifying the operation of the load balance*

Don't put a web farm into production unless you've tested that it will perform as expected. You should intentionally "break" a server and verify that the load balance flips to the good server.

That's easy. I like to test my load balance this way during a maintenance window every couple months to ensure its proper operation. I start by placing a web page in the default website called NLB.htm, which has the computer name of the server (such as Web1). Then do the following:

1 Connect to the web address of the load balance with a browser: http://www.MyNLB.com/NLB.htm.

2 Record the name of the server displayed in the web browser. This is the server you're currently connected to in the load balance.

3 Turn off (not shut down) or remove the cable from the network interface of the server you're connected to.

4 Refresh the browser. A new web page should be displayed by the functioning server saying that the load balance successfully redirected the browser.

If the test is successful, bring the "failed" server back online and check to make sure all servers converge. If the test isn't successful, check your configuration again to make sure that all servers can converge before the test begins. Remember, if they can't converge before the test, then the load balance won't function properly.

To get a good feel for how the load balance works and the troubleshooting involved, try the lab before you finish your lunch!

13.5 *Lab*

I would like you to deploy a new website to a web farm using Microsoft NLB. Make sure you have two additional servers for this lab as described in chapter 1. In this lab, those servers are named Web1 and Web2.

TRY IT NOW

In case you didn't get a chance to perform the Try It Now sections, I repeat them here for your convenience. Once complete, you can start the lab with task 1.

1 Make a PowerShell Remoting connection to your two other VMs. Windows Server 2012 has PowerShell Remoting enabled by default, so it should work. But if you're using Windows Server 2008 R2, you may need to run the Enable-PSRemoting cmdlet on the remote server first.

2 Install the NLB feature and Web Server (IIS) role on your additional web servers.

3 Create your own load balance on your two additional VMs. This process may take around 5 minutes to complete.

4 If you built your NLB earlier in the chapter, check the status of the load balance and verify that it's converged. You can use the graphical Network Load Balancing Manager or PowerShell.

TASK 1

Configure the load balance of the two servers. Use 192.168.3.100 as the cluster IP address. Add this IP address to DNS using an A record named www.

TASK 2

Create a local folder structure C:\sites\www. In the www folder, add a default.htm web page. Deploy the folder and the web page to the two servers using PowerShell.

TASK 3

Using PowerShell Remoting, create an application pool and a website named Web-BikezDefault on the two servers. Verify that the website works by testing, using the browser on your domain controller: http://www.webBikez.com.

TASK 4

On each server, add a web page named NLB.htm. The page should contain the computer name of the local host to help identify the unique server during NLB testing.

TASK 5

To test the load balance you created, open the browser on your domain controller and type the address http://www.WebBikez.com/NLBhtm.

Based on the computer name displayed in the browser, turn off the corresponding VM. Refresh the browser to see a new web page displayed—this time with the remaining server's computer name.

13.6   *Ideas to try on your own*

In chapter 11 you learned how to enable remote management of web servers so you could use the IIS manager. When you get a chance, enable the remote management of the web servers in your load balanced environment.

Building a web farm with Application Request Routing

A simple load balancer such as Microsoft NLB is great for preventing downtime due to a failing web server, but as your websites on a server grow in number, you need something with more intelligence. Websites themselves may fail, as an application pool stoppage, without shutting down the entire server. In these cases an application layer (layer 7) load balancer such as Microsoft's Application Request Routing (ARR) is an excellent choice for many web farms. ARR (which is free) can detect a failure to an individual website or application pool and then switch to a new website on a different server that's functioning. ARR also provides detailed health monitoring and logging information along with easy management for a large web farm.

ARR is much more than a load balancer. It acts as a manager of the servers in a load balance and helps in provisioning new sites and application frameworks and caching content to increase performance. ARR includes rich health monitoring tools, live URL testing, and performance statistics logging that far exceed the capabilities of NLB. The drawback (if there is one) to ARR is that it requires an additional web server to act as the load balancer—similar to using a hardware load balancer such as a Big-IP F5. Because ARR offers many more features and a better load balancing environment, it's also more complicated to configure and manage.

But don't let that scare you away from ARR! You'll start at the beginning in this chapter using ARR in its simplest form to replace Microsoft NLB. Once you learn how to install, create, and configure the web farm, you'll learn how to monitor the health of your new farm. Over the course of the next several chapters, you'll experience more of ARR's features.

The first section starts with a look at the requirements and installation of ARR.

14.1   *Installing ARR*

Microsoft NLB provides fault tolerance by detecting when a server no longer responds to a heartbeat (something like ping). This works well at the machine level if an entire server crashes. ARR works at the application layer, meaning it can test specific URLs (HTTP requests) to detect whether a website or application has failed and redirect those requests to a functioning server.

To achieve this ARR acts as a request manager, directing the customers' HTTP requests to the available website, as shown in figure 14.1.

Above and beyond

One of the most common questions I hear is: "Should I use a layer 7 hardware load balancer instead of ARR?" Other hardware and software load balancers (such as Big-IP F5 or Cisco Pix) are great solutions that support load balancing for many purposes beyond IIS. I've certainly used many of these and find them to be excellent solutions. The reason I prefer ARR is because it was written specifically for IIS by Microsoft and is a lightweight solution that can grow to web farms of any size. It's tightly integrated into IIS and provides many more features (such as provisioning) than basic load balancing. You'll experience many of those features in later chapters, so before you go out and buy a hardware load balancer, finish the book and give ARR a try.

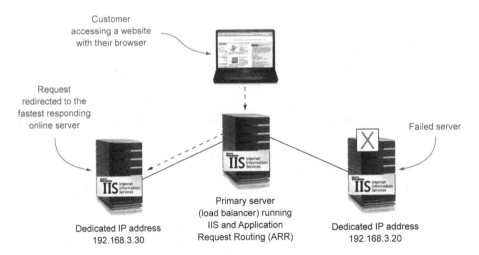

Figure 14.1   Application Request Routing as a load balancer redirecting requests

ARR uses URL Rewrite rules to route the requests (remember chapter 12?) to the correct server and website. This is a fast, lightweight approach to load balancing that ensures great performance even as your web farm grows.

14.1.1 *Requirements for Application Request Routing*

ARR is software that runs on a dedicated server, so if you're going to run ARR, you'll have to add another server, either physical or virtual, that will act as the load balancer. For most companies this is a minor expense compared to a hardware-based load balancing solution. You'll also need the following:

- Server operating systems supported: 2008, 2008 R2, and 2012.
- IIS versions supported: 7, 7.5, and 8.
- IIS installed prior to installing ARR.
- During the installation of ARR, additional requirements—such as the Web Farm Framework (discussed in chapter 19) and URL Rewrite—will be automatically installed: I mention this because you'll notice it during the installation process.

Let's take a look at the installation process and the addition of ARR.

14.1.2 *Installing Application Request Routing*

Installing ARR is as simple as many of the components you've installed throughout this book. It's a free download from www.iis.net and can be easily installed using the WebPI, which you'll perform in the next Try It Now section.

After the installation using WebPI, a new icon will appear under the IIS section in the IIS manager. This icon is for viewing and managing performance-enhancing cache settings (discussed in chapter 19). The important thing for this chapter is the addition of the Server Farms folder in the navigation pane, as shown in figure 14.2.

The Server Farms folder is where you'll spend most of your time in this chapter. This is where you'll create your new load balance.

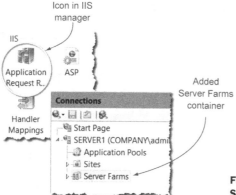

Figure 14.2   The new ARR icon and Server Farms folder in the IIS manager

TRY IT NOW Before installing ARR make sure you remove the NLB you installed in chapter 13. Here in this chapter use your domain controller as the ARR control server. Install ARR to the domain controller and verify you have the Server Farms folder added to the IIS manager. (Remember, you may have to close and reopen the IIS manager.)

With ARR installed on the *control* server, you're ready to build a new load balance. No additional software is needed on the web servers that are running your websites. The control server only needs to be able to see them (by IP address or host name) on the network.

In the next section you'll build a simple web farm (load balance) using ARR.

14.2 Creating a web farm with ARR

I said you'd build a load balance with ARR in its simplest form. That doesn't mean that the load balance you build here won't be useful for real production—in fact, quite the opposite. In this chapter I don't focus on the many additional features ARR includes, such as automated provisioning, the Web Farm Framework, and multiple web farms. We'll save those for later. In this section your focus is on how easy ARR makes it to build a load balance.

TRY IT NOW As in chapter 13, the web servers hosting the websites should have IIS installed and a test page that displays the host name of the server in place. Again, I prefer to put a web page in the default website for testing, such as http://hostname/NLB.htm, or make a default.htm to keep the URL simple, such as http://hostname.

The control server (the one with ARR) is the load balancer, so DNS should have an A record that points to the IP address of the control server. This is where all HTTP requests need to be directed. See chapter 13 for review if needed.

With ARR installed on the control server and the web servers hosting the websites in place, let me show you how to create the load balance. Then you can try it in the Try It Now section.

14.2.1 Creating a load balance with ARR

Creating the load balance using the IIS manager and ARR is quick and simple, as I mentioned. This is a good time to use the graphical IIS manager to perform the tasks.

Let's create the container for the first load balance.

Above and beyond

It's possible to perform these tasks with PowerShell using a *snap-in* (similar to a module of cmdlets) called the Web Farm Framework (WFF). The version of WFF that installs with ARR doesn't yet have this snap-in—it's something you'll add in a later chapter—but in the case of configuring the load balance, the graphical tool is a great solution.

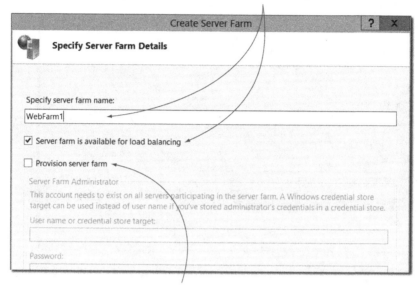

Specify a name for the new
load balance and select the new
farm for load balancing.

This feature sets up the web
farm for automatic provisioning
(discussed in chapter 19).

**Figure 14.3 Creating the server
farm (web farm) for the load balance**

CREATING A NEW WEB FARM

To create the web farm container that holds the individual servers and the configuration of the load balance, open the IIS manager and right click the Server Farms folder to create a new farm.

Enter a name for the web farm, as shown in figure 14.3, and select the farm to perform load balancing. ARR supports managing more than one load balance. The name of the load balance can be as simple as Web Farm or it can be more related to the websites that will be inside the farm. In that case, a name that describes the sites is a good choice, such as BikeShop for the WebBikez shop websites.

The next step is to add the web servers that are to be members of the load balance.

ADDING SERVERS TO THE WEB FARM

You can deploy the websites before or after the load balance is created. In chapter 19 you'll see how to provision websites and components using ARR.

You'll add the web server by host name or IP address, as shown in figure 14.4.

At this point you need to add a URL Rewrite rule that directs customer HTTP requests to the load balance. You'll see this rule in more detail shortly. But the wizard will offer to create this rule for you automatically, as shown in figure 14.5. For single web farms with one or two websites, the automatically created URL works well.

Add the host name or IP address of the
web servers that are to be members of the
load balance and click add.

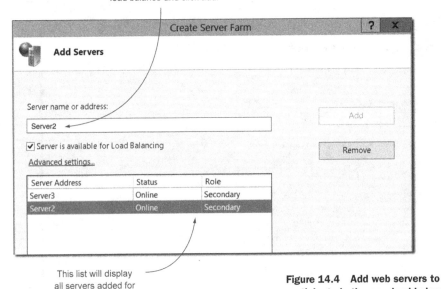

This list will display
all servers added for
the web farm.

**Figure 14.4   Add web servers to
participate in the new load balance.**

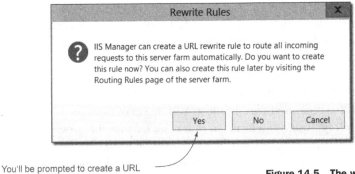

You'll be prompted to create a URL
Rewrite rule. For a single web farm with one
or two websites choose Yes. It can
be altered later for more complicated scenarios.

**Figure 14.5   The wizard offers to
create a URL Rewrite rule automatically
to redirect HTTP requests.**

Above and beyond

In more complicated (larger) load balance environments, the automatically created
rule is too basic, and you'll want to create your own. I cover that in chapter 19, but
for your environment you may not need to add the additional complexity, and this
solution works great.

The web farm is created using the default configuration (explored in the next section), but the web farm is functioning as a load balance at this point. Take a few minutes and set it up for yourself.

TRY IT NOW Create a new web farm and add the two web server VMs that you created for the lab environment.

Believe it or not, you're done. See? ARR makes creating a load balance fast and simple. When you select the new web farm in the IIS manager, you'll see a series of management icons, as shown in figure 14.6.

Although I won't go through all of them in this chapter, there are a few you'll want to check to make sure that the load balance is configured correctly and that you can monitor the performance and statistics of the farm. You'll do that in the next section. First I'll show you how to test the current default configuration.

TESTING THE WEB FARM

With the default configuration, the new web farm is load balanced and will work similarly to the Microsoft NLB you examined in chapter 13. Using the default website, you can once again add a web page with the computer name of the local server, connect to the load balanced website using the cluster IP address or URL, and power off the active server. When you refresh the browser, you'll receive the web page from the new active web server.

I perform this quick test now to make sure the load balance is working before I start changing the configuration. That way it's easier to troubleshoot if something goes wrong: I know it worked with the default configuration, so I must have made a mistake with one of my new configuration changes.

TRY IT NOW Before we continue examining and changing the default configuration of the web farm, perform a quick test of the load balance to make sure it's working.

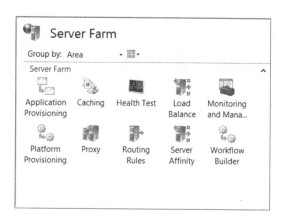

Figure 14.6 The configuration icons for the new web farm

With the web farm performing its load balancing operations successfully, let's examine the default configuration and take a look at some of the changes to the configuration you may want to make for your environment.

14.3   *Configuring Application Request Routing*

The default configuration created during the installation of the web farm works well for many environments. In this section you'll examine some of the default settings of the URL Rewrite and load balance and view the options you may want to change.

Let's start by examining the default URL Rewrite rule that was created automatically.

14.3.1   *Examining the URL Rewrite rule*

During the creation of the web farm, the wizard offers to create a URL Rewrite rule that redirects all HTTP requests that the ARR server receives to the load balance. This request is then subject to the load balancing algorithm (described shortly) that determines which physical server to send the request to.

You can view the default rule in the URL Rewrite icon of the IIS manager. (If you don't remember URL Rewrite, see chapter 12.) The default rule matches all URLs and has an action condition that points the requests to the correct web farm. Figure 14.7 shows the two sections of the default rule created by the wizard.

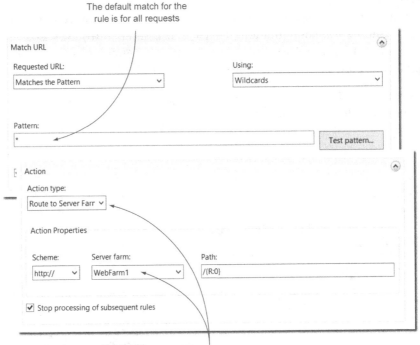

The default match for the rule is for all requests

Notice the action is to route the requests to the server farm listed in the Action Properties

Figure 14.7   The default URL Rewrite rule redirects all HTTP requests to the web farm.

For simple environments with a single web farm and a few websites, this rule works well. ARR supports managing more than one web farm and can handle thousands of websites. In cases of larger and more complex environments, this rule is too simple. In fact you may want to create your own rules that point specific websites to specific web farms. An example would be to create a redirection rule similar to those in chapter 12. An HTTP_HOST condition for www.company.loc may have an action that redirects the requests to WebFarm1, whereas www.BikeShop.Com may have an action that redirects to WebFarm2, but for now, for a single farm, the default rule works well.

> **WARNING**   I find that making changes to the existing rule causes problems, so if I need to make changes, I delete the default rule and create my own.

Similarly the default load balance settings work well in a smaller environment. But let's take a look at those settings to be sure.

14.3.2 *Changing the load balancing algorithm*

One of the benefits of using ARR is the ability to control the load balancing algorithm that ARR uses to redirect requests. This algorithm controls how servers are selected to receive a new inbound request.

You have several algorithm options to choose from. I'll show you the more common ones first, and then you can experiment when you get to the lab. To locate the load balance options, select your new web farm in the IIS manager. In the Load Balance options page, click the Load Balance icon, and the default option will be displayed, as shown in figure 14.8.

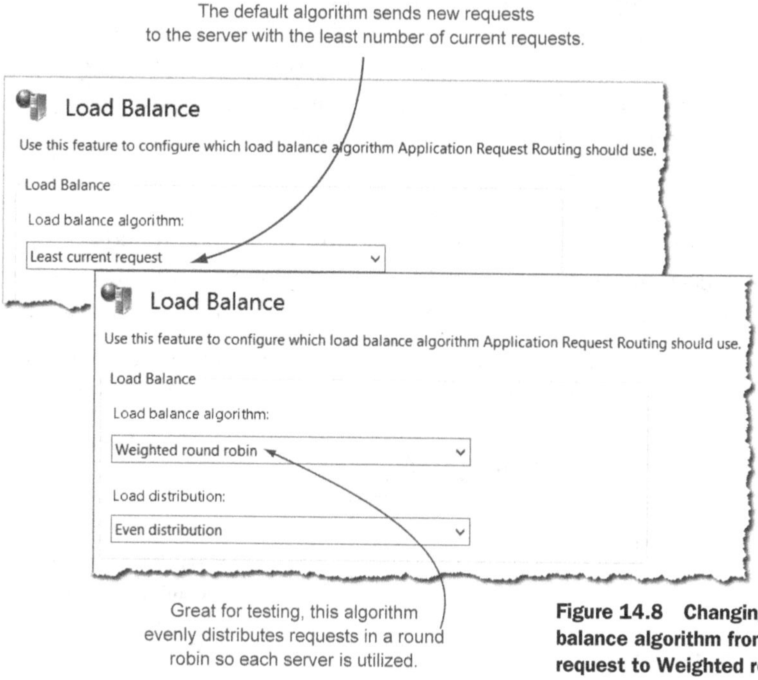

The default algorithm sends new requests
to the server with the least number of current requests.

Great for testing, this algorithm
evenly distributes requests in a round
robin so each server is utilized.

Figure 14.8   Changing the default load balance algorithm from Least current request to Weighted round robin for testing

The default algorithm is Least current request, which means ARR will route new requests to the web server with the least number of current requests. This is a good option that balances the request load among your servers.

I don't often need to change the default except when I'm testing to see if the load balance is working. The challenge in testing the default option is that it's hard to put enough load on the first server so that it moves requests to the next one. I like to change the algorithm to Weighted round robin, with an Even distribution, when testing to see the load balance switch between servers. The round robin algorithm sends requests to servers in a sequence rather than based on workload. As an example, when I open a browser to test the load balance using http://www.company.loc, the URL for my default website, it connects me to the first server available. Then as I press F5 (sometimes several times) to refresh the browser, it switches (round robin) to the other servers in the load balance.

By doing that, I can visually see that each server is responding by the changing display of the host names, as shown in figure 14.9. This is a simple testing method, but it works well.

After I finish testing I normally return the algorithm to its default setting of Least current request, because I find it works well in most situations. There are additional algorithms to choose from. Most of them are for special environments and lie outside the scope of this book, but here are a few you might find useful:

- *Weighted round robin*—ARR distributes requests in round robin fashion, switching from one server to the next. In general, unless you specifically want a round robin, other algorithms are better.
- *Weighted total traffic*—ARR distributes requests based on size in bytes so that each server is servicing the same amount of data. The server that currently has the least amount of request data is the next server to receive a new request. This is one of my preferred options when working with websites that produce large amounts of data, such as streaming video and audio.
- *Least current request*—This is the default setting. ARR distributes request traffic to the server that currently has the least number of requests. This works well for websites that don't produce heavy content like video and audio.
- *Least response time*—This is more like the traditional load balancing model. It distributes requests to the fastest responding server and is similar to NLB.

After checking the configuration of the load balance, it's time to start monitoring its health and statistics. In the next section you'll look at the health monitor.

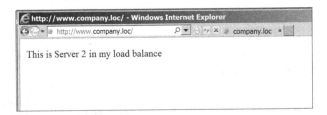

Figure 14.9 Browser displaying the unique web page that contains the host name of the local server for testing

14.4   Logging and health monitoring with ARR

Once your load balance is established, you should monitor its performance and health to ensure it's functioning the way you want. ARR includes health testing and monitoring tools to make this task easier.

This section covers the basics of the health monitoring statistics with ARR and is an important building block for future chapters. Let's perform some health tests for the load balance.

14.4.1   Checking the health of the load balance

In addition to monitoring the status of the web servers in the farm, ARR can specifically monitor the health of a URL, such as your primary website. It verifies which nodes (servers in the load balance) are serving the URL. If a server fails to respond, it's marked as unhealthy, and requests aren't sent to it. When the server returns online and is healthy again, requests to that URL can be sent to it once again.

The Health Test icon for your web farm in the IIS manager is where all that happens. You enter the URL that you want tested at the top, along with the frequency of the test. The default is to test the URL every 30 seconds and to wait for a response (timeout) of 30 seconds, as shown in figure 14.10.

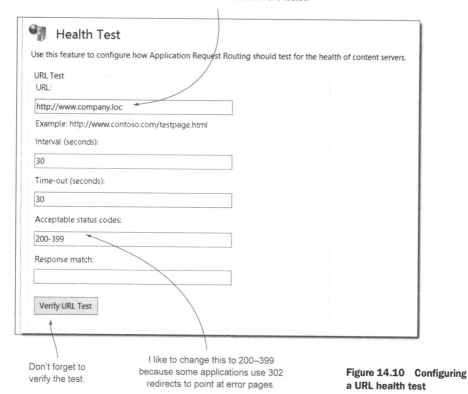

Figure 14.10   Configuring a URL health test

ARR automatically replaces the URL domain with the IP address of each of the nodes so that every server in the farm is tested. You should verify the URL test—to make sure there are no typos—by clicking the Verify URL Test button at the bottom of the form, and then apply the changes. You can see the health of the nodes in the health monitoring statistics discussed shortly.

With the settings in figure 14.10, if you stop the website on one host, it will be listed as unhealthy in about 30 seconds. ARR won't send requests to it until it becomes healthy again.

Let's take a look at the health monitor, where you can see the health of your nodes and the current statistics of your web traffic.

14.4.2 *Health monitor statistics*

ARR includes a great health monitoring application to which we'll return often in the next several chapters. For now, let's take a look at the traffic statistics and the health of the nodes in the web farm.

In the IIS manager, under your web farm folder, is a Health Monitoring icon. It displays information about the health of your nodes (available or not) along with statistics about the number of current requests and response times that each node is handling, as shown in figure 14.11.

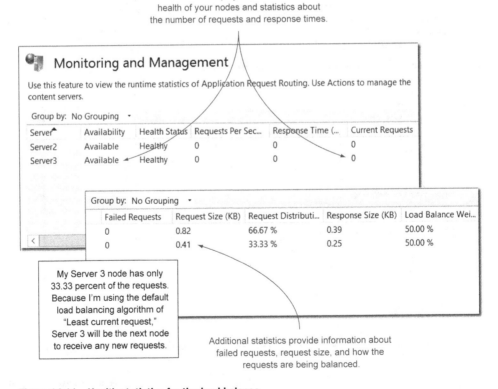

Figure 14.11 **Health statistics for the load balance**

Additional statistics specific to how the requests are being load balanced are displayed, such as request size and request distribution. By monitoring these statistics you can determine whether your load balance is functioning properly and handling the requests in a rapid manner.

This chapter has included a lot of information, but once you try it a couple of times, you'll see why I like ARR so much. We'll explore more features of ARR in later chapters. I think you'll find it to be a great solution. To make sure you have all the information for the next chapter, try the lab before you finish lunch.

14.5 Lab

This lab is similar to the one you did in chapter 13. I want you to deploy a web farm using ARR. Make sure you have two additional servers for this lab, as described in chapter 1. In this lab, those servers are named Web1 and Web2.

TRY IT NOW

In case you you didn't get a chance to perform the Try It Now sections, I repeat them here for your convenience. Once complete, you can start the lab with task 1.

1. Before installing ARR make sure you remove the NLB you installed in chapter 13. Here in this chapter use your domain controller as the ARR control server. Install ARR to the domain controller and verify you have the Server Farms folder added to the IIS manager. (Remember, you may have to close and reopen the IIS manager.)

2. As in chapter 13, the web servers hosting the websites should have IIS installed and a test page that displays the host name of the server in place. Again, I prefer to put a web page in the default website for testing, such as http://hostname/NLB.htm, or make a default.htm to keep the URL simple, such as http://hostname.

3. The control server (the one with ARR) is the load balancer, so DNS should have an A record that points to the IP address of the control server. This is where all HTTP requests need to be directed. See chapter 13 for review if needed.

4. Create a new web farm and add the two web server VMs you created for the lab environment.

TASK 1

If you didn't get a chance to do this earlier in the chapter, install ARR on your domain controller. This will become the control server for ARR.

TASK 2

Using the wizard, add a new web farm named WebBikezShop to ARR and include the two web servers Web1 and Web2.

TASK 3

Add a DNS record for the URL www.WebBikez.com that points to the IP address of your domain controller, the ARR control server.

TASK 4

Add a web page to Web1 and Web2 in the default site that contains the computer name of the local server. This will be used for testing.

TASK 5

Configure the load balance algorithm for Weighted round robin.

TASK 6

Configure the health test with the URL www.WebBikez.com and a 15-second interval with a 15-second timeout.

TASK 7

Open a browser on the domain controller with the URL www.WebBikez.com. Test and verify the load balance by turning off the first server that responds to the request. Check the Monitoring and Management page to see the server change its status to unhealthy.

14.6   *Ideas to try on your own*

Combine the information you've learned so far by deploying additional websites and web pages to the load balance using PowerShell. Also, if you haven't tried this yet, enable remote management and confirm you can manage the servers Web1 and Web2 using the IIS manager on your domain controller.

High availability for
ARR using Microsoft NLB

In chapter 14 you began using Application Request Routing (ARR) as the load balancer for your IIS web servers. Imagine what would happen if the ARR server went offline. You'd lose the entire load balance, and customers wouldn't be able to access any websites. Protecting ARR from failure is just as important as protecting your websites.

In this very short chapter you'll see how using Microsoft NLB is a great solution for protecting your ARR load balancers in case one should fail. You already have almost all the information you need to make this work from chapters 13 and 14. In this chapter I help you tie it together.

This is a short chapter, but don't underestimate its importance. If you lose your ARR server, the entire web farm fails. You need to protect your ARR server and provide failover capabilities.

In this chapter I describe the concept by using Microsoft NLB to load balance two ARR servers. If you want to follow along with the Try It Nows, you'll need to build another VM for the new ARR server and join it to your domain. You can do that now or read the chapter to get the concept and wait until the lab.

15.1 Adding affordable high availability

ARR doesn't have any failover or high availability features built in to the product. It's up to you to provide those capabilities. Many larger implementations use a hardware-based—and expensive—load balancer for this; fortunately you can also use the free load balancer NLB from Microsoft. Whichever you choose, the concepts are the same.

Making ARR highly available requires two ARR servers instead of one, as shown in figure 15.1. The ARR servers themselves are placed into a load balance by using a hardware load balancer or Microsoft NLB. This does increase your hardware costs (another ARR server), but it's worth it if one of those servers should fail.

Let's look at the requirements for creating a highly available ARR environment.

15.1.1 Requirements for a highly available ARR

To achieve a highly available ARR environment, you'll need an additional load balancer. As discussed in previous chapters, this can be a hardware load balancer such as a BIG-IP F5. Again, I get the question all the time: "If I have a hardware load balancer, would I even use ARR?" My answer is yes, ARR provides many features specific to IIS, and I think it's the best solution. But when you need to protect ARR and the functionality it's providing from failure, a good hardware load balancer is a great choice.

What do you do if you don't have an available hardware load balancer lying around? Microsoft recommends (and I agree with the recommendation) that NLB is perfect for this situation. As you've already seen, NLB is easy to configure, and its limitations don't impact the ARR environment. It makes for a great, affordable solution.

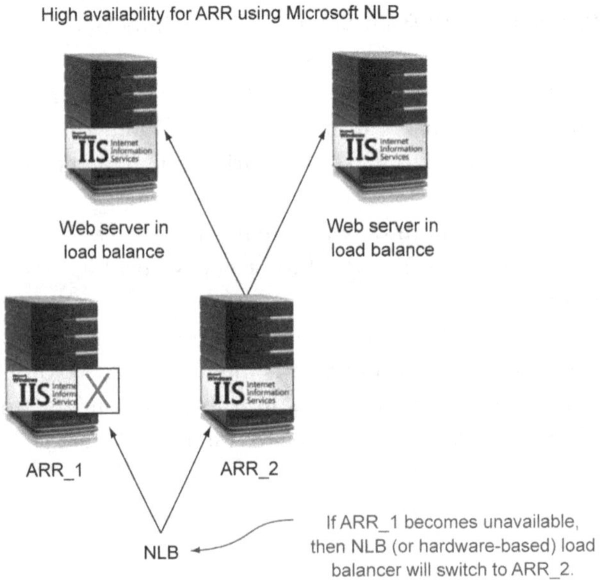

High availability for ARR using Microsoft NLB

Web server in load balance

Web server in load balance

ARR_1   ARR_2

NLB   If ARR_1 becomes unavailable, then NLB (or hardware-based) load balancer will switch to ARR_2.

Figure 15.1   Two ARR servers with an additional load balancer such as Microsoft NLB

If you've worked with Microsoft Clustering services, you can use it in place of NLB. It does provide better health monitoring statistics than NLB, but I find, if I'm lacking a hardware load balancer, NLB is the easiest and works well.

One more requirement is very important: the two ARR servers need to share their configuration with each other. Doing that is a simple process—I discuss it in chapter 16. You can use Shared Configurations for IIS for many purposes. I chose to place that discussion after this chapter and before some of the other chapters that need it. I remind you of turning on Shared Configuration for ARR in chapter 16. By sharing their configuration, the two ARR servers will be synced with each other so that changes made on one are reflected on the other.

In this chapter I have chosen to use NLB to protect two ARR servers. Let me run down the installation process for you.

15.1.2 Installation of NLB for ARR

Believe it or not this section is more of a review than anything else. If you worked through chapters 13 and 14, you already know how to set this up, but this time you'll be performing it on the ARR servers instead of the web servers. Let's review the process just to make sure.

The first step is installing ARR on a second server to be used in the load balance. I'll use PowerShell and PowerShell Remoting to install the NLB feature on the two ARR servers and then configure the load balance for NLB. The following example creates a PowerShell Remoting session to the two ARR servers and installs the NLB feature:

```
PS> $sessions = New-PSSession -ComputerName Arr1, Arr2

PS> Invoke-Command -Session $Sessions {Import-Module ServerManager}

PS> Invoke-Command -Session $Sessions {Add-WindowsFeature NLB}
```

TRY IT NOW If you built the extra VM, make sure to join it to your domain and add IIS and ARR. From one of your VMs, connect and install NLB on the two ARR servers using the cmdlets from the preceding code.

Once again I can use the NLB cmdlets to create the load balance and add the second server to the load balance:

```
PS> New-NlbCluster -HostName ARR1 -InterfaceName Ethernet -ClusterName ARR -
    ⇒ClusterPrimaryIP 192.168.3.200 -SubnetMask 255.255.255.0 -
    ⇒OperationMode Multicast

PS> Get-NlbCluster -HostName ARR1 | Add-NlbClusterNode -NewNodeName ARR2 -
    ⇒NewNodeInterface Ethernet
```

TRY IT NOW Complete the Microsoft NLB configuration using the New-NlbCluster and Add-NlbClusterNode cmdlets. This is a good time to put the cluster IP address into DNS as well.

At this point NLB is almost completely configured to protect your ARR servers in case one fails. In chapter 17 you'll complete this by adding the ARR servers to a Shared Configuration—but it's not time to do that yet, so don't jump ahead.

Let's make sure NLB is working correctly by checking the Network Load Balance Manager.

15.1.3 *Monitoring NLB: a quick review*

NLB doesn't have all the health monitoring tools that ARR does, but then again it really doesn't need much. It's important, both during the initial configuration of NLB and on occasion while it runs (once a month), that you check to make sure that both nodes are online and converged.

You can use the NLB Manager to connect to the ARR load balance and check the nodes or use the PowerShell cmdlet `Get-NlbClusterNode` from the NetworkLoadBalancingClusters module, as shown in figure 15.2.

> **TRY IT NOW**   Check the convergence of the load balance using both the GUI and the `Get-NlbClusterNode` cmdlet.

With all the nodes converged, I like to test NLB by intentionally failing one of the servers. But we have one more step to accomplish in chapter 16 before you should try that.

All the labs in this book have been built around a specific setup that you created in a virtual environment, and each lab has built on the previous. As you can tell from this chapter, providing high availability to ARR means that you would need some extra

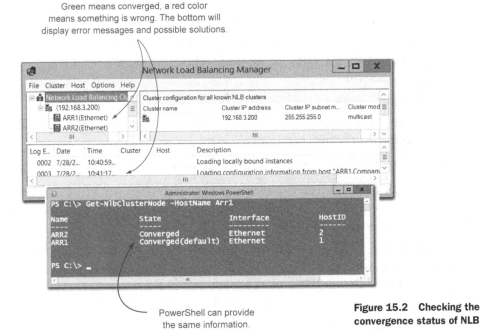

Green means converged, a red color means something is wrong. The bottom will display error messages and possible solutions.

PowerShell can provide the same information.

Figure 15.2   Checking the convergence status of NLB

virtual machines. I wrote the lab for this chapter to be completely independent of all other labs. If you have the time and resources to build an extra virtual machine to test the NLB for ARR, I highly recommend it. If not, go ahead and start the next chapter. You can always return later and try out the lab at another time.

15.2 Lab (optional)

This lab is optional because it requires that you build a new VM as a second ARR control server for the load balance. If you have the resources and time, you should try this out if you intend to use ARR.

TRY IT NOW

In case you didn't get a chance to perform the Try It Now sections, I repeat them here for your convenience. Once complete, you can start the lab with task 1.

1 If you built the extra VM, make sure to join it to your domain and add IIS and ARR. From one of your VMs, connect and install NLB on the two ARR servers using the cmdlets from the code (earlier in the chapter).
2 Complete the Microsoft NLB configuration using the `New-NlbCluster` and `Add-NlbClusterNode` cmdlets. This is a good time to put the cluster IP address into DNS as well.
3 Check the convergence of the load balance using both the GUI and the `Get-NlbClusterNode` cmdlet.

TASK 1

Create a new VM and install the Windows server operating system of your choice. Name the computer ARR2 and join it to your domain.

TASK 2

Install Microsoft NLB on both ARR control servers—your domain controller and the new ARR2 server. Configure NLB to load balance between the two servers, as you did in chapter 13.

TASK 3

At this point, don't attempt to test the ARR load balance. You need to perform a configuration change that's discussed in chapter 16. When you reach that chapter, you'll share the configuration between the two ARR servers so that they're identical.

15.3 Ideas to try on your own

If you're currently running a production web farm environment, examine your current load balancing solution. Is it hardware-based? If so, what kind is it and who's responsible for its configuration and maintenance? Is the load balancing solution highly available in case the hardware fails?

If you currently don't have a load balancing solution, consider building a test environment, matching your current production environment, that uses ARR.

Sharing content and configuration to the web farm

Regardless of the load balancing and high availability technology you choose, supplying the web content to your websites becomes a challenge as your web farm grows. So far in this book you've had locally stored content (website files) on the web server for each of your websites. That becomes challenging in a web farm when you need to update or add to those files—you'll find yourself running around copying files to each server in the farm. This chapter focuses on ways to make this process more manageable by automating the file copy process using PowerShell or Microsoft's Distributed File System.

Content doesn't have to be locally stored; it can be centralized in a single location and shared to all the web servers in the farm. This method creates a *content server* that the websites access for the website files and works well for both small and larger web farms. An increase in complexity is involved, so this solution may not be for everyone. But you'll have a chance to decide for yourself.

This chapter focuses on three options for making your web farm content easier to manage. You'll share website content to the farm from a single location using a network share and also using Microsoft's Distributed File System (DFS).

By the end of this chapter you'll have these options in your arsenal for managing content in your web farm. Let's get started with deploying that content with PowerShell.

16.1 Sharing content for a web farm using PowerShell

Over the years several methods of adding and updating website files on web servers in a web farm have been developed, some with scripts using various scripting languages, some using commands such as Copy or Robocopy. All of these try to achieve the same goal: quickly adding and updating website files on multiple servers.

Remember, each web server in your web farm needs the same websites and website files in order to provide fault tolerance. You can achieve that in two ways: one is to make sure each server maintains a local copy of the website files that are updated; the other is to create a central repository (content server) that holds all the content in one location that each server shares. In this section, you'll discover two different methods of handling local copies of the websites:

- Manually deploy local content using PowerShell
- Automate the deployment with a PowerShell script

Let's start with a manual deployment of website content to multiple servers using PowerShell.

16.1.1 Manually deploying local-stored content using PowerShell

Manual deployment of web content is nothing more than a file copy. In fact you could achieve the same results in this section by using the Copy or Robocopy commands. PowerShell adds more flexibility in scripting automation, though, and is frankly easier to use.

You've already seen the basic PowerShell commands in chapter 13 when you initially deployed website content and created new websites for the load balance. Let's do a quick review and try it out again. Then you'll put these commands into a script for simple automation of the process.

DEPLOY (COPY) WEBSITE FILES

If you have a small web farm that rarely needs to have its content updated, then this manual process—you have to run the commands—works well. If your farm grows or you need to update content more often, you can automate these commands (which you'll do shortly) to reduce your workload.

I'll create a simple scenario with a new website so you can try this. You have two web servers in a load balance, named Web1 and Web2. On your local computer you have the folder C:\sites\WebBikezPhotos that contains the website files for a new website. Using PowerShell you can copy that content to all the web servers in the farm and then create a new website.

You start by creating a variable that contains the names of the web servers, like this:

```
PS> $Servers = 'Web1', 'Web2'
```

Then, using the Copy-Item command in PowerShell, you copy the folder structure to each of those web servers:

```
PS> $servers | foreach{Copy-Item -Path c:\sites\* -Destination \\$_\c$\sites
    -Recurse -Force}
```

You can copy specific sites or entire folders that contain multiple sites, as I've done.

TRY IT NOW   Create a new folder C:\sites\WebBikesPhotos on your domain controller (DC) and place a simple default web page in the folder that identifies the website. You can even place some of your favorite photos into the folder for fun. Deploy the folder to the servers in the web farm.

Once the content is copied to each of the web servers in the farm, you need to create the new Photos website.

CREATE A NEW WEBSITE
Using PowerShell to create a new application pool and website for the Photos content is the fastest way:

```
PS> $Sessions = New-PSSession -ComputerName Web1, Web2
```

```
PS> Invoke-Command -Session $Sessions {New-WebAppPool -Name
    WebBikezPhotospool}
```

```
PS> Invoke-Command -Session $Sessions {New-Website -Name Photos -HostHeader
    Photos.WebBikez.com -PhysicalPath C:\sites\WebBikezPhotos -
    ApplicationPool WebBikezPhotospool}
```

TRY IT NOW   Using the preceding commands create a new website and make sure you can access the site and the default web page you created.

As you've seen in earlier chapters, you can also deploy certificates and set up remote management, but let's keep the focus on the content and websites for this chapter.

UPDATING WEBSITE CONTENT
In the future if you update the web pages on your computer, you'll run the copy process again to update the files on the remote computers. Make sure to fully test the updated website content before you deploy to a production web farm:

```
PS> $Servers = 'Web1', 'Web2'
```

```
PS> $Servers | foreach{copy-item -Path c:\sites\* -Destination \\$_\c$ -
    Recurse -Force}
```

What if you need to update website content often and for several websites? I like to put those commands in a script so it's easier to run (less typing). Let's look at automating this example.

16.1.2 *Automating with PowerShell scripts*
One of the reasons I like to use PowerShell instead of older commands is that it's so much easier to automate PowerShell commands. In its simplest form, PowerShell scripting involves taking commands that you've manually run and putting them into a script file—similar to old DOS batch files. That creates a script that performs automation.

> **Above and beyond**
>
> You can further enhance those scripts by providing parameters and help information; you can even turn your script into its own PowerShell cmdlet (advanced function). The topic of advanced functions is more than we can cover here. It's a PowerShell tool-making topic covered extensively in *Learn PowerShell Toolmaking in a Month of Lunches* by Don Jones and Jeffery Hicks (Manning, 2012).

A PowerShell script is a text file with the extension .ps1. You can create the text file using any text editor of your choice, such as Notepad or the built-in PowerShell ISE. Figure 16.1 shows a script file named Update-Content.ps1 in which I typed the copy commands into the script.

Anytime I need to update the files on the web servers in the farm, I can run the script from a PowerShell prompt, as in the following example:

```
PS> C:\scripts\Update-Content.ps1
```

NOTE You need to have a script execution policy that permits you to run scripts. By default PowerShell doesn't permit this, so change your policy. You can read more about this in the help files in PowerShell's About _Execution_Policy.

This simple script makes the process much easier, and you can quickly deploy new content to both a test environment and your production environment.

TRY IT NOW Create your own version of the preceding script. Change the default web page in your local C:\sites\WebBikezPhotos folder and run the script to deploy the changes out to the web farm.

This process does have its challenges. If you make a mistake and forget to update one of the web servers, it will be out of sync and deliver the customer old content. Also this process requires that you initiate the copy process.

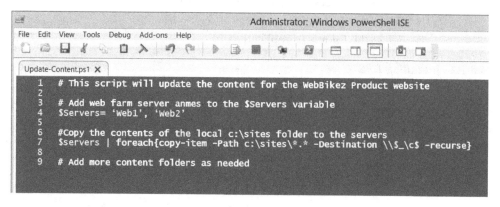

Figure 16.1   A simple copy script to deploy new content to web servers

There's another method of synchronizing your web servers' content: using Microsoft's Distributed File System Replication.

16.2 *Sharing content using Distributed File System (DFS)*

Microsoft's Distributed File System is designed to synchronize folders across file servers and has been around for a long time. No doubt you've run across it in your IT pro career. IIS can take advantage of DFS to synchronize website content across web servers in a web farm. Although it's slightly more complicated to configure than the simple script from the previous section, it overcomes a couple problems with the script.

There are two drawbacks to the copy script:

- The copy process doesn't delete or remove files. That leaves old content out on your servers and increases disk usage. You can fix that by writing better scripts and scheduling updates using PowerShell, but it requires a much greater understanding of scripting.
- The web farm content is only updated when you run the script. If you make a mistake, you could have web servers that don't get updated and have old content.

Microsoft DFS overcomes these drawbacks by continuously updating the folders of your choice on each web server. If you delete a file or folder from one web server, it will be deleted from the others. As you add and update files, DFS keeps all servers synchronized. Sounds like a magical solution, and it's one of my preferred solutions, but it requires additional configuration on all the web servers in the farm.

DFS is used for many network situations beyond IIS and has extensive configuration options. I'll focus on the configuration of DFS for web servers in a farm. For a more complete discussion of DFS, check out www.TechNet.com.

I want you to wait for the lab before you try this; it will help you to see the complete process first. Here's the process for configuring DFS for a web farm:

1 Install DFS to the web servers.
2 Create a replication group.
3 Add web servers to the replication group.
4 Select the replication topology and schedule.
5 Select the folders to replicate.

16.2.1 *Installing DFS*

DFS is a role that must be installed on each of the web servers in the farm that will synchronize content. You can install DFS using the graphical Server Manager or PowerShell. DFS has many components to support features outside of IIS. The one you want for your web servers is called DFS Replication.

In the graphical Server Manager for Windows Server 2008 R2, DFS Replication is located under the role File Server/Distributed File System. On Windows Server 2012 the role is located under File and Storage Services/File and ISCSI services. I find this difference too complicated to remember, so I prefer using PowerShell to install the role because it's the same on both Windows Server 2008 R2 and Server 2012.

To install the DFS Replication role and Management tool on a local web server:

```
PS> Add-WindowsFeature FS-DFS-Replication, RSAT-DFS-Mgmt-Con
```

To install DFS on remote web servers in the farm using PowerShell Remoting:

```
PS> Invoke-Command -ComputerName Web1, Web2 {Add-WindowsFeature -Name FS-DFS-
    ➥Replication}
```

After the roles have been installed, DFS is configured using the DFS Management tool and by creating a new replication group.

16.2.2 *Creating a replication group*

The DFS Management tool contains a wizard that walks you through the process of configuring replication between folders on each web server. The process begins by creating a new replication group. A *replication group* is a collection of web servers that replicates based on settings you provide to the wizard.

To start the wizard, open the DFS Management tool and select New Replication Group, as shown in figure 16.2.

The wizard will prompt for configuration information to complete the process. Remember that DFS can be used for many tasks outside of IIS, so some of these options won't be necessary for your web servers. I'm only showing the ones you need for IIS. In figure 16.3 you can see how to select the type of replication group desired. For web servers sharing content, the best option is Multipurpose.

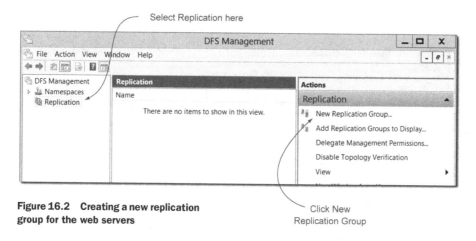

Figure 16.2   Creating a new replication group for the web servers

For IIS shared content
this is the best option.

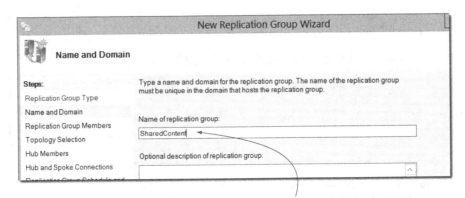

New Replication Group Wizard

Replication Group Type

Steps:

Replication Group Type

Name and Domain

Replication Group Members

Topology Selection

Hub Members

Hub and Spoke Connections

Replication Group Schedule and Bandwidth

Select the type of replication group to create.

◉ Multipurpose replication group

This option configures replication between two or more servers for publication, content sharing, and other scenarios.

◯ Replication group for data collection

This option configures two-way replication between two servers, such as a branch server and a hub (destination) server. This allows you to collect data at the hub server. You can then use backup software to back up the data on the hub server.

Figure 16.3   Select Multipurpose replication group for sharing website content

DFS supports multiple replication groups, so each group needs a name. In this example, all the website content for the farm is located under folders in C:\sites, so I named the group SharedContent, as shown in figure 16.4.

After the replication group is created, the wizard will continue to walk you through the process by letting you select which web servers should be members of the group.

16.2.3 Adding web servers to the replication group

You need to add the web servers that will share (replicate) content to the replication group. The wizard provides a simple form to select the servers for the group. If you try to add a server to this form, and it doesn't have the DFS role installed, you'll receive an error.

New Replication Group Wizard

Name and Domain

Steps:

Replication Group Type

Name and Domain

Replication Group Members

Topology Selection

Hub Members

Hub and Spoke Connections

Type a name and domain for the replication group. The name of the replication group must be unique in the domain that hosts the replication group.

Name of replication group:

SharedContent

Optional description of replication group:

Figure 16.4   Creating the name for the replication group

Create a name for the replication group. This group will replicate your files to each web sever.

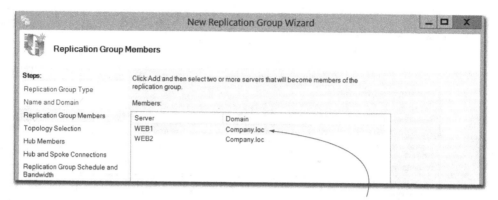

**Figure 16.5   Adding web servers
to the replication group**

Using the Add button at the bottom
of the page, add all the web servers that will
replicate site content with each other.

Figure 16.5 shows how you add servers to the replication group.

You can return to the DFS management tool later to add or remove web servers from the list. As your web farm grows, add the new servers, and the website content will be automatically replicated.

16.2.4   Selecting the replication topology and schedule

If you've worked with Active Directory site topologies, this next step in the process will be familiar. If you haven't, a *replication topology* controls how content will be replicated to the web servers in the replication group. There are three options:

- *Full mesh*—You can make a change to the content on *any* web server, and it will be replicated to all other servers in the replication group. This is best for small web farms of ten servers or less because of the two-way replication.
- *Hub and spoke*—One server is designated as the hub server. You make all your changes to the hub, and then those changes are replicated out to the other servers. Unlike full mesh, if you make changes to *any* of the other servers, those will be overwritten when the hub replicates out. Hub and spoke is best for larger farms because it reduces network traffic.
- *Custom*—You can create your own custom topology for DFS—however, this is unnecessary for web farms both large and small. Full mesh or hub and spoke are the best options.

The wizard provides the replication options for you to select, as shown in figure 16.6. You can schedule replication to occur at specific times on specific days. That reduces the network traffic during business hours if you have a large collection of files in DFS. Web server content is small enough that it normally doesn't require this type of scheduling, and in fact it could cause the web servers in the farm to be not fully up to date.

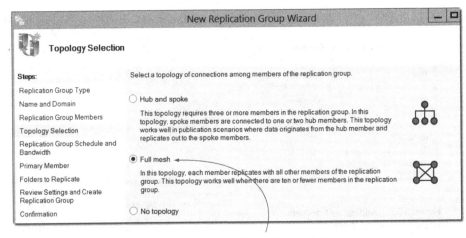

Figure 16.6   Selecting the replication topology based on the size of the web farm

For less than ten web servers in the group, choose full mesh, if larger, then hub and spoke is best.

The best option is to replicate continuously to make sure any changes are made immediately, as shown in figure 16.7.

Now that the replication topology and schedule have been configured, the last steps involve selecting the folders (content) you want to replicate to all the web servers in the farm.

This is the best option for replicating web content. Scheduling content updates can cause website mismatches in a farm.

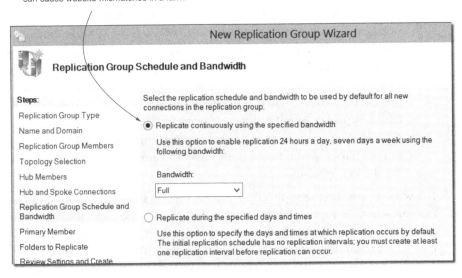

Figure 16.7   Selecting continuous replication for web server content

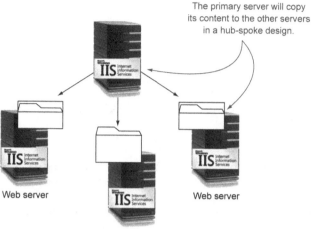

Figure 16.8   Hub and spoke design

16.2.5   *Selecting the folders to replicate*

The time has arrived to select the content that will be replicated across all the web servers in the farm. In this example all my content for all the WebBikez websites is located under C:\sites, so I only need to add one folder to the replication.

The wizard prompts for a primary server. In a full mesh topology, this is the server that initially contains the content that will be replicated out to the other servers. After the initial replication, changes made to *any* server will be fully replicated. If the topology selection is hub and spoke, content will always be replicated from the primary to the other servers, as shown in figure 16.8. If you make changes on a non-primary server, those changes will be overwritten.

The wizard provides a dropdown box to select the primary server, as shown in figure 16.9.

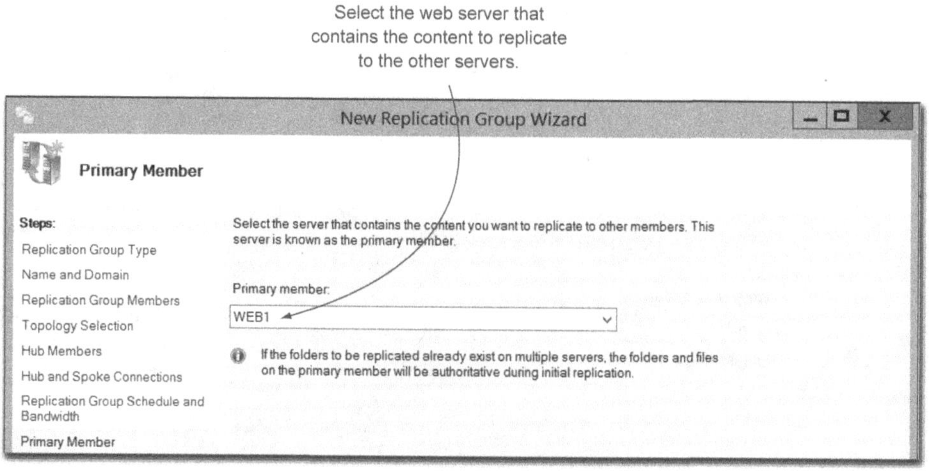

Figure 16.9   Selecting the primary server that contains the initial content to be replicated

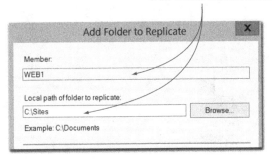

The primary server contains the files to initially replicate. Specify the location of the website folders and files.

Figure 16.10 Choosing the folder to replicate to the replication group

Once the primary server is selected, choose the folder that you want replicated to all other servers in the replication group, as shown in figure 16.10.

The last step in the wizard is to specify into which folder location on the non-primary servers to copy the content. You can choose all the remaining target servers and type the directory (folder) location that you want the content copied to, as shown in figure 16.11. When replication completes, you'll have the new folder and all its content on each web server.

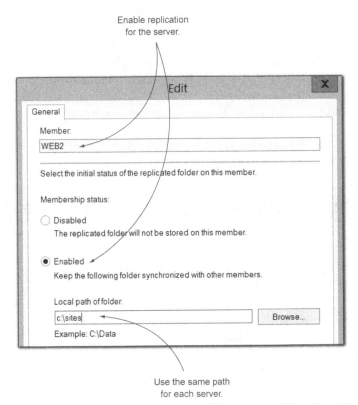

Enable replication for the server.

Use the same path for each server.

Figure 16.11 Setting the folder location on the target servers

When the wizard has completed, you'll be notified that replication will begin when Active Directory informs the servers of the changes through a Group Policy update. This could take several minutes. If you're as impatient as I am, you can force the Group Policy update on each server, so DFS starts replicating content, by typing the following command:

```
PS> GPUpdate /Force
```

Within a moment you'll see the folders and website files appear on each server—but only if you try out the lab at the end of this chapter. I would have you do a Try It Now, but this process takes several minutes for you to perform, so wait until the lab.

As you add or remove files to the folder on any server, they're automatically updated on every server in the farm. Microsoft DFS is a great way to share content between web servers and keep the content up to date.

16.3 *Sharing content from a single location*

The previous two sections demonstrated how to share and update locally stored content between web servers in a web farm. Whether you choose to manually do that with PowerShell and script or have the local content updated continuously using Microsoft DFS, you'll greatly reduce mistakes and management time spent updating content.

Another approach to sharing content with web servers in a farm is to centralize, or store your content in one location, and then have the websites access that content across the network. Here are some of the advantages to this approach over locally-stored content:

- Content is stored in one location making updates easy.
- You can easily store content for hundreds of websites, creating a *content server.*
- It reduces the local storage requirements for each web server.

I have to be honest—this is my personal favorite in most cases, and I'll use this same concept in the next two chapters to make the web farm even easier to manage. You may ask, "Well, if this is your favorite, then why didn't we start with it?" The answer is simple: although it's easy to configure, there's a danger that must be addressed if you should lose access to the content server. By not having local content, if the content server fails, then all websites fail. There's a way to protect against this, and I'll give you direction on how to handle it. Let's get started with the easy part: using content for your websites from a central location.

16.3.1 *Creating a network share*

All your website content can be stored in a central location—a file server—that shares that content to your websites. Each website is configured to access this remote content. That means you no longer need to have locally stored content and therefore can reduce the complexity of your web farm by avoiding Microsoft DFS.

Back in chapter 5, when you first started creating websites, I explained that a website needs access to the physical web pages, which are stored locally. You configured a

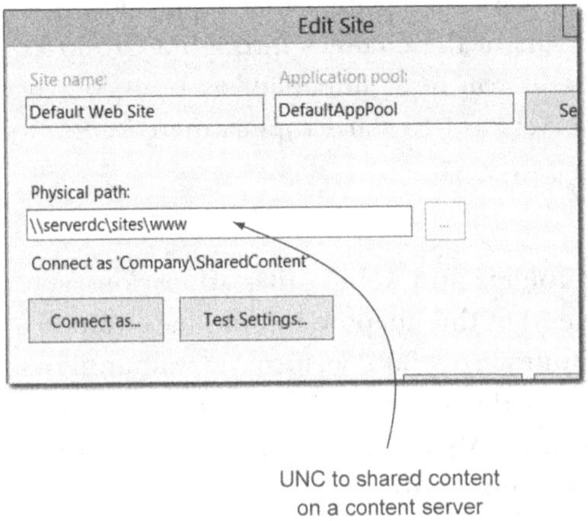

Edit Site

Site name: Application pool:

Default Web Site   DefaultAppPool   Se

Physical path:

\\serverdc\sites\www   ...

Connect as 'Company\SharedContent'

Connect as...   Test Settings...

Figure 16.12   Configuring a UNC path for the website files

UNC to shared content
on a content server

physical path when you created the website to those files. The physical path doesn't need to point to a local folder. It can point to a network share—Universal Naming Convention (UNC)—as shown in figure 16.12.

In this example I created a simple network share on a file server and copied all the website files to that share. The websites on web servers in the farm can access those files through the network by connecting to the share.

TRY IT NOW   Using the IIS manager examine the basic settings for one of the websites you created earlier in the book. Note that the physical path points to a local folder. In the upcoming lab you'll change this to a network share.

As with any other file share you've set up in your network environment, you can create a user account and assign permissions to the share. You'll do this shortly in the lab, but for the demonstration here I created an account in Active Directory called SharedContent. The beauty of this solution is that your web servers don't have to be members of the AD domain—you could as easily create a local account and assign permissions. After typing the UNC to the share, click the Connect As button to enter the user account to use to access the share, as shown in figure 16.13.

Specify an AD or local user
with credentials and permissions
to the share.

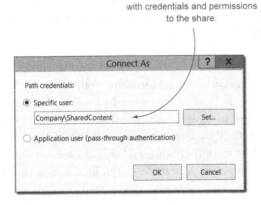

Connect As   ?   X

Path credentials:

⦿ Specific user:

Company\SharedContent   Set...

◯ Application user (pass-through authentication)

OK   Cancel

Figure 16.13   Setting an AD or local account with permissions to the network share

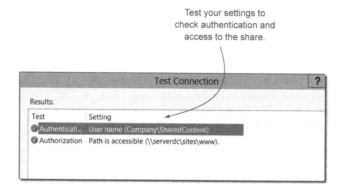

Test your settings to
check authentication and
access to the share.

Figure 16.14 Testing the account to verify access to the website files on the network share

After setting the account, click the Test Settings button to make sure that the website can authenticate to the network share and access the UNC path specified, as shown in figure 16.14.

Each website on each server is configured to get its website content from this network share. Any changes you make to the content immediately affect all servers in the web farm. This method of sharing content is easier to manage because you only need to update the content in one location, and it reduces complexity because you don't need replication products like Microsoft DFS.

The pain-point here, as I mentioned, occurs if something happens to that single content server providing all the web pages for your websites. Imagine losing access to that content. That's why, if you're going to use a content-sharing tactic like this, you need to make sure the content is highly available.

Above and beyond

The biggest risk to sharing content over a network share to a web farm is the possible loss of the content server. If the content server fails, then all the web servers in the farm lose access to the web pages.

This is why, as much as I prefer this option for sharing content, you need to evaluate whether this is a good option for you. To provide high availability to the content server, you need to cluster the file services on the file server. That requires two file servers, configured and running the Microsoft Cluster service.

If you've performed this task, you know it's not a small undertaking. It requires extensive knowledge of Microsoft clustering and possibly costly hardware. Configuring a cluster is more than I can cover here, but here's a reference to a step-by-step guide if you want to experiment in your lab environment: http://mng.bz/rYXK. You can install a cluster on physical computers or virtual machines, so you have plenty of options to work with.

I have you try a network share for content in the lab, but keep in mind that if you're going to use it for production, you need to make sure that content is always highly available.

It's time to put away your lunch sack, wash up, and try the lab, where you'll build your own content-sharing solution.

16.4   Lab

In this lab you'll try the different methods of deploying content to servers in a web farm. You don't need to have a load balancer, Microsoft NLB, or ARR configured on your VMs for this lab, but if you do, all the better.

TRY IT NOW

In case you didn't get a chance to perform the Try It Now sections, I repeat them here for your convenience. Once complete, you can start the lab with task 1.

1   Create the new folder C:\sites\WebBikesPhotos on your DC and place a simple default web page in the folder that identifies the website. You can even place some of your favorite photos into the folder for fun. Deploy the folder to the servers in the web farm.

2   Create your own version of the automation script. Change the default web page in your local C:\sites\WebBikezPhotos folder and run the script to deploy the changes out to the web farm.

3   Using the IIS manager, examine the basic settings for one of the websites you created earlier in the book. Note that the physical path points to a local folder. Shortly you'll change this to a network share.

TASK 1

Create three folders on your domain controller under C:\sites, named Website1, Website2, and Website3. Add some files to each of these folders. These will be copied to the web farm servers during this lab. They won't become websites, so you can place any files you want into the folders—just put at least a few in there so you can see that the copy process works.

TASK 2

Create a PowerShell script that will copy the C:\sites\Website1 folder and all its contents to your two web servers. Run the script and verify that the folders and files appear on the web servers.

TASK 3

Install the DFS Replication role and DFS Management console on your domain controller. This will become a primary server in a DFS replication group.

TASK 4

Install the DFS Replication role on your two web servers.

TASK 5

Using the DFS Management tool, create a replication group with the following settings:

- Multipurpose Replication group named SharedContent
- Members of the group: domain controller and the two web servers
- Full mesh topology that replicates continuously
- Primary server: domain controller
- Folders to replicate: C:\sites\Website2

TASK 6

Run GPUpdate on all servers and verify that replication has occurred. Each server should now have the C:\sites\Website2 folder and its contents.

TASK 7

Create a central content location for one of the websites you created in a previous chapter. Start by sharing the C:\sites folder on your domain controller. Create an AD user named SharedContent and give it read permissions to the folder.

TASK 8

Using a website created in a previous lab, or using the default website on one of your web servers, edit the basic site settings and change the physical path to the UNC for the network share. Set the Connect As option for the user SharedContent and test the website.

16.5 *Ideas to try on your own*

If centralized content is your goal, then take some time to learn and work with Microsoft clustering so you can provide a highly available content server. You can use the two web server VMs and try the step-by-step guide on TechNet (http://mng.bz/Clqo).

Sharing IIS
configurations
for a web farm

In chapter 16 you explored sharing website content to the web farm to reduce overhead and management when updating web files. You can use the same technique to make the configuration of websites and bindings across the web farm automatic and simple.

Each IIS server in a web farm can be configured to use a single set of configuration files. When you create a new website or binding, it's automatically created across every server in the farm. Imagine adding servers to the farm—instead of configuring the sites on each new server, the process occurs automatically with shared configurations, making scaling your farm a breeze.

Each server is configured to use a single set of configuration files stored on a clustered network share or in DFS, as shown in figure 17.1.

The process for configuring Shared Configurations isn't complicated, although it can be tricky when you need to add new software, such as from WebPI, that requires binaries to be installed. This chapter covers the different configurations using a network share and DFS. It also shows you how to master the installation of additional products and avoid common problems and issues.

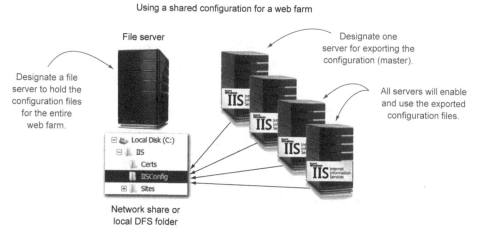

Figure 17.1 Shared configuration for the web farm

Let's start by working through the process of setting up a Shared Configuration. In this chapter you'll configure Shared Configurations using a network share and try it out using DFS. You'll also learn the process for performing staggered installations of new components with Shared Configurations.

17.1 Configuring Shared Configurations

The configuration files that you want to share between servers in the farm are the applicationHost.config and administration.config files mentioned back in chapter 6. These files contain the entire configuration for the server: the websites, application pools, and bindings you want to share. They don't contain the individual website settings normally stored in the web.config, but I come back to that in a bit.

The reason this technique works is because the IIS team at Microsoft removed server-specific information from these configuration files. Any number of servers can successfully use the same set of configuration files. Changes made on one web server will automatically occur on all other web servers in the farm. That means adding a new website or changing a binding can be performed on only one server.

Things that aren't shared include specific changes to a website stored in the web.config files for the website or application, such as compression settings. You need to make sure that the web.config files are kept in sync across web servers, but if you centralized your content as described in chapter 16, you don't have to worry. Recycling an application pool or resetting a web server isn't synchronized across all servers in the farm either. You can safely recycle an application pool without shutting down the entire site!

> **NOTE** Although bindings are synchronized, certificates aren't. You'll need to deploy, install, and configure the certificates as described in chapter 9 or use the new IIS 8 feature of centralized certificates described in chapter 18.

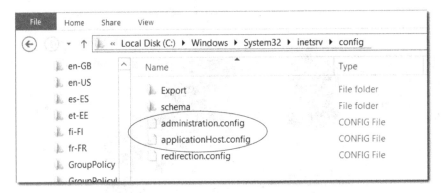

Figure 17.2   Location of the default configuration files

The configuration files that you want to share are located in the default location of C:\Windows\System32\inetsrv\config\, as shown in figure 17.2.

The two files, administration.config and applicationHost.config, are the ones that will be shared to the farm. The redirection.config file contains the information for the Shared Configuration and is unique to each server. It won't be part of the configuration.

> **TRY IT NOW**   Using File Explorer or PowerShell, locate the default folder for the configuration files.

You have two methods to share these files with the entire farm: network share or DFS. Let's start with my preferred method—over a clustered network share, where you'll export and configure the Shared Configurations.

17.1.1 *Configuring Shared Configurations using a clustered network share*

You created a network share for content sharing in chapter 16, and you can do the same thing for sharing configuration files. One set of configuration files is stored on a network share, and each server is pointed to those files. If you make a change on a web server (such as adding a new website), the change automatically occurs on every other server.

This is easy to set up and requires not much additional work other than configuring IIS for the Shared Configuration—however, a devil is lurking that the unaware administrator might miss: a server failure.

As in chapter 16 with shared content, you must take special care to ensure that if the server hosting the configuration files fails, there's a backup. Creating the share on a clustered file server is the most common way to prevent a single point of failure. Remember, your web servers need those configuration files, and to lose them because of a server failure could potentially take down the farm. The IIS team was pretty smart about this. They designed IIS to run from cached copies of the configuration files in the event the server holding the Shared Configurations failed. If that happens, you'll want to get the network share back online quickly—something as simple as an IIS reset will cause the web server to use the local configuration files and behave improperly.

> **Above and beyond**
> Configuring a file server cluster is different for each version of the server OS. For this reason, and because of the complexities of clustering, it's more than we can cover here. At www.TechNet.com you'll find plenty of documentation to get you started based on your version of the server OS.

Configuring a Shared Configuration between your web servers begins by selecting a web server in the farm as the *master*. The master is the server that the configuration files are exported from to the network share. All settings needed for the entire process are located at the server level in the IIS manager in the Management section, as shown in figure 17.3.

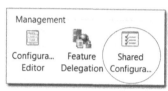

Figure 17.3 The Shared Configuration icon is located in the Management section.

I show you how to export the initial configurations from the first server (the master) to the network share, and then you can try it out.

17.1.2 *Exporting the configurations from the first (master) web server*

In a web farm using Shared Configurations, it helps to designate a master, or primary, server. This is nothing more than the server you'll export the configuration from to the network share that all the other servers use. I generally select the first server I bring in to the web farm as the master, but you can choose whichever you like. You can change your mind anytime; it's an arbitrary choice, not one written into the software.

You want to set up a few things before you proceed to export the configuration. You should do the following:

- Create a network share on a clustered file server.
- Create a user account and assign it Read/Write (Change) permissions to access the network share. This account will be used by each of the web servers in the farm. It can be an Active Directory account or a local account if the farm is outside your internal network.
- I always add Domain Admins to the network share with Full permissions and remove the Everyone group.

For the figures in the rest of the chapter, I created a network share on a computer named DC, called IISConfig, to hold the configuration files. I also created a user named IISConfig and a password.

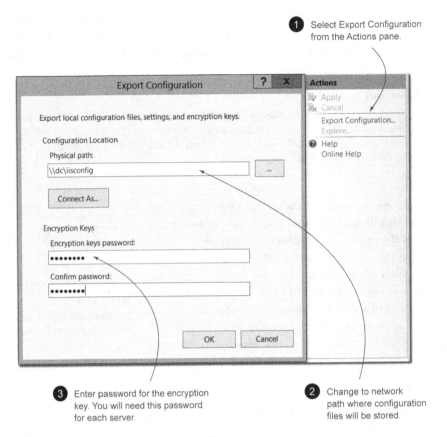

Figure 17.4   **Exporting the configuration files**

TRY IT NOW   Let's get your network share set up. Create a folder structure on your domain controller (DC) to hold the IIS configuration files. Create an AD user named IISConfig. Share the folder and add Change permissions for IIS-Config. Also add Domain Admins with Full control. This is a good time to select which of your two web servers will be the master.

To export the configuration files from your master to the network share, open the Shared Configuration feature under the Management section on the master web server.

On the right side of the screen, under the actions pane, select and double-click Export Configuration. That launches the form displayed in figure 17.4.

The next step is to supply the network path to the network share created earlier. Click the Connect As button and specify the user with Change permissions to the folder, as shown in figure 17.5.

The encryption key is the last thing to deal with before exporting the configuration. Think about this: the application pool identities and custom credentials you create will need to be accessible by each web server in the farm. You don't want these sent across the network in clear text, so the encryption key creates a secure method of storing and using these credentials and is stored in a file, as shown in figure 17.6.

It's important not to forget the encryption password because you'll need it when you join each web server to the farm. You can delete the encryption key file because it's not needed after you join all web servers to the farm. Remember the password in case you want to join additional servers or make changes.

The exported configuration files on the network share will be accessed by all web servers in the farm, including the master server. I discuss backing up IIS in a later chapter, and the configuration files on the network share (along with shared content files) are the files to back up in case of a complete server failure.

> **TRY IT NOW** Using the master web server you designated earlier, export the configuration files to the network share you created on the domain controller.

The next step in the process is to enable each of the web servers to use the newly exported configuration files on the network share.

Figure 17.5 Specifying the user account with Change permissions to the network share

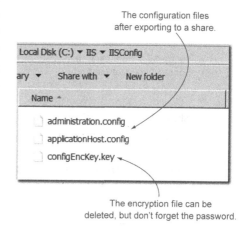

Figure 17.6 The exported files on the network share

17.1.3 Enabling Shared Configurations

After the master server has exported its configuration to the network share, the last step is to enable each web server to use the new configuration files.

On each web server, open the Shared Configuration icon under the Management section to enable and configure the feature, as shown in figure 17.7.

After supplying the network path and user account, you're prompted for the encryption key. The server may appear to be using the new configuration files on the network share, but it's still using the local Administration.config until you perform an IIS reset:

```
PS> IISRESET
```

Click to
enable Shared
Configuration.

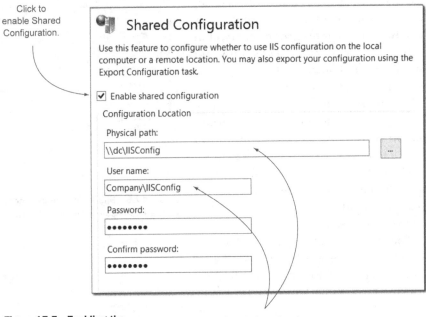

**Figure 17.7 Enabling the
Shared Configuration feature**

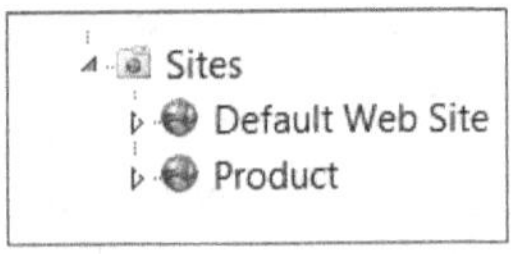

Supply the network
path and credentials.

For each web server in the farm, enable and configure
Shared Configuration and perform an IIS reset. Any additional websites, applications, or bindings created on one
server will now automatically appear on all servers, as
shown in figure 17.8. Keep in mind you'll need the encryption key for each server added.

> ▲ ⬚ Sites
>   ▷ ⬢ Default Web Site
>   ▷ ⬢ Product

**Figure 17.8 New websites
and other configurations will
automatically appear on all
servers.**

A lot of admins like to delete the local copies of the configuration files to prevent confusion and to prevent backing up the wrong files. Although I've done this, I usually
don't take the time to delete the local files because it's unnecessary. I prefer to clearly
document the shared configuration settings to prevent confusion. I also check that
the backups are performed on the network share rather than locally and remind you
of that in chapter 20.

> **TRY IT NOW** Enable the Shared Configuration settings on your master server
> and one additional web server. When you create a new site on the master
> server, note that it automatically appears on the other.

Using a network share on a clustered file server isn't the only way to use Shared Configurations. If you set up DFS as described in chapter 16, that's an option as well.

Let's take a look at using DFS next.

17.1.4 *Configuring IIS for Shared Configurations using DFS*

DFS is a great replication technology for shared content, as discussed in chapter 16. You can also use it for Shared Configurations. I'd be remiss if I didn't tell you that a lot of admins prefer DFS because it's easier than setting up a clustered file server.

I tend to prefer clustered file servers and network shares if my web farm is for internal clients such as with Microsoft SharePoint. With clustered file servers I know exactly where my content and configuration are located, the system is easier to back up, and my back end network already has several clustered servers. In the middle tier, adding clustered servers for an outside-accessible web farm is more expensive and complicated than using existing internal resources, so DFS clearly shines because it doesn't require additional servers and is fairly simple to get working.

The benefit of DFS is that each server maintains a local copy of the configuration instead of using a network share. If something should occur, and DFS fails, the web server continues to use the local copy and can withstand a complete IIS reset or server reboot. This small advantage over a single server network share is removed if you cluster the network share.

In the lab you'll have a chance to use the DFS configuration you created earlier for a Shared Configuration. Before you try that, let's look at adding components to a web farm that's using Shared Configurations.

17.2 *Installing components with Shared Configurations*

Installing additional features with WebPI or a standalone product is a simple process when working with a standalone web server. When the web servers in a farm are sharing their configurations, it becomes a little more challenging.

When you install new software components, binaries and other configuration files need to be installed on each server. You don't want the servers using a Shared Configuration during the installation and possibly corrupting the shared files. When you need to install a new software product to IIS servers in a farm, you need to temporarily disable the Shared Configuration. There are two simple procedures to accomplish this goal: the *all-at-once* and *staggered* approaches. Let's start with the first one, the one I call the all-at-once method.

17.2.1 *Installing new software using all-at-once*

The all-at-once approach is the easiest of the two installation methods and in many cases it's the fastest. I like this approach when using PowerShell to install the software quickly, but it does have a couple drawbacks:

- The web farm will become unavailable for the time it takes to complete.
- You run the risk of crashing all the servers or causing corruption if the install fails.

Spend time testing in a lab environment before you do this!

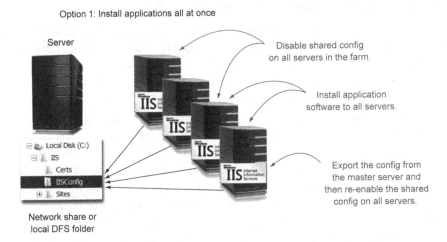

Figure 17.9   Performing software installs using the all-at-once process

Why would I even mention this approach? Because some of the web farms you may work on have maintenance windows for which this practice would be perfectly acceptable. In other cases, the web farm may be a testing platform or development platform that's not publicly accessible and therefore would cause no business outage.

Imagine you need to install a new software component for IIS, which has additional binaries and other configuration files, to the servers in your web farm. (You'll do that in chapter 19 with the ARR helper from WebPI.) Each server needs a copy of the binaries and any local configuration changes that need to be made. To do that you need to remove all servers from the Shared Configuration, install the software, and then re-enable the Shared Configuration, as shown in figure 17.9.

Here's a summary of the all-at-once installation process:

- Remove (disable) all servers from the Shared Configuration. You'll be prompted to copy the network configuration as the new local configuration.
- Apply (install) the new software on each server.
- On the master server, export the new configuration back to the network, as described earlier in this chapter.
- Join (enable) all servers to use the new network Shared Configuration.

Again, keep in mind that this process can cause the entire web farm to fall out of service until the servers have rejoined the Shared Configuration. If uptime is important, as in a publically available farm, then a staggered installation approach is best.

17.2.2   *Installing new software using a staggered approach*

A staggered install is the process I use most of the time when installing new components or software that require additional binaries and configurations on each server. It can be a little confusing at first, but the process is easy to master after you've done it once or twice.

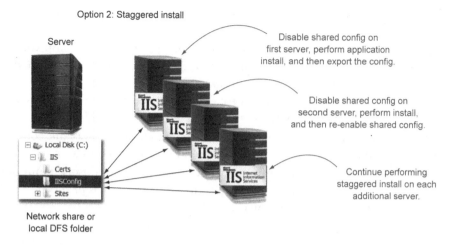

Option 2: Staggered install

Disable shared config on first server, perform application install, and then export the config.

Disable shared config on second server, perform install, and then re-enable shared config.

Continue performing staggered install on each additional server.

Network share or local DFS folder

Figure 17.10 Performing a staggered installation of software

In the staggered install, the software is installed on only one server at a time. If there's a problem with the new software installing correctly, you can stop the installation process without destroying the entire farm, as shown in figure 17.10.

Here's a summary of the staggered installation process:

- Remove (disable) the master server from the Shared Configuration. You'll be prompted to copy the network configuration as the new local configuration. (Remember to perform an IIS reset.)
- Apply (install) the new software on the master server.
- After the software is successfully installed on the previous server, remove the next server from the Shared Configuration and install the software.
- Continue with each server, one at a time, until the software has been successfully installed.
- On the master server, export the new configuration back to the network, as described in section 17.1.2 earlier in this chapter.
- Join (enable) all servers to use the new network Shared Configuration.

The staggered installation process takes a little longer than the all-at-once process, but it's safer, in particular for business-critical web farms.

17.3   Lab

In this lab you'll create a Shared Configuration between your web servers and add a new website to test that it's working properly. Having the servers in a load balance (NLB or ARR) isn't required for this lab.

TRY IT NOW

In case you didn't get a chance to perform the Try It Now sections, I repeat them here for your convenience. Once complete, you can start the lab with task 1.

1   Using File Explorer or PowerShell, locate the default folder for the configuration files.

2   Let's get your network share set up. Create a folder structure on your domain controller to hold the IIS configuration files. Create an AD user named IISConfig. Share the folder and add Change permissions for IISConfig. Also add Domain Admins with Full control. This is a good time to select which of your two web servers will be the master.

3   Using the master web server you designated earlier, export the configuration files to the network share you created on the domain controller.

4   Enable the Shared Configuration settings on your master server and one additional web server. When you create a new site on the master server, note that it automatically appears on the other.

TASK 1

On your domain controller, create a folder structure to hold the Shared Configurations. If you created a structure in the last chapter for shared content, you can use the same structure. For example, create the folder C:\IIS\IISConfig.

TASK 2

If you didn't perform this in the Try It Now, create a new Active Directory user with the name IISConfig. This user will be used to assign permissions to the share in the next task.

TASK 3

Share the IISConfig folder and assign the following permissions:

- Domain Admins: Full control
- IISConfig: Change
- Remove the Everyone group

TASK 4

On the master server, create two additional websites. These websites can use shared content or local. The bindings aren't important for this exercise, so you can assign different port numbers.

TASK 5

Export the master server's configuration to the network share. Verify that the configuration files are located on the share.

TASK 6

Enable the Shared Configuration on the master and then on the other server. Verify that the websites you created on the master have appeared on the other server. Congratulations! You have a Shared Configuration.

17.4   *Ideas to try on your own*

When you get a chance, try using DFS for the Shared Configuration. This is a common approach unless you have a clustered file server available. In chapter 19 you'll install additional software and be required to perform a staggered install. If you like, try that out now using a component (such as the ARR helper) from WebPI.

Using the central certificate store for certificate management

Certificate management—the installing, revoking, and binding of certificates—is truly an ongoing management headache. You saw in chapter 9 that working with certificates on remote servers can be challenging, even with PowerShell to help automate the process. Remember the process of deploying and installing the certificates to each web server and then creating an SSL binding for each website? Add to that the challenge of searching through all those servers to determine when the certificates will expire and need to be replaced. If you want to reduce your management time and make the whole process much simpler, the new IIS 8 feature called the central certificate store (CCS) is for you.

The central certificate store is a simple concept, almost exactly the same as you saw in chapters 16 and 17 on sharing content and configuration: store all the certificates on a clustered network share and then have the website bindings point to those certificates instead of locally installed ones. Need a new certificate? Put it in the network share. Need to check for expiring certificates? Look in the network share. If you're already using shared content and configurations, you already have everything you need to make this work, as shown in figure 18.1.

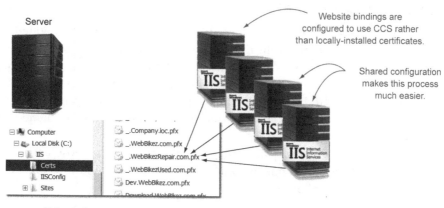

Figure 18.1 **Using the central certificate store (CCS) for certificate management**

CCS works for standalone web servers, web servers in a load balanced web farm, and web servers on a farm that are sharing configurations. To participate in CCS, the only requirement is that all web servers must be running Microsoft Server 2012 and IIS 8. If you're looking for an excuse to upgrade your web servers, you've found the best reason.

As with the last two chapters, you start with a clustered network share. You create a user account that has Read permissions to access the network share. You can use one of the accounts you created for shared content or Shared Configurations, but I prefer to create a special one for CCS, such as IISCert. This user account is needed during the configuration of CCS.

Once the network share is accessible by the other web servers using the user account, you'll be able to set up certificates in a central location. You finish this off by setting the bindings on the remote servers to use the new certificate store. Let's get started with configuring the central store.

> **NOTE** I realize you may not have Windows Server 2012 and IIS 8 on your VMs. Because of that, there are no Try It Now sections in this chapter. I describe in detail the entire process, so if you get a chance to use Server 2012, you can refer back to this chapter. I include a complete lab to help you through the entire process.

18.1 Installing and configuring the central certificate store

Each website configured with an HTTPS binding can use certificates that have been installed locally or that are in the certificate store located on a network share. The websites can be on standalone web servers or part of a web farm.

With so much experience in this concept from the last two chapters, let's dive immediately into storing and naming your certificates for CCS.

18.1.1 *Storing and naming certificates*

Remember chapter 9, when you configured a website for SSL? You added an HTTPS binding and selected the locally installed certificate for the website. When you enable a site for CCS, the process is a little different. Rather then look for a locally installed certificate, CCS checks the configured network share for the certificate. CCS locates the correct certificate by using the host name of the website binding (the URL the user types) and finding a certificate file that has the exact same name as the host header plus the .pfx extension.

For example, suppose you have two websites with the host names www.WebBikez.com and www.MyCompany.com. The certificates should be stored in the network share with the following names:

- www.WebBikez.com.pfx
- www.MyCompany.com.pfx

The file extension is important—the certificate needs to be a .pfx. When you purchase a new certificate, you get the .pfx from the certificate vendor. If you already have certificates installed on a web server that you want to use in CCS, you can export the certificates to make a .pfx file. You can review how to export a certificate in chapter 9.

> **NOTE** Wildcard certificates (*.MyCompany.com) should be named with an underscore to replace the wildcard character: _.MyCompany.com.pfx.

As you add websites that need SSL, create or purchase new certificates and place them into the network share. The next step in the process is to install the CCS component on your web servers and then configure CCS and your websites.

18.1.2 *Installing CCS on a local web server*

The installation process is simple and can be accomplished using the graphical management tools or PowerShell. In this section I describe the process of installing CCS on a local web server using the GUI so you can see how the process works. The last section covers how to perform these tasks on remote web servers using PowerShell, including my favorite: Server Core on Windows Server 2012.

You must install the Centralized SSL Certificate Support feature on your web server before you can use the certificates on a network share. You can use the graphical Server Manager or the `Install-WindowsFeature` cmdlet in PowerShell:

```
PS> Install-WindowsFeature Web-CertProvider
```

When the new feature is installed, a new Centralized Certificates icon appears under the Management section of the IIS manager, as shown in figure 18.2.

Each web server that has secured websites needing access to the certificates on the network share will need to be configured for CCS. The CCS icon opens a form for the configuration. This form contains many familiar options, such as the

Figure 18.2 The CCS icon in the Management section

network path to the share and the user account required for permissions to access the share, as shown in figure 18.3.

You click the Enable Centralized Certificates check box to enable the centralized certificates and then select the network physical path to the shared certificates. The user account specified should have Read permissions to the share so that CCS can use the certificates.

At the bottom of the form is a place to specify a private key. When you export a certificate to a .pfx, you have the option of specifying a password, and most admins supply one. If the .pfx has been created with a password, you need to specify that here in the form so it can be used with CCS.

If the configuration and the private key password are set correctly, you're rewarded with a list of the available certificates, as shown in figure 18.4.

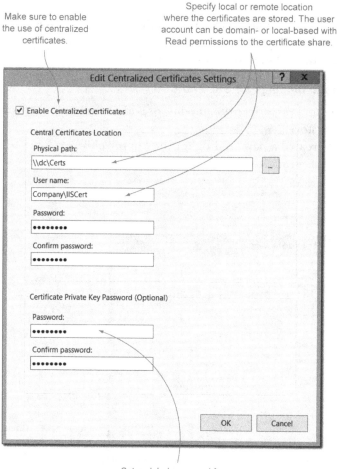

Make sure to enable the use of centralized certificates.

Specify local or remote location where the certificates are stored. The user account can be domain- or local-based with Read permissions to the certificate share.

Set a global password for .pfx certificate files created with a password.

Figure 18.3   Configuring CCS on each web server

Available certificates
in the store

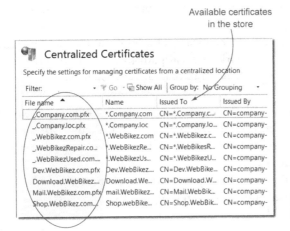

Figure 18.4   Enabled
certificates for CCS

This scrollable screen also contains other useful information, such as when the certificates will expire. Managing certificates has never been easier, but you still need to set the SSL bindings for the websites to use the certificates.

18.1.3   Creating the website bindings for SSL and CCS

The last step in the process is to create, modify, or add a new binding to your website that uses the central store.

In figure 18.5 I created a new binding for the Shop.WebBikez.Com site using the option for the central certificate store.

Type the host name. The
certificate filename should match
the host name with a .pfx extension.

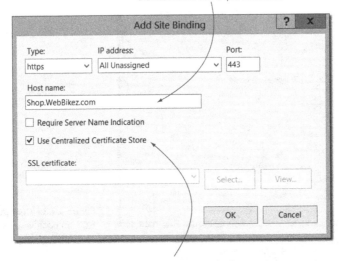

Figure 18.5   Creating a
binding using the central
certificate store

Select this option. This is required
for the binding to access the central
certificate store.

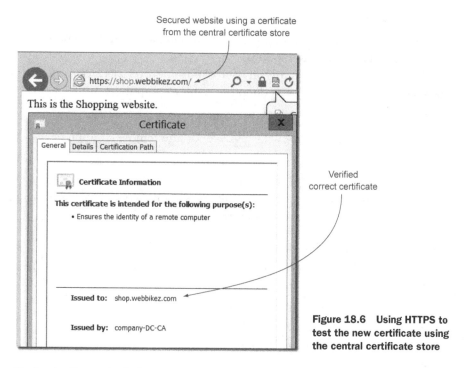

Secured website using a certificate
from the central certificate store

Verified
correct certificate

**Figure 18.6 Using HTTPS to
test the new certificate using
the central certificate store**

Notice in figure 18.5 that the SSL Certificate setting is blank. That's because all certificate requests will now be sent to the store for this website. If there's a certificate file in the store with the name Shop.WebBikez.Com or a wildcard certificate _.WebBikez.Com, then SSL will work.

Test the new certificate using the central certificate store, as shown in figure 18.6. The process of enabling and using CCS on a local server is fairly easy. But what if you need to enable and configure this on remote servers? That's where the challenge begins because you can't do this through the IIS manager. Even with remote management enabled, there's no icon or other way to do it. If you have a web farm or remote servers, you can accomplish all this using PowerShell, as explained in the next section.

18.2 Using CCS on remote web servers

At the time of this writing, the graphical IIS manager can't enable and configure CCS on a web server that you can't physically (or RDP) access. If you're using Server Core, then even RDP won't help, because you don't have a graphical manager anyway.

In this case the only solution is to use PowerShell. I'll show you the same process covered in the preceding section, only this time using PowerShell. Let's get started by installing the central provider component on a remote server and taking a look at the cmdlets that become available.

18.2.1   *Installing CCS on remote servers*

By now you know what's coming next—the installation of the component on remote servers using PowerShell Remoting.

When you're ready to do this on your Windows Server 2012 VMs, you start by creating a PowerShell Remoting session to the remote computers:

```
PS C:\> $Sessions = New-PSSession -ComputerName server2,server3
```

Install the CCS feature (Web-CertProvider) on the remote computers:

```
PS C:\> Invoke-Command -Session $Sessions {Install-WindowsFeature Web-
    ➥CertProvider}
```

And that's all there is to the installation—to as many web servers as you want for CCS. The next task is to enable and configure the feature.

18.2.2   *Enabling CCS on remote servers*

The IIS team at Microsoft created six cmdlets to assist in enabling and configuring the central certificate store on the web server:

- Clear-WebCentralCertProvider
- Disable-WebCentralCertProvider
- Enable-WebCentralCertProvider
- Get-WebCentralCertProvider
- Set-WebCentralCertProvider
- Set-WebCentralCertProviderCredential

The cmdlets are fairly self-explanatory and have help files, but here's an example of using the Enable-WebCentralCertProvider cmdlet to enable and configure CCS on a local web server:

```
PS> Enable-WebCentralCertProvider -CertStoreLocation \\dc\cert -UserName
    ➥company\IIScert -Password P@ssw0rd -PrivateKeyPassword P@ssw0rd
```

Here's where it gets tricky, as I mentioned at the beginning of this section. The Enable-WebCentralCertProvider cmdlet has a parameter called –CertStore-Location that accepts a network share for the certificate location. The problem is that the cmdlet attempts to verify the share location before it writes the information to the Registry. In PowerShell Remoting this causes a multi-hop issue: you're connected to a remote computer that's trying to connect to a remote computer, and that's not supported by default. I'm sure at some point the IIS team will fix the cmdlet, but until they do, here are two ways around the problem: enable CredSSP or add the entries to the Registry manually. Because enabling CredSSP has other security implications, I like to edit the Registry to solve this issue.

Above and beyond

If you're deep into PowerShell, you can enable CredSSP, enable CCS, and then turn off CredSSP. The process of enabling CredSSP and the security implications it has is more than we can cover here, but if you already know how to do this, then it's a quick solution. If you're not deep into PowerShell or don't understand the security implications, then I don't recommend it. Stick to the simple process I outline here to modify the Registry directly.

To enable CCS on remote web servers:

```
PS> Invoke-Command -Session $Sessions {Set-ItemProperty -Path
    HKLM:\SOFTWARE\Microsoft\IIS\CentralCertProvider\ -Name Enabled -Value
    1}
```

To set the share location of the certificates:

```
PS> Invoke-Command -Session $Sessions {Set-ItemProperty -Path
    HKLM:\SOFTWARE\Microsoft\IIS\CentralCertProvider\ -Name
    CertStoreLocation -Value \\DC\CertStore}
```

You can't set the username and password directly to the Registry, but the `Set-WebCentralCertProvider` cmdlet will take care of the rest:

```
PS> Invoke-Command -Session $Sessions {Set-WebCentralCertProvider -Password
    P@ssw0rd -UserName Company\certuser -PrivateKeyPassword P@ssw0rd}
```

At this point you can add or change web bindings on the remote servers to use the central certificate store with the IIS manager. I demonstrate that with PowerShell in chapters 16 and 17, but there's one more issue that will cause a problem.

18.2.3 *Web bindings for CCS on remote servers*

I'm going to tell you this up front: currently the best way to enable web bindings using CCS is to follow the process in the IIS manager I covered at the beginning of the chapter. You can connect to the remote servers using IIS remote management and set the bindings for your websites.

At the time of this writing, configuring the bindings using PowerShell—or any other method I've found—isn't complete, so I won't waste your time. When there's a complete solution, I'll post it on MoreLunches.com. Until then remote manage the bindings using the GUI, as shown in figure 18.7.

You may find yourself making this change on a lot of websites. If you have a web farm using Shared Configurations, the process is much simpler.

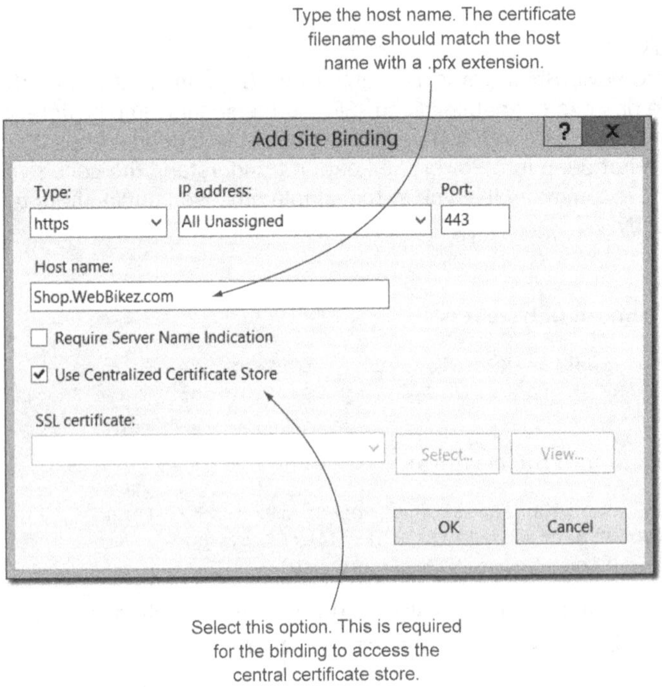

Type the host name. The certificate
filename should match the host
name with a .pfx extension.

Add Site Binding   ? X

Type: IP address: Port:
https   ∨   All Unassigned   ∨   443

Host name:
Shop.WebBikez.com

☐ Require Server Name Indication

☑ Use Centralized Certificate Store

SSL certificate:

                              ∨   Select...   View...

                                           OK   Cancel

**Figure 18.7 Setting the
binding through remote
management with the GUI**

Select this option. This is required
for the binding to access the
central certificate store.

18.2.4 Using CCS with Shared Configurations

This topic is much too short for an entire section because you already know the
answer. If you're using Shared Configurations from chapter 17 in a web farm, then the
central certificate store is your best friend. You already have the shared folder location
and a user account for the certificates. The rest is pure magic.

To use CCS in a web farm with Shared Configurations, do the following:

- Install the `Web-CertProvider` component to each web server. This doesn't
  require a staggered install.
- Enable and configure the central certificate store on each server using the
  PowerShell commands discussed in section 18.2.2.
- Add or change bindings on the master server using the IIS manager. Those
  new bindings are automatically configured on all servers using the Shared
  Configuration.

18.3 Lab

In this lab you can use the web farm with Shared Configuration from chapter 17 or try
it the first time on a standalone server. The following are the tasks you should perform.

TASK 1

On your domain controller, create a folder structure to hold the certificates for the central certificate store. If you created a structure in chapter 17 for Shared Configurations, you can use the same structure. As an example, create the folder C:\IIS\IISCert.

TASK 2

Create a new Active Directory user with the name IISCert. This user will be used to assign permissions to the share in task 3.

TASK 3

Share the IISCert folder and assign the following permissions:

- Domain Admins: Full control
- IISCert: Read
- Remove the Everyone group

TASK 4

Export a certificate for one of the secured websites you've already created or create a new one. Save the exported .pfx to the network share as <hostname>.pfx. (For information on exporting the certificate, see chapter 9.)

TASK 5

On a standalone web server or the master server in your web farm, install the Web-CertProvider component.

TASK 6

Enable and configure the central certificate store on the web server and add or modify the website HTTPS binding to use the certificate on the store.

18.4 *Ideas to try on your own*

The central certificate store is an immediate time saver when working with secured websites. The challenge you face in implementing this in production is that your web servers need to be running IIS 8. Consider your existing environment and start the discussion around upgrading to IIS 8 to take advantage of this feature.

Once you have IIS 8, add CCS to your environment for easier certificate management. If you have an existing web farm, add CCS and start moving your certificates into the store.

Web farm provisioning with the Web Farm Framework

Whether you're hosting multiple websites for customers or a single mission-critical website for your business, provisioning (deploying), scaling, and managing your growing web environment can be challenging. Consider the difficulty of adding a single new server to a load balanced web farm. That requires you to install components and platforms to support the web applications—the additional management of websites, bindings, certificates, and content—which make adding a server or website a complicated and lengthy process.

In this chapter I discuss a solution that involves the technologies and concepts you've been working with from chapters 14–17. By using Microsoft Application Request Routing (ARR), combined with the additional components Web Farm Framework (WFF) and Web Deploy, you can achieve an automated provisioning process for rapid (elastic) scaling and site management.

WFF is a collection of additional features, including PowerShell cmdlets, that makes the process of deploying and maintaining a web farm faster and easier to manage. You can use WFF with ARR for load balancing or without ARR if you have your own load balance solution.

WFF also offers administrators a collection of management tools to provide many of the WFF features:

- One-step automated server provisioning
- Automated deployment of new platforms to the web farm
- Automated application deployment to the farm
- Advanced status and trace logs

I only list a few of the features, but in a nutshell, fully implementing WFF makes administering an IIS web farm fast and easy.

I can't take you through every aspect of WFF, but this chapter will get you up and running and show you how to avoid many pitfalls. You'll implement the Web Farm Framework, build a new web farm using WFF, and manage the farm.

Before you dive into your lunch and this chapter, I need to change a few of the rules you've been following as you read this book. First, this chapter has no real lab at the end. ARR and WFF take much longer than a lunch period to get installed and configured, so I've included the full lab in the last chapter as your final exam. Second, I didn't include any Try It Now sections in this chapter. You need a new, clean virtual environment with additional VMs, and I don't want you to erase yours right now in case you still want to work with previous chapters. For now, let me demonstrate ARR and WFF to you and then you can use this chapter as a reference when you're ready to try it out in the final exam.

One last note before you begin: the components discussed in this chapter are always growing and changing to include new features and support. WFF is one of the most exciting areas in IIS. It's possible that by the time you read this chapter, some changes may have occurred and improvements been made. Although the concepts and process that I outline here will remain the same, you may expect some additional features and changes to the screens shown in the figures in this chapter. But have no fear—everything you need to know about updates, improvements, and more can be found on www.iis.net. Enter *Web Farm Framework* into the search bar or go directly to the download at www.iis.net/downloads/microsoft/web-farm-framework.

19.1 Implementing the Web Farm Framework with ARR

The architecture for WFF with ARR is similar to the ARR architecture you worked with in chapter 14. Some important changes have been made to both the terminology and functionality of the servers in the web farm to accommodate the provisioning and scaling features. In this section you'll install WFF and configure the control server. Once complete, you'll designate and configure your primary and secondary servers for the web farm.

The control server, shown in figure 19.1, is the server with the WFF and ARR components. This server is used to create and manage the web farm, perform the load balancing, and provide log and tracing information for the web farm. As in chapter 14, this is the server that receives the client web requests and then distributes them to the web farm.

The primary and secondary servers provide the websites and content for the web farm. You'll install the new components and platforms on the primary server using

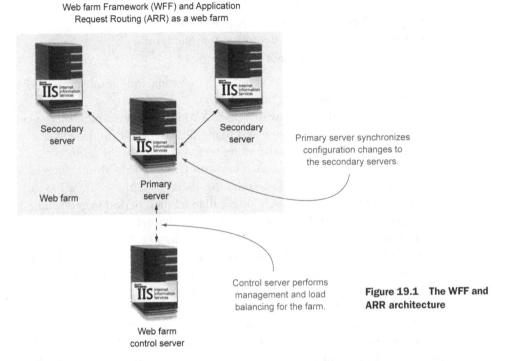

Figure 19.1 The WFF and ARR architecture

WebPI. The secondary servers synchronize with the primary, getting the configuration changes, the new components, and the web applications. This is similar in concept to the Shared Configuration and content you experienced in chapters 16 and 17, but without the manual processes involved. The automated deployment and synchronization from the primary to the secondary servers is the magic sauce in removing the complicated workload from your hands.

It's important to keep in mind that you can't fudge on this architecture. This isn't a time to try and combine roles such as making the control server also a primary server. The primary and secondary servers synchronize their configuration files and will include website information, bindings, web application settings, application pool settings—all the things needed to provide your content. The control server doesn't have this information and needs its own configuration files. The moral of the story: don't cheat.

Although I don't discuss it here in this chapter, the control server can be load balanced to provide failover protection. I cover load balancing in chapter 15 and want to remind you of it so you can protect the control servers.

Let's get started configuring the environment for a WFF and ARR web farm.

19.1.1 Configuring the environment

The requirements to run WFF are the same requirements you already experienced using this book. WFF works on Windows Server 2008, 2008 R2, and Server 2012. Let's look at a couple of tasks you should perform before installing WFF.

WINDOWS FIREWALL SETTINGS

If you're using the Windows Firewall, you need to open some additional ports to support WFF. You may in fact already have these open for other applications, but it's important to check. In the Windows Firewall settings, verify under the Core Networking settings that the following Firewall Groups are open:

- Remote administration
- File and printer sharing

These need to be open on each server in the web farm, including the control server.

MANAGEMENT ACCOUNT

You need to create an account that has local administrative privileges on each of the web farm servers. This account is required for automated application and platform installs, along with the synchronization process. There are two ways to accomplish this:

1. If the web farm servers are members of Active Directory, create an Active Directory user (IIS_Prov) and make the user a member of the Domain Admins group.
2. If the web farm servers are standalone, create a local user that's a member of the local Administrators group on each server.

Once the administrative account has been created, the next step is to install IIS on the control and web farm servers.

INSTALL IIS ON THE CONTROL AND WEB FARM SERVERS

All servers will need IIS, and if you don't already have it installed, you'll be able to quickly install it using PowerShell. You don't have to worry about all the additional components you might need because you'll install them using WFF later. Here's an example you can use when you're ready to perform the install:

```
PS> Invoke-Command –ComputerName Controller, Primary, Secondary1, Secondary2
    ➥{Add-WindowsFeature –Name Web-Server -IncludeManagementTools}
```

When IIS is installed, you'll be ready to install and configure WFF, along with ARR, on the control server.

19.1.2 *Installing and configuring the control server*

The control server is the key to the entire web farm, and it's the one you'll spend most of your time getting installed and configured. At the time of this writing, the process is a little cumbersome. You need to install separate components in the correct sequence to avoid running into brick walls. This section gets you through these pitfalls, but keep in mind that newer versions of these components may exist when you try this, and the process may change.

The following is a list of the components—and versions—I downloaded for this section. When you download these, if you encounter a version difference, you should check the instructions in the download area to see if the installation order has changed.

- Web Deployment Tool 2.1
- Web Farm Framework 2.2 (with Web Deploy 2.0)
- Application Request Routing 2.5

I'll show you the process of getting these components properly installed on the control server.

INSTALLING WFF AND ARR ON THE CONTROL SERVER

Most of the installation process on the control server entails getting components from WebPI. The first step is to make sure you've installed WebPI on the control server, as I've discussed before. You need to pay attention to the version of WebPI that's installed. The current version is 4.5, and it can't install the correct version of the WFF. I'm sure that will be fixed in a later release.

If you have WebPI version 4 or later, you need to also install version 3 for the installation of the WFF component. You can download and install the Web Platform Installer 3.0 from http://mng.bz/69oG.

Once you've installed WebPI 3 on the control server, you're ready to install the components for WFF and ARR. Here are the steps:

1 Open WebPI and install the Web Deployment Tool 2.1.
2 Download and install the Web Farm Framework 2.2 from http://mng.bz/2mlG. You must have WebPI version 3 or this component won't install. WFF will also install Web Deploy 2.0 automatically.
3 Open WebPI and install Application Request Router 2.5.
4 If desired (and you'll get additional cmdlets for doing this), install Web Deploy 3.0 from WebPI.

After the installation is complete on the control server, I prefer to reboot the server. This isn't required, but I like to make sure I have a clean start before continuing.

Now that the installation is complete, you need to perform a few post-installation tasks.

POST-INSTALLATION BEST PRACTICES

The control server running ARR will be directing web requests to the web farm, as mentioned in chapter 14. I'll cover a few IIS configuration tasks that will improve the control server's response to and performance of these requests. Although these post-installation tasks aren't required, they're considered best practices for the controller. First the application pool for the default website will shut down its worker process in 20 minutes. That means the new requests could fail while waiting for a new worker process to launch. In the Advanced Settings of the default application pool, change the Idle Time-out Setting to 0, as shown in figure 19.2. This will stop the worker process from shutting down.

The default application pool will recycle on a regular interval of 29 hours. When the pool recycles, web requests can be lost, so I prefer to stop the application pool from automatically recycling. In the Recycling Settings for the default application pool, clear the check boxes for the Recycling Conditions, as shown in figure 19.3.

Set the Idle Time-out to 0 to keep the worker process running.

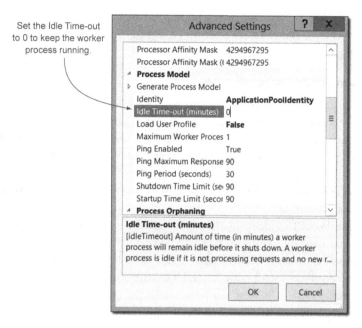

Figure 19.2 Disabling the Idle Time-out

Clear the check boxes to disable the app pool recycling.

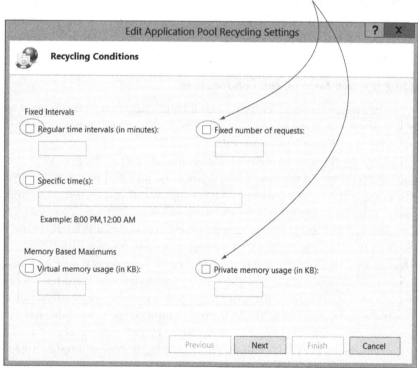

Figure 19.3 Disabling the default application pool recycling

With the control server configuration complete, the next tasks are to configure the primary and secondary servers. There isn't much left to do, and then it will be time to create the new web farm.

19.1.3 Preparing the primary and secondary servers

The bulk of the installation occurs on the control server, leaving some minor tasks for the primary and secondary servers. Remember that the primary server will be the one where new components and platforms will be installed and then synchronized out to the secondary servers. Because of this, you can only have one primary server in a web farm.

You can install components directly to the primary server using WebPI, so the only task remaining for the primary server is to make sure you've installed WebPI. At this point, you can use WebPI to download and install the additional components and platforms your web farm will need, but WFF will let you do this from the control server using new management tools (which I demonstrate later in this chapter).

Although the secondary servers don't need any additional software installed, this is a good time to make sure you have an administrative account for these servers as described at the beginning of this section. When you create the web farm, you'll need this account.

19.2 Building the web farm

If you tried the lab for chapter 14, creating and configuring the web farm is almost identical to the tasks you performed in that lab. In this section I'll show you some minor differences to the process.

19.2.1 Creating the web farm on the control server

After all the chapters you and I have been through together in this book, I'm sure you know the answer to this question: what tools do I need to create and manage a web farm? Answer: a GUI tool and PowerShell.

I applaud the IIS team at Microsoft for continuing to add support for management through PowerShell. In the case of WFF, you may not need to script deployments and provisioning because WFF handles that for you. But if you're someone who needs to automate processes beyond WFF or web farm implementations, PowerShell makes the automation easier. I won't bore you with everything you can do, but let me introduce you to both the PowerShell and GUI environment you can use with WFF.

During the installation of the Web Farm Framework, a PowerShell snap-in with additional cmdlets to create and populate a web farm was included on the control server. *Snap-ins* are the older form of modules to extend PowerShell functionality and are loaded a little differently than the WebAdministration module that you've seen throughout this book. The name of the snap-in is `WebFarmSnapin`, and it can be loaded using the PowerShell cmdlet `Add-PSSnapin`, as shown in figure 19.4.

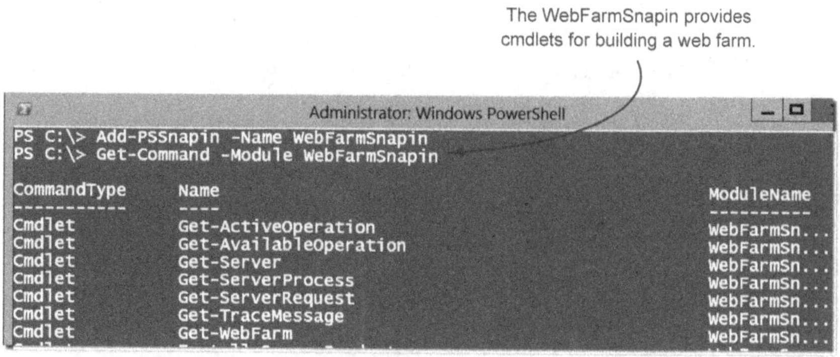

The WebFarmSnapin provides cmdlets for building a web farm.

```
                          Administrator: Windows PowerShell            _ □
PS C:\> Add-PSSnapin -Name WebFarmSnapin
PS C:\> Get-Command -Module WebFarmSnapin

CommandType      Name                                      ModuleName
-----------      ----                                      ----------
Cmdlet           Get-ActiveOperation                       WebFarmSn...
Cmdlet           Get-AvailableOperation                    WebFarmSn...
Cmdlet           Get-Server                                WebFarmSn...
Cmdlet           Get-ServerProcess                         WebFarmSn...
Cmdlet           Get-ServerRequest                         WebFarmSn...
Cmdlet           Get-TraceMessage                          WebFarmSn...
Cmdlet           Get-WebFarm                               WebFarmSn...
```

Figure 19.4   Loading the WebFarmSnapin for PowerShell management and automation

Use `Get-Command` to receive a list of available cmdlets. You can then use `Get-Help` to learn about and see examples of the cmdlets that interest you. I'll use a couple of these shortly when I create the web farm.

> **NOTE**   Additional cmdlets are available for managing provisioning when you install Web Deploy 3. These are located in the snap-in `WDeploySnapin3.0` and can be added using the same method as the `WebFarmSnapin`.

For your first time setting up WFF and ARR, the IIS manager is the best choice because you can see what's happening in this complicated environment and the options that are available. The IIS manager has a new navigation feature and new actions for the web farm, as shown in figure 19.5.

To create a new web farm that uses the provisioning and load balancing of WFF and ARR, select Create Server Farm from the actions pane and fill out the web farm details, as shown in figure 19.6.

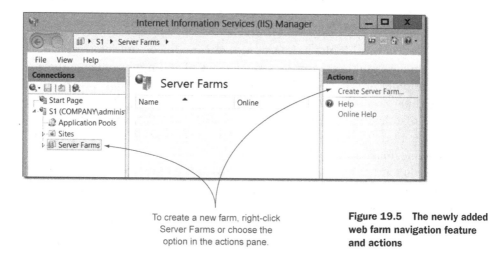

To create a new farm, right-click Server Farms or choose the option in the actions pane.

Figure 19.5   The newly added web farm navigation feature and actions

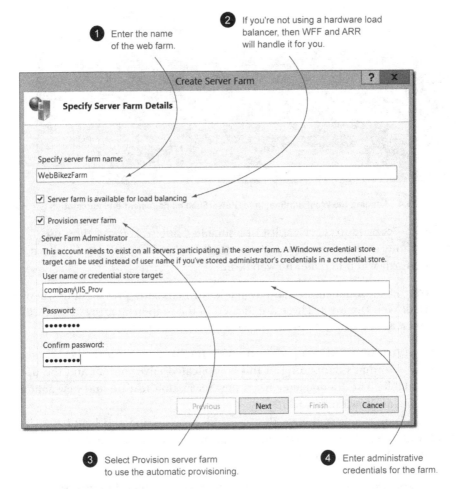

Figure 19.6 Specifying the name of the web farm, load balancing, and provisioning account

You need to provide the web farm with a name for organizational purposes because you can have multiple farms on a single controller. I prefer to name the web farm for the customer or primary application. In larger hosting web farm environments, where several websites for different customers are being hosted, I tend to create a web farm name that describes the farm's location rather than the customer's. Remember from chapter 14 that the web farm name is part of the URL Rewrite rule, so if you change the name, make sure to check the rule.

If you want ARR to perform the load balancing tasks, you need to select that option when filling out the details for the farm. If you're using a hardware load balancer for the web farm servers, remove the check box.

To get the features of the automated provisioning and elastic scaling, check the Provision server farm check box.

The last information to provide is the administrative account you created to manage the web farm servers. This can be an Active Directory account if your web servers are joined to your domain, or a local administrative account on the individual web servers.

The last step is adding the web farm servers—both the primary and secondary servers—to the farm. The wizard guides you to that, as you'll see in the next section, and you can always add additional servers as your web farm grows. Next I'll show you how to add the web farm servers.

19.2.2 *Adding the primary and secondary servers*

After you create the web farm, the wizard will guide you in adding the primary and secondary servers for the web farm. You can always add and remove servers later in the IIS manager or with PowerShell, so don't worry if you don't get them all added at once.

In the wizard I start by adding the server I want designated as the primary server. Add the server name and check the check boxes for load balancing and primary, as shown in figure 19.7.

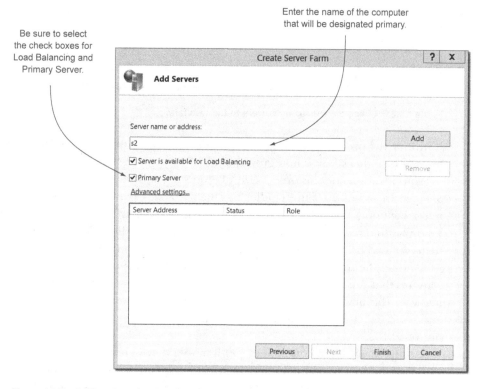

Be sure to select the check boxes for Load Balancing and Primary Server.

Enter the name of the computer that will be designated primary.

Figure 19.7 Adding the primary server to the web farm

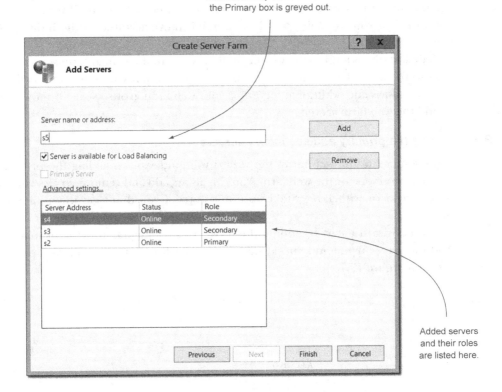

Figure 19.8   Adding the secondary servers to the web farm

Continue the process by adding the secondary servers. Note in figure 19.8 that the Primary Server check box is now greyed out.

You can automate this process with PowerShell and the cmdlets from the WebFarm-Snapin. In figure 19.9 the cmdlet New-WebFarm has parameters for everything you need, including the web farm name and the management credentials. In my example I supply the credentials using the Get-Credential cmdlet. The parameter –Enable turns on load balancing, and –EnableProvisioning enables the provisioning.

Adding the web farm servers is as easy with PowerShell. The New-Server cmdlet requires that you specify the name of the web farm that will receive the servers and the name of the new server. The –IsPrimary parameter designates the primary server, and –Enable specifies that the servers are part of the load balance, as shown in figure 19.10.

At this stage, when completed, you'll have a new web farm running WFF and ARR with load balancing and automated provisioning capabilities. Although the management and tasks are similar to ARR (discussed in chapter 14), you now have the new provisioning icons in the IIS manager. Let's briefly check those out.

Figure 19.9   Creating a web farm using PowerShell and the WebFarmSnapin cmdlet New-WebFarm

19.3   *Managing the web farm*

Managing the new web farm is similar to the concepts and technologies you've already seen in previous chapters, but now the management is more automated and easier. The control server contains additional icons and actions to assist in component and platform installation, along with better tracing and monitoring tools. In this section I'll show you those, but I don't want you to lose sight of how this whole thing works.

The control server is using ARR (and URL Rewrite) to send web requests to the web farm and load balance those requests, as shown in figure 19.11. You saw this in chapter 14. Those icons and settings are still the same.

You also experienced the ease of management with Shared Configurations in chapter 17. The concept is the same here except you don't have to set up any additional configurations on each server. The primary server is the place where you create websites and web applications and install additional components and platforms. Then those things are synced out to the secondary servers, in a manner similar to the concept of Shared Configurations.

My point is that you know more about managing WFF with ARR than you may think. You're ready to go and can start getting your sites up and running. If you're

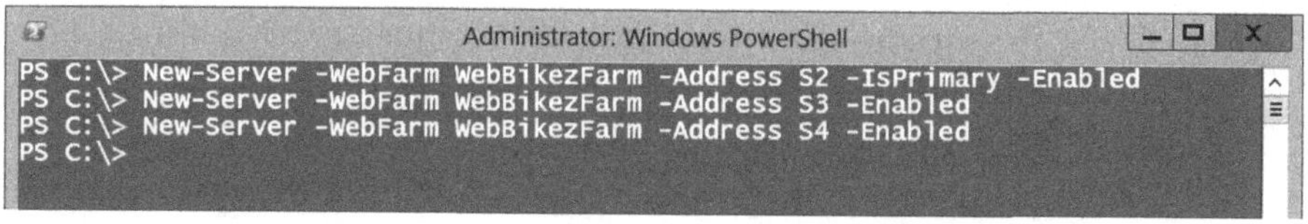

```
PS C:\> New-Server -WebFarm WebBikezFarm -Address S2 -IsPrimary -Enabled
PS C:\> New-Server -WebFarm WebBikezFarm -Address S3 -Enabled
PS C:\> New-Server -WebFarm WebBikezFarm -Address S4 -Enabled
PS C:\>
```

Figure 19.10   Adding primary and secondary servers to the new web farm

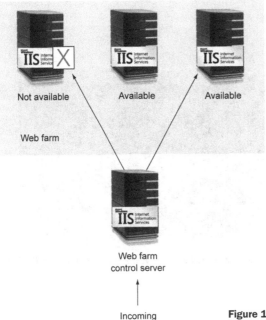

Not available   Available   Available

Web farm

Web farm
control server

Incoming
web request

Figure 19.11   ARR using URL Rewrite to route the web request to an available web server in the farm

using Windows Server 2012, you can include the central certificate store for your certificate management. Content can be shared, as in chapter 16, or stored locally on the primary and secondary servers for top performance. The Web Deploy snap-in even has cmdlets to help copy and keep the content up to date across all your web farm servers.

The IIS manager has some helpful new built-in tools now that you're using the automated provisioning to help you out. You can use them from the control server. I want to introduce a few of them, including performing actions across the entire farm, adding new components, and monitoring the farm.

19.3.1 Using the tools under the actions pane

The graphical IIS manager contains several new actions to assist you in managing the farm. Most of what you need is under the actions pane, as shown in figure 19.12. The actions pane provides several farm-related actions:

- *Take Server Farm Offline*—For maintenance tasks such as service pack updates.
- *Reboot Server Farm*—Resets IIS and is sometimes needed after a new platform installation and for other troubleshooting.
- *Repair Server Farm*—Resynchronizes the servers in the web farm. Useful for troubleshooting, adding/removing a new server from the farm, or installing new applications. The automatic sync times can be changed, as discussed shortly.

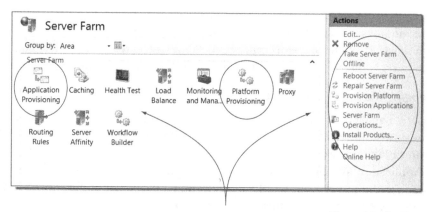

New additions to the ARR
tools to manage the farm

**Figure 19.12 New management
tools for the web farm**

- *Provision Platform and Applications*—Deploys new platforms and applications to the entire farm. This removes the need for you to perform the installation of an application or platform on each server individually.

In addition to the actions discussed previously, one of my favorites is a management tool listed in the actions pane as Server Farm Operations. This tool helps in performing several management tasks related to the entire web farm, as shown in figure 19.13.

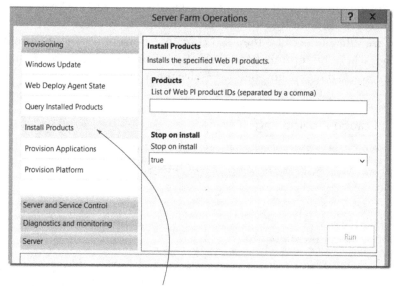

These tasks can be performed
for the entire web farm.

**Figure 19.13 Server Farm Operations
performs several tasks for the entire farm.**

Server Farm Operations is the main management tool and helps perform Windows updating tasks, software queries, and diagnostics. Almost everything you need to perform, such as platform provisioning and WebPI product installations, can be done from here. No need to run around to all the web servers anymore.

19.3.2 Changing the provisioning settings

The IIS manager includes icons that permit you to change the application and platform provisioning settings. You can disable automatic provisioning and set the synchronization time, as shown in figure 19.14.

Application and platform provisioning normally require that the server be taken offline for the installation, but if you know that a particular application doesn't need an IISreset, you can clear those check boxes.

Along with new farm management tools, monitoring has been improved for the server in the web farm.

19.3.3 Monitoring the web farm

In chapter 14 you explored the load balancing monitor tools. Those still exist and should be checked for load balancing issues and performance. With WFF when you select the server's navigation container, the web farm operations, alerts, and provisioning status are displayed, as shown in figure 19.15.

This additional monitoring support includes event messages that can help troubleshoot a problem. In figure 19.15 the servers are attempting to perform an AddServer operation. The trace messages show an error during the process. Many of these trace messages are valuable because they also contain actions to correct the problem. You should check here often to make sure the farm is functioning normally, and if not, check the trace to discover how best to resolve the problem.

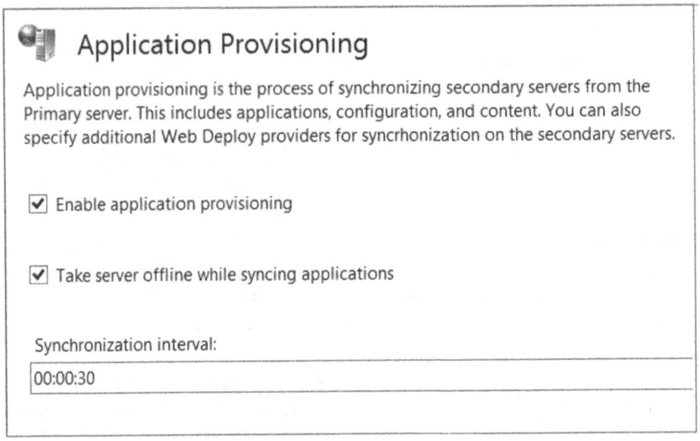

Application Provisioning

Application provisioning is the process of synchronizing secondary servers from the Primary server. This includes applications, configuration, and content. You can also specify additional Web Deploy providers for syncrhonization on the secondary servers.

☑ Enable application provisioning

☑ Take server offline while syncing applications

Synchronization interval:

00:00:30

Figure 19.14 The default provisioning settings for applications and platforms

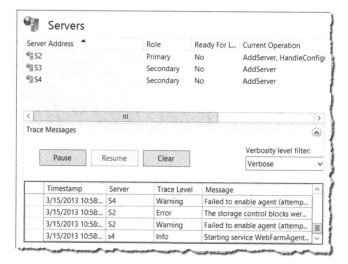

Figure 19.15   Monitoring the web farm status

19.4   Lab

To perform the implementation of ARR and WFF would require you to scrap your current lab environment. I don't want you to do that until the end of the last chapter in case you still want to work with other chapters first. When you're ready to test this out in a clean environment, go to chapter 21 for your final exam.

19.5   *Ideas to try on your own*

The best idea I have for you is to build this environment and get some websites running. But don't do this now. When you're ready, go to chapter 21 and tackle the final exam.

Disaster recovery for IIS

I hope this isn't the first chapter you started to read when you picked up this book. I know that in the middle of a crisis, sometimes you turn immediately to the information you hope will help. This isn't that chapter.

Here's why: disaster recovery for IIS is a planning process, not an immediate fix for a failure. Part of this planning process requires that you fully understand the web environment you're responsible for so you know *what* needs to be recovered in the event of a failure. To help accomplish that—and to become successful at disaster recovery—I hope you've been reading through the book, one chapter at a time, over your lunch, because then you'll understand IIS and have a better understanding of *what* needs to be protected.

The best disaster-recovery planning starts with avoiding the disaster in the first place. I've focused almost a third of this book on high-availability solutions that will protect you from a server failure. No matter what size web environment you're working with, you must implement some form of high availability, even if it's only two servers in a simple Microsoft Network Load Balance with a Shared Configuration. Products such as the Web Farm Framework and Application Request Routing are excellent, free solutions for this.

The hardest part of disaster-recovery planning is realizing that the concepts are the same for everyone, but the implementation is completely different. For example, I can tell you to back up your website content, but I can't tell you the step-by-step process for it because I don't know what backup software you're using. As you read through this chapter, keep in mind that I'm alerting you to the things you need for disaster recovery—but you'll have to determine how to best acquire them.

The second part of preparing for disaster recovery is understanding the cost of failure. Does your company lose money if its website goes down? If so, how much per hour? Disaster recovery for IIS isn't difficult, nor is it expensive, but parts of your network infrastructure could impact IIS, such as losing your internet connection. These networking issues require money to make your network redundant. They can be expensive. Understanding how much your company is willing to spend on those issues is important as you make your disaster-recovery plans.

In this chapter I take you through the important areas in IIS to back up and recover when you're planning your disaster-recovery process. Then I show you how to get a good backup for the day you need to restore.

Let's get started by looking at what might go wrong.

20.1 Analyzing your environment for disaster recovery

The first step is to outline and diagram your environment so you have a complete understanding of the components you need to protect. Do you have a single web server with a single website? Or do you have a large WFF and ARR load balance with 14 servers and hundreds of websites? This is the critical operational path: understanding all the components in your environment that might affect your customer's web experience. Once you've taken this step, then I take you through common points of failure to watch for with IIS.

Using the knowledge you've gained in this book about IIS and how it works, you know you need to document and understand your environment. Let me help you get started.

20.1.1 The critical operational path

Whether you're planning disaster recovery for a new implementation or an existing one, understanding and documenting the entire communication and operational path is essential to knowing what kinds of failures might occur and what you need to plan to avoid or recover from them. As I've mentioned, I find that a good network diagram—such as the one given in chapter 2—helps to understand this critical path.

Here are some things you want to make sure you've documented:

- Where are your internet connection(s) and routers, and is there any redundancy? If you have only one connection to the internet, and you lose that connection, does it hurt your business? If so, is it worth getting another connection installed?
- Who hosts your outside DNS, and how do you access it to add and change A records for websites?
- Do you use internal DNS for internal websites? If so, is that DNS server redundant?

- Are there network devices (such as switches) that might fail and cause a web outage? Is it worth the extra cost to make those redundant?
- What server hardware platform are you running IIS on? Are you virtualizing your web servers with VMware or Hyper-V? If so, have you looked at the recovery features included with those products?

I think you get the idea. Document the path from the customers outside your network all the way to the website they're using and see if you have any room for redundancy. If not, then plan what to do when the disaster occurs. Find out who's responsible for fixing the problem, what that person's phone number is, and how long it should take to repair. This is often referred to as a *Service Level Agreement* (SLA). Although small companies generally have verbal SLAs, such as *I can recover the server in four hours*, larger companies often document these SLAs in their disaster-recovery planning, including the responsible parties and their contact information.

20.1.2 *Determining points of failure in IIS*

When it comes to IIS and your web environment, the most common failure is losing an entire web server. Let's face it: it's easier to avoid a complete outage than to recover a server from failure. Let me review a few ways to avoid causing a critical outage:

- Implementing a load balance
- Implementing a load balance with Shared Configuration and Shared Content
- Implementing WFF and ARR for elastic automated provisioning

A simple load balance would prevent a complete outage of your web environment, but recovering the server is more challenging than it needs to be. For example, suppose a web server had a hard disk failure. Imagine the process of recovering that server and putting it back into the load balance. You'd need to reinstall the operating system, install IIS, install the additional components, platforms, and application-specific software, recreate the websites, the bindings, and so on—*arrrg*!

A load balance where you're sharing the content and the configuration makes it much easier to recover a server. Install the OS and IIS and turn on Shared Configuration—this gets all the websites and bindings back, along with access to the content—and you're back in business.

The best approach to handling server failures and recovery is with the full WFF and ARR implementation discussed in chapter 19. Adding and removing a server is as easy as adding it to the web farm. The new server is automatically provisioned, and you don't need to do anything else. That's simple, fast, server-failure recovery—and because it's in a load balance with other servers, you avoided the web outage altogether.

Besides a complete server failure, other things could go wrong on your web server, most of which could be resolved with a simple backup (I go through backing up IIS in a moment). Here are some other common failures to think about:

- *Corruption of the IIS configuration files*—This rarely occurs, but it's possible. This kind of corruption could impact all your websites, and you'd repair them by restoring the configuration files.
- *Corruption of web application-specific configuration files such as web.config*—This does occur from time to time and could be the result of an application update or a hacker attacking the application. If you maintain a backup of your web applications and their configuration files, you can easily recover the corrupted configuration file.
- *Loss or corruption of content*—Keep in mind where your web content's being stored. Is it local, or is it shared from a clustered server or other content service? Your content should be backed up regularly so that, in the event of corruption or loss, you can easily restore it.
- *Loss or corruption of web components and platforms*—Although uncommon, one or more of the applications or platform components could become corrupt. This can occur if the component is updated. In most cases you can remove and reinstall the component.

As you can see from the general cases I've outlined, the most common recovery technique if you aren't using WFF and ARR is to restore the corrupted data from a backup. Let's look at how to get a good backup.

20.2 Back up the critical components and data

Backing up an IIS server isn't as complicated as most administrators think. You know the truth behind IIS: everything about your websites, bindings, and applications is in the XML configuration files. XML files are text files, which means you can copy them to a safe location, or even to a USB drive. Most administrators use a third-party backup tool because they make it easy to manage the backup process. Regardless, the important thing is to back up the IIS configurations, the website files and configurations, and any other content you have to support those websites. In this section I show you the critical configuration components, explain how to quickly and easily perform a backup/restore, and give you a few notes about planning your disaster recovery as well as recovering from a failure.

Let's start with the critical components and locations so you can point your backup software to the right place.

20.2.1 Determining your critical components to back up

The following is a reminder list of the configuration files and their locations—if you're using a Shared Configuration, be sure to back up the network share that holds the configuration files:

- The files applicationHost.config, administration.config, and redirection.config are located at C:\%windir%\System32\inetsrv\config. These are the most critical files to be sure you've backed up because they contain the information about your websites and configuration settings.

- The web.config files are application configuration files and are stored with your website content. Be sure to back up your website content and all the configuration files. If you're using Shared Content, point your backup software to the network share that's hosting the content.

- IIS keeps its own backup of applicationHost.config in C:\inetpub\history. In fact, every time you make a change to an IIS configuration, it makes a backup and stores the last ten versions. I like to back up this folder, too.

You can use a third-party backup program to handle all of this, including the recovery in the event of corruption or failure. I'll show you one common way of backing up these configuration files using a built-in IIS command.

20.2.2 *How to back up and restore IIS*

I normally have a third-party backup program do this task, but I like to be able to get a quick copy of my configuration files before I make any changes to a system.

Before PowerShell became the standard management tool across all product platforms, IIS had its own command-line tool. Although I don't use that tool in this book—or in real life anymore—I *do* use it for the task of making a quick backup of configuration files. You can use PowerShell and script your own solution, but the older command is easier to use. The command, AppCmd.exe, is located in C:\%windir%\System32\inetsrv. Here are examples that use the command to back up and restore your configuration files.

The following example will create a backup of your configuration files:

```
c:\%windir%\System32\inetsrv\appcmd.exe add backup "MyBackup"
```

Here's an example to restore from a backup:

```
c:\%windir%\System32\inetsrv\appcmd.exe restore backup "MyBackup"
```

Here's how to delete a backup:

```
c:\%windir%\System32\inetsrv\appcmd.exe delete backup "MyBackup"
```

Here's an example of getting a list of backups currently stored on the system:

```
c:\%windir%\System32\inetsrv\appcmd.exe list backup
```

Now that you know what to back up on an IIS server, you're almost ready to start your own disaster-recovery planning process. But first let's look at a few things that commonly get missed.

20.2.3 *What you may have missed*

Besides the configuration files, there are other pieces to your puzzle that may need to be part of your backup and restore strategy. Often administrators miss backing up the certificates that are needed for HTTPS and other custom components that may have been added by developers. The key here is to make sure you document and back up anything that wasn't part of the out-of-box experience. Let's talk about a few items that are often missed.

CERTIFICATES

Using IIS 8 and the new central certificate store makes backing up your certificates a snap because they're all in one place. Until you're able to use this feature, each of your web servers will contain the certificates you need for your HTTPS sites, and you don't want to lose them. Many admins skip this part, and when they lose a server they find themselves buying new certificates.

You should be proactive in making sure you have copies of your certificates locked in a safe place. Chapter 9 shows you how to export a certificate to a .pfx file. If you lose a server, you can reinstall the certificates quickly and easily. As you look around your web servers, you should document the website bindings that require certificates, the certificates they're using, and make sure to have a backup of them.

THE REGISTRY

Most third-party backup software will back up your Registry—normally when recovering IIS and your websites, you don't have to worry about the Registry. The challenge comes if you (or another admin) have made changes to the Registry with regard to IIS. Generally that's not recommended for most web servers because many of those settings can be handled directly through IIS and the configuration files.

The Registry contains settings for HTTP.SYS and other components, and if they've been changed you need to make sure you get a system state backup (most third-party software easily handles that). For a complete list of Registry settings (and there are hundreds), check out the Microsoft support article at http://support.microsoft.com/kb/954864.

CUSTOM COM AND .NET COMPONENTS

If you installed additional components with WebPI, recovering those is as easy as running WebPI again. Some web applications are written using custom COM and .NET components created by the developers. These are usually installed as additional .dlls that are registered with the system.

Custom .dlls should be part of your backup process, along with the instructions on how to reinstall them if a failure occurs. Many custom applications have an installer to handle this, but some require you to copy the .dlls to the server and register them using RegSrv32.exe. I don't know which applications you're using or how you got them installed, so this might require a little research on your part. One way to quickly tell if this is an issue is to build a test environment with your web applications running on them. If you needed to install or register any specific components to get the website to function, then you know you need to back those up along with the website files.

If your web servers and applications are part of a web farm, then you've increased your availability and can handle losing a server or website. But that doesn't mean you shouldn't have a backup plan for emergencies. Let me give you some planning tips and ideas for a web farm.

20.2.4 *Planning disaster recovery for web farms*

If you're using a web farm with a load balance (and you should be), I recommend being careful when planning your backup and recovery. Remember that the configuration files and content may in fact be located in a Distributed File System or on a network share. Don't back up the wrong thing. I keep the following important questions in mind when I plan for backup and recovery in a web farm:

- Does the web farm use Shared Configuration? Where are those files located?
- Where's the website content located? Locally? Or is it shared through DFS or a network drive?
- What additional components (application and platform) need to be installed on a web server to support its applications?
- Is there an ARR or a control server? If so, are its configuration files backed up separately from the web farm server's?

I still recommend that the best disaster-recovery option in the event of a server failure is WFF and ARR, with automatic provisioning. Because they're free, they're worth considering and testing.

20.2.5 *Recovering from a failure*

It all boils down to this: you get a phone call that the website's down or a web server failed—what do you do? This isn't the time to try out your recovery options for the first time.

I know it sounds basic, and you probably already do this, but test and document your recovery process before a failure happens. You may have a complicated web environment, so make sure to test for multiple types of failures and how to recover from them.

I find that for smaller web environments, a virtualized test environment works well for testing disaster recovery. That doesn't always work well for larger environments, and developers often create a full replica of the production environment. Keep in mind that a good test environment is used for testing applications and new components as well as for disaster recovery. It's common to have a development environment, a test environment, and a production environment that are as identical as possible.

The best test environment exactly matches the production environment. This match prevents surprises when you roll out new applications and offers you the chance to fully test your recovery capabilities.

20.2.6 *Don't forget to monitor*

Monitoring the operations of your websites and servers can sometimes be as complicated as the disaster recovery process, should something fail. Throughout this book, and notably in chapters 6 and 8, I gave you some tactics to get started on monitoring your environment. Let me give you a list to remind you of the tools you have at hand and then I'll conclude with some additional tools you might be able to use:

- *Ping test*—Even the simplest ping test can help you identify when a website becomes unavailable. Although Ping.exe isn't the best tool, PowerShell includes `Invoke-WebRequest`, which allows you to specify a particular website and port to test.
- *Check your logs*—Using a tool like LogParser or PowerShell, you can check the responses of your websites. I also like to watch for application pool recycling, which can indicate a problem with an application. Although it may not crash my server, it's resetting my website and could be causing issues with my customer.
- *Failed Request Tracing (FRT)*—Sometimes the only way to know you're having issues is by trapping and noticing the problem. FRT is a great way to isolate problems that may turn into larger issues.
- *Process Explorer and Monitor*—It's not only for security. Process Explorer and Process Monitor can help diagnose response problems and memory leaks that may be occurring from custom application components.
- *Your web farm statistics*—If you're using the Microsoft ARR and WFF, you're provided with many health monitoring statistics. Check these often to see whether a site is causing a failover.

Monitoring the state of your servers can involve more than tools for IIS. Many companies employ complete monitoring packages, such as Microsoft's System Center Operations Manager (SCOM), that can provide reports and statistics on how the servers and roles like IIS are behaving. Such analytical tools can warn you before an outage occurs and even help drill down to the exact problem. Tools like SCOM also monitor the entire server and infrastructure—a slow response to a website could be caused by a network traffic issue. These advanced monitoring tools can identify those root causes.

The drawback to the more advanced tools is that they aren't free and they require additional knowledge and installation. Larger companies, many of which already have extensive monitoring tools, can easily add the web infrastructure to the monitoring list. If you have a smaller environment, then something as simple as `Invoke-WebRequest` in PowerShell might be the answer you need:

```
PS>Invoke-WebRequest -URI HTTP://www.company.loc
```

You can drill further into `Invoke-WebRequest`, but even in its simplest form you could script several sites and return the status codes:

```
PS>Invoke-WebRequest -URI HTTP://www.company.loc | Select-Object -Property
   ➥StatusDescription
```

However you decide to monitor your web environment will be based on the tools you have and the scale of the environment you need to monitor. I generally start simple, monitoring for outages with `Invoke-WebRequest`, and build my monitoring based on the tools available.

20.3   Lab

For this lab I want you to throw caution to the wind and destroy a web server. Take one of the lab VMs that you've been working on and make a backup of the configuration files.

I want you to then delete—yes, delete—the applicationHost.config file from C:\%windir%\System32\inetsrv\config. Restart the server and see if any of the websites still work. They won't.

Now recover the configuration files and test the websites again. Explore the IIS manager and note that everything came back.

20.4   Ideas to try on your own

High availability and disaster recovery are the most important tasks a web administrator can perform. Companies that rely on their websites for business and branding need to be able to withstand failure and recover from disaster. Because your environment is different from mine, I want you to document, plan, and test for disaster recovery. Examine and document your environment and try different scenarios for both high availability and recovery.

The final exam 21

I have one more challenge for you. Equipped with the knowledge and experience you've gained from this book, build a complete, highly reliable web environment—from scratch. This chapter is fairly short and doesn't require a whole lunch to read, but as a lab it's big and complicated—it may take several hours or even days to complete, over the course of several lunches. You can come back to this lab anytime, or create your own challenge. This chapter is meant to give you something to shoot for if you want to try to put it all together. Go ahead and give it a quick read, and when you're ready, fire up some VMs and give it a try.

If you take this challenge, keep in mind that you'll likely get stuck and run into problems. Use these problems as opportunities to try out the resources discussed in previous chapters. Explore the forums and the internet for answers. Refer back to sections in this book when you need to and don't be afraid to make mistakes. I've learned the most by breaking things.

This "final exam" requires a new set of VMs—and perhaps some additional ones—to support the WFF and ARR high availability. The first section takes you through the requirements for those VMs, and the last section is the lab.

You can change the lab to suit your own needs, and I encourage you to explore different setups. My solution to this lab will be on MoreLunches.com, along with the rest of the lab answers from this book.

21.1   *The lab setup*

This lab requires that you start your virtual environment from scratch. You can remove all the work you've completed by uninstalling IIS and deleting your web content, or rebuild your VMs. I enjoy experiencing the whole process, so I prefer to build the VMs from scratch. I encourage you to go beyond your current VM setup if your hardware allows. In other words, three VMs are fine for this lab, but four or five would create a better experience.

You'll be implementing a highly available web environment using WFF and ARR, discussed in chapter 19. If you only have three VMs, your environment will be similar to figure 21.1. The ARR control server will be installed on the Active Directory domain controller; the remaining two VMs will be used as primary and secondary servers. Choose the Windows operating system you prefer, but if possible consider using Windows Server 2012.

If you have the capacity and want to experience a more realistic approach, then a larger lab environment is for you. If so, you'll need five VMs, as shown in figure 21.2.

When you've chosen your lab environment and you've built a clean set of VMs, start the challenge in the next section. The lab assumes a domain name of Company.loc, but you can install Active Directory with whatever domain name you like.

21.2   *Your lab challenge*

You've been contracted by WebBikez.com to build a highly reliable web farm for its growing website. You need to design and implement a web farm using the Web Farm Framework and Application Request Router as both the load balancing and automated provisioning solutions. The bike shop has provided you with the following information about the company's needs.

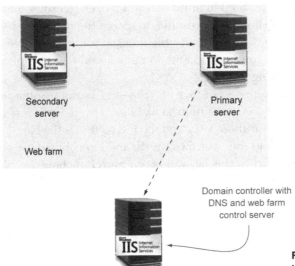

Figure 21.1   The small
lab environment

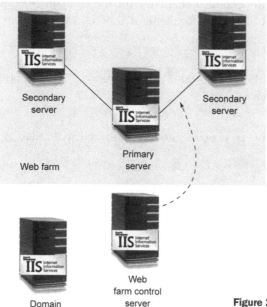

Figure 21.2 A large lab environment gives the most realistic experience.

WEBSITES

The company has three websites that need to be highly available. All three need ASP and ASP.NET to support their applications. Two of the websites are publicly available and should allow anonymous access, but the third is a shopping site and should require that users log in. The company wants the shopping site protected with SSL. The websites are as follows:

- www.Company.loc—This is the default website in IIS.
- Product.Company.loc—This is the company product catalog.
- Shop.Company.loc—This is the secured shopping site.

The content for these websites should be centrally located and shared to the websites during the initial development phase.

WEB FARM

The company needs a highly reliable web farm. They'd like to use the features of IIS to accomplish that. Please implement WFF and ARR to provide this environment. (Hint: chapter 19.)

MANAGEMENT

The company needs to be able to manage all web servers through the remote management capabilities in IIS. The IIS manager on the control server should have a connection to each web server so that the administrator can view them and make changes if necessary.

Certificate management will become a challenge for the company—both locating and replacing certificates. You'll have to implement the central certificate store to make this process easier (only if you're using Server 2012).

DISASTER RECOVERY

Provide a process to back up the content and configuration of the IIS, both for the control server and the web farm servers.

VERIFICATION

Demonstrate the disaster recovery process and the failover capabilities of the load balance.

Never the end 22

It's been a long road to get to this point in the book. You've almost reached the end, but certainly not the end of IIS. You've gone beyond the basics, you've learned and experienced IIS administration, and you're equipped with the knowledge to go further to support your web administration career. This short chapter won't take you a whole lunch to read, but hopefully you'll return to it often when you're looking for additional resources to help you work with IIS.

I include books and websites that will help you go beyond this book to advance your skills in PowerShell, and I offer additional IIS references. In this chapter I want to point you in the right direction to find out more about IIS to support your environment and become a better web administrator. I'll try not to ramble, but let's talk about the inadvertent IIS administrator one more time.

22.1 Resources for the inadvertent IIS administrator

The inadvertent IIS administrator has a busy work day, often spent putting out fires, and in some cases putting out fires he or she started. If you're an IIS administrator, you're probably responsible for many products and applications on your network and don't have much spare time. Although the goal of this book is to help a new IIS administrator learn the ropes, the learning never ends. It's time for you to explore and advance your IIS and web knowledge even further.

When I'm stuck and need more information, the following sites are where I go to talk with other administrators and find resources. Although this isn't an exhaustive list, these are my favorites:

- *IIS.NET (www.iis.net)*—This website contains the latest information about IIS. You should check it often. Many administrators ignore this site because it's hard to search and find information, but that's because it's packed with tons of information. You should spend some time looking around. You'll find thousands of articles that go deep into information about the components and operation of IIS. Often the solution to my problem is some nugget of information I found on IIS.NET. Not only do IIS team members post articles, but MVPs and other IIS experts also post to the site. You get both the Microsoft approach and the real-world experience of thousands of people. If you have a question that you can't find the answer to, jump into the forums and post it. Don't be afraid—the responders are professionals working just like you and they want to help. Eventually you may take the time and answer a few questions as well.

- *PowerShell.org (www.PowerShell.Org)*—If you're working with PowerShell and IIS, trying to automate tasks, working with Server Core and remote servers, attempting to make heads or tails out of the web administration cmdlets, and so on, then you should stop by the PowerShell and IIS forums. Along with several other PowerShell administrators, I monitor the forums and look forward to answering questions. I learn as much from you and your questions as I do from working with IIS. Stop by and share your PowerShell/IIS experience and help other inadvertent PowerShell/IIS administrators.

- *The Web Platform Installer*—WebPI is often updated with the latest and greatest web components, many of which you could spend hours hunting down on the internet. WebPI is an overlooked resource for admins trying to install the new components demanded by today's applications. You should open and check out the spotlighted new additions to keep yourself familiar with what's available. Make sure to update your WebPI version (currently at 4.5) at www.iis.net.

- *Search engines*—Google and Bing are my best friends when I'm working with IIS. Regardless of application or platform, you'll find a vast wealth of knowledge spread out on blogs from all over the world. Type in your problem starting with *Microsoft IIS*, and you'll find your answer.

- *Books*—A couple books on my bookshelf go deeper into areas of IIS and make great reference material. I have a tremendous amount of respect for the authors and I follow their blogs to learn from their experiences. Here they are, one for IIS 7 and one for IIS 8. Enjoy.
  - *Professional IIS 7* by Kenneth Schaefer, Jeff Cochran, Scott Forsyth, and Rob Baugh (Wrox, 2008)
  - *Professional Microsoft IIS 8* by Kenneth Schaefer, Jeff Cochran, Scott Forsyth, and Dennis Glendenning (Wrox, 2012)

- *Books for developers*—I wrote this book for anyone who needs to learn how to administer IIS. I teach the topic often and have had many developers as students. The information in this book is often just what they needed to help clarify some part of their deployment or management process. Sometimes they need to go deeper than an admin would normally go, and for that I recommend starting at www.iis.net. If you mean to drill down into a technology such as PHP, MVP, or even Azure, then check out www.manning.com for books on those web development technologies.

■ *PowerShell books*—The book you're holding in your hands isn't a PowerShell book. PowerShell is an amazing tool for real-time management and automation. I couldn't be successful in today's world without it, particularly when I'm working with large IIS implementations. Here are the books that I think will help you the most to learn to use PowerShell to its fullest:

– *Learn Windows PowerShell 3 in a Month of Lunches, Second Edition* by Don Jones and Jeffery Hicks (Manning Publications, 2012)

– *Learn PowerShell Toolmaking in a Month of Lunches* by Don Jones and Jeffery Hicks (Manning Publications, 2012)

– *PowerShell in Depth* by Don Jones, Richard Siddaway, and Jeffery Hicks (Manning Publications, 2013)

– *PowerShell Deep Dives* edited by Jeffery Hicks, Richard Siddaway, Oisin Grehan, and Aleksandar Nikolic (Manning Publications, 2013)

Keep moving forward and learning as much as you can about IIS. It's a great career being the inadvertent IIS administrator.

22.2 DevOps: the ever-changing job of the IIS administrator

I'm often asked by administrators if I think they should learn how to build web applications, become a developer, and sink into the guts of the web. On the flip side, I teach IIS to many developers who ask the same question about learning administration. The truth is, to be the most effective, administrators and developers should learn a little about each other.

Being effective working with IIS means you should understand the needs and challenges that both the administrators (formerly known as operators) and developers face. By bridging the gap we become smarter, more effective and efficient, and better at problem solving in an ever-growing web environment. This is known as *DevOps*.

Does that mean that after reading this book you should run out and buy an ASP.NET book and learn to build a website? Why not? Even if you learn only a little, it'll help you understand more about the applications and requirements that are needed with IIS.

If you've never programmed or scripted before, my recommendation is to get started on the DevOps path with PowerShell. Not only will you be able to manage IIS better, you'll also start to learn the thinking process of a programmer through the scripting and automation you create.

If you're fortunate enough to work in an environment where you have web developers on staff, why not take them to lunch, become friends, and learn from them? You might be surprised; they'll probably have as many questions for you as you have for them.

I find the more I understand about the IIS architecture—the guts inside that make it go—the better I become at solving problems. This book isn't designed to be a "deep dive" into the internal workings of IIS, but as you work with it you'll find additional knowledge helpful. Many resources offer this information, and a good place to start is on IIS.net.

THE INADVERTENT IIS ADMINISTRATOR,
JASON

IIS PowerShell cheat sheet

No one (including your author) knows what your particular PowerShell needs will be when working with IIS. Fortunately PowerShell is designed to be flexible. This chapter is a collection of my favorite PowerShell commands that I keep around. Each of these is explored elsewhere in this book, but here they are together for your reference. The list is always growing and changing, but this is a good start for your own cheat sheet.

Getting a list of IIS components
```
PS> Import-Module ServerManager #only required for PowerShell v2
PS> Get-WindowsFeature -Name *web*
```

Installing IIS
```
PS> Import-Module ServerManager #only required for PowerShell v2
PS> Add-WindowsFeature Web-Server
```

Testing a default installation
```
PS> Start iexplore http://<ServerName>
```

Importing and viewing cmdlets for IIS
```
PS> Import-Module WebAdministration
PS> Get-Command -Module WebAdministration
PS> Get-Command -noun web*
PS> Get-Help *web*
```

Viewing a website
```
PS> Get-WebSite -Name Default*
PS> Get-Childitem -Path iis:\sites
PS> Get-Childitem -Path c:\inetPub\wwwroot
```

Navigating to application pools

```
PS> Set-location IIS:\appPools
PS> Get-Childitem
```

Getting information about application pools

```
PS> Get-Item -Path IIS:\appPools\defaultAppPool
PS> Get-Item -Path IIS:\appPools\defaultAppPool | Format-List -Property *
```

Creating application pools

```
PS> New-WebAppPool -Name BikeTestPool
```

Changing a website to a new application pool

```
PS> Set-ItemProperty -Path 'IIS:\Sites\Default Web Site' -Name
    ApplicationPool -Value BikeTestPool
```

Getting a list of worker processes

```
PS> Get-WmiObject Win32_Process -filter 'name="w3wp.exe"'
PS> Get-WmiObject Win32_process -filter 'name="w3wp.exe"' | Select-Object
    Name, ProcessId, @{n='AppPool';e={$_.GetOwner().user}}
```

Restarting an application pool

```
PS> Restart-WebAppPool -Name BikeTestPool
```

Setting application pool settings (managed runtime)

```
PS> Set-ItemProperty -Path IIS:\appPools\TestBikePool -Name
    ManagedRuntimeVersion -Value v4.0
```

Setting application pool recycling settings (recycle time)

```
PS> Get-ItemProperty -Path IIS:\AppPools\DefaultAppPool -Name
    recycling.periodicRestart.time
PS> Set-ItemProperty -Path IIS:\AppPools\DefaultAppPool -Name
    recycling.periodicRestart.time -Value 3.00:00:00
```

Setting application pool recycling settings (schedule)

```
PS> Get-ItemProperty -Path IIS:\AppPools\DefaultAppPool -Name
    recycling.PeriodicRestart.schedule.collection
PS> clear-ItemProperty -Path IIS:\AppPools\DefaultAppPool -Name
    recycling.PeriodicRestart.schedule.collection
PS C:\> set-ItemProperty -Path IIS:\AppPools\DefaultAppPool -Name
    recycling.PeriodicRestart.schedule.collection -Value @{value='06:00:00'}
```

Viewing events for application pools

```
PS> Get-Eventlog -LogName System -Source WAS
```

Getting the application pool identity

```
PS> Get-ItemProperty -Path IIS:\AppPools\MyTest -Name
    ProcessModel.IdentityType
```

Setting an application pool identity (example for NetworkService)

```
PS> Set-ItemProperty -Path IIS:\AppPools\MyTest -Name
    ProcessModel.IdentityType -value 2
```

Setting your own custom application pool user account as the identity

```
PS> Set-ItemProperty -Path IIS:\AppPools\MyTest -Name
    processmodel.identityType -Value 3
PS> Set-ItemProperty -Path IIS:\AppPools\MyTest -Name processmodel.username -
    Value Administrator
PS> Set-ItemProperty -Path IIS:\AppPools\MyTest -Name processmodel.password -
    Value P@ssw0rd
```

Creating websites

```
PS> New-Item -ItemType Directory -Path c:\PoshTestSite
PS> New-WebAppPool -Name PoshTestSitePool
PS> New-Website -Name PoshTestSite -Hostheader Posh.Widget.Com
    -PhysicalPath c:\PoshTestSite -ApplicationPool PoshTestSitePool
```

Setting static compression for a server

```
PS> Get-WebConfiguration -filter system.webserver/urlcompression
    -PSPath iis:\ | fl *
PS> Get-WebConfigurationProperty -filter system.webserver/urlcompression
    -PSPath iis:\ -name doStaticCompression
PS> set-WebConfigurationProperty -filter system.webserver/urlcompression
    -PSPath iis:\ -name doStaticCompression -value True
```

Getting and setting static compression for a site

```
PS> Get-WebConfiguration -filter system.webserver/httpcompression -PSPath
    iis:\ | fl *
PS> set-WebConfigurationProperty -filter system.webserver/urlcompression
    -PSPath 'IIS:\Sites\Default Web Site' -name doStaticCompression
    -value true
PS> Get-WebConfigurationProperty -filter system.webserver/httpcompression
    -PSPath iis:\ -Name maxDiskSpaceUsage | fl *
PS> set-WebConfigurationProperty -filter system.webserver/httpcompression
    -PSPath iis:\ -Name maxDiskSpaceUsage -Value 100
```

Adding dynamic compression

```
PS> Add-WindowsFeature -Name Web-Dyn-Compression
```

Changing directory browsing

```
PS> Get-WebConfigurationProperty -filter system.webserver/directorybrowse
    -PSPath iis:\ -Name enabled
PS> Set-WebConfigurationProperty -filter system.webserver/directorybrowse
    -PSPath iis:\ -Name enabled -Value true
```

Getting and setting the Default Documents

```
PS> Get-WebConfiguration -Filter system.webserver/defaultdocument/files/add -
    -PSPath iis:\ | select value
PS> Add-WebConfiguration -Filter system.webserver/defaultdocument/files -
    -PSPath iis:\ -Value 'jason.htm' -AtIndex 3 #If no index specified it
    places it at the top
```

Adding IIS 6 compatability mode

```
PS> Add-WindowsFeature web-mgmt-compat -IncludeAllSubFeature
```

Adding ASP and ASP.Net

```
PS> Add-WindowsFeature -Name Web-ASP
PS> Add-WindowsFeature -Name Web-ASP-Net
PS C:\> Get-WebConfiguration -filter system.webserver/asp -PSPath iis:\ |
    format-List *
```

Adding CGI

```
PS> Add-WindowsFeature -Name Web-CGI
```

Listing all log files for every website

```
PS> Get-childitem -Path C:\inetpub\logs -filter *.log -recurse
```

Listing all HTTP requests that occurred at 9:00 p.m.

```
PS> Get-childitem -Path C:\inetpub\logs -filter *.log -recurse | Select-
    String -SimpleMatch "21:00"
```

Listing all requests from clients to a particular URL

```
PS> Get-childitem -Path C:\inetpub\logs -filter *.log -recurse | Select-
    String -SimpleMatch "MySite/TestPage.asp"
```

Listing all requests to/from a particular IP address

```
PS> Get-childitem -Path C:\inetpub\logs -filter *.log -recurse | Select-
    String -SimpleMatch "10.211.55.30"
```

Adding Failed Request Tracing

```
PS> Add-WindowsFeature web-http-tracing
```

Getting a list of authentication mechanisms

```
PS> Get-WebConfiguration -Filter /system.WebServer/Security/authentication |
    foreach-Object{$_.sections}
```

Getting anonymous authentication settings

```
PS> Get-WebConfigurationProperty -Filter system.WebServer/security/
    authentication/anonymousAuthentication -PSPath IIS:\  -name enabled |
    select-Object value
```

Disabling/enabling anonymous authentication for the entire web server

```
PS> Set-WebConfigurationProperty -Filter system.WebServer/security/
    authentication/anonymousAuthentication -PSPath IIS:\  -name enabled -
    Value false
```

Enabling/disabling anonymous authentication for a website or application

```
PS> Get-WebConfigurationProperty -Filter system.WebServer/security/
    authentication/anonymousAuthentication -PSPath IIS:\  -name enabled -
    Location mysite
PS> Set-WebConfigurationProperty -Filter system.WebServer/security/
    authentication/anonymousAuthentication -PSPath IIS:\  -name enabled -
    Value False -Location MySite
```

Adding Windows authentication

```
PS> Add-WindowsFeature Web-Windows-Auth
```

Getting information about Windows authentication settings

```
PS> Get-WebConfiguration -Filter system.WebServer/security/authentication/
    windowsAuthentication | Format-List *
PS> Get-WebConfigurationProperty -Filter system.WebServer/security/
    authentication/windowsAuthentication -name enabled |
    select-Object value
```

Enabling/disabling Windows authentication

```
PS> Set-WebConfigurationProperty -Filter system.WebServer/security/
    authentication/windowsAuthentication -name enabled -Value true
```

Enabling/disabling Windows authentication per site or application

```
PS> Get-WebConfigurationProperty -Filter system.WebServer/security/
    authentication/windowsAuthentication -name enabled -Location mysite |
    select-Object value
```

Adding basic authentication

```
PS> Add-WindowsFeature Web-Basic-Auth
```

Getting configuration information about basic authentication

```
PS> Get-WebConfiguration -Filter system.WebServer/security/authentication/
    BasicAuthentication | Format-List *
PS> Get-WebConfigurationProperty -Filter system.WebServer/security/
    authentication/BasicAuthentication -name enabled | select value
```

Enabling/disabling basic authentication

```
PS> Set-WebConfigurationProperty -Filter system.WebServer/security/
    authentication/BasicAuthentication -name enabled -Value true
```

Enabling/disabling basic authentication per site or application

```
PS> Set-WebConfigurationProperty -Filter system.WebServer/security/
    authentication/BasicAuthentication -name enabled -Location mysite |
    select-Object value
```

Installing certificates

```
PS> certutil -p P@ssw0rd -importpfx c:\shop.Company.com.pfx
```

Adding an SSL binding

```
PS> New-WebBinding -name shop -Protocol https -Port 443 -IPAddress
    192.168.3.201 -SslFlags 0}
```

Binding a certificate to a website

```
PS> $Cert=Get-ChildItem -Path Cert:\LocalMachine\My |
    where-Object {$_.subject -like "*shop*"} |
    Select-Object -ExpandProperty Thumbprint
PS> Get-Item -Path "cert:\localmachine\my\$cert" |
    New-Item -path IIS:\SslBindings\192.168.3.201!443
```

Installing Remote Management to multiple computers using PowerShell Remoting

```
PS> $Session=New-PsSession -ComputerName web1,web2
PS> Invoke-Command -Session $Session -ScriptBlock {Add-WindowsFeature Web-
    Mgmt-Service}
PS> Invoke-command -Session $Session -FilterScript{Set-ItemProperty -Path
    HKLM:\SOFTWARE\Microsoft\WebManagement\Server -Name
    EnableRemoteManagement -Value 1}
PS> Invoke-command -Session $Session -FilterScript {Set-Service -name WMSVC -
    StartupType Automatic}
PS> Invoke-command -Session $Session -FilterScript {Start-service WMSVC}
```

Installing a new certificate for Remote Management

```
PS> Invoke-Command -session $session {$cert=Get-ChildItem -Path
    Cert:\LocalMachine\My | where {$_.subject -like "*company*"} | Select-
    Object -ExpandProperty Thumbprint}
PS> Invoke-Command -session $session {Import-Module WebAdministration}
PS> Invoke-command -Session $session {remove-item -Path 0.0.0.0!8172}
PS> Invoke-Command -Session $session {get-item -Path
    "cert:\localmachine\my\$cert" | new-item -path
    IIS:\SslBindings\0.0.0.0!8172}
```

Installing Microsoft NLB to multiple servers

```
PS> $Sessions=New-PSSession -ComputerName Web1, Web2
PS> Invoke-Command -Session $Session {Install-WindowsFeature Web-server, NLB}
PS> New-NLBCluster -Hostname Web1 InterfaceName Ehternet -ClusterName web -
    ClusterPrimaryIP 192.168.3.200 -SubnetMask 255.255.255.0 -
    OperationMode Multicast
PS> Get-NlbCluster -HostName Web1 | Add-NlbClusterNode -NewNodeName Web2 -
    NewNodeInterface Ethernet
```

Adding DNS records for websites

```
PS> Add-DnsServerResourceRecordA -name www -ZoneName company.loc -IPv4Address
    192.168.3.200 -ComputerName DC.company.loc
```

Deploying simple websites to a web farm

```
PS> $Servers= 'Web1', 'Web2'
PS> $servers | foreach{copy-item -Path c:\sites\*.* -Destination \\$_\c$ -
    recurse}
```

Making new sites on a web farm

```
PS> $Sessions=New-PSSession -ComputerName Web1, Web2
PS> Invoke-Command -Session $Session {New-WebAppPool -Name BikeShop-pool}
PS> Invoke-Command -Session $Session {New-Website -Name BikeShop -HostHeader
    www.BikeShop.loc -PhysicalPath C:\sites\BikeShop -ApplicationPool
    BikeShop-pool}
```

Installing the central certificate store

```
PS> Install-WindowsFeature Web-CertProvider
PS> Enable-WebCentralCertProvider -CertStoreLocation \\dc\cert -UserName
    company\IIScert -Password P@ssw0rd -PrivateKeyPassword P@ssw0rd
PS> Set-ItemProperty -Path HKLM:\SOFTWARE\Microsoft\IIS\CentralCertProvider\
    -Name Enabled -Value 1
PS> Set-ItemProperty -Path HKLM:\SOFTWARE\Microsoft\IIS\CentralCertProvider\
    -Name CertStoreLocation -Value \\ServerDC\CertStore
PS> Set-WebCentralCertProvider -Password P@ssw0rd -UserName Company\certuser
    -PrivateKeyPassword P@ssw0rd
```

Lab setup guide

This chapter gives you some additional options and instructions for your own lab setup to work with this book. I think you'll find that the lab environments I describe aren't difficult to build and will be very useful as testing environments while you work through the book and try new ideas for your own production environment.

The only software you'll need is a copy of Server 2008 R2 or Server 2012. If you don't have a licensed copy available, you can download a 180-day free trial from Microsoft at http://mng.bz/Wvv0.

In this chapter you'll see several options for a standalone client and selecting a virtualization platform, as well as instructions for building the basic and extended environments. Let's get started with the advantages and disadvantages of using a standalone client.

24.1 Using Windows 7 or Windows 8 as a standalone client

Keep in mind that to experience this book, the complexities of the IIS product, and the network and DNS configurations for IIS to the fullest, using a single client operating system is not the best choice. I spend considerable time showing how to work with IIS on a network that includes domain controllers and DNS servers—as you would in real life. Without that experience, you'll have additional troubleshooting challenges and mistakes. But if you're an IT pro who already has this experience, there's no reason to waste your time. For chapters 1–12, you can get a lot out of the

book by running IIS on your client operating system without needing additional virtualized servers.

Remember that the labs are written for a server-based environment, so the steps
won't match your standalone client, but the screenshots and the basic instructions will
all be the same.

To install IIS on a Windows 8 client operating system, open Control Panel, choose
Programs, and select Turn Windows Features on or off. Check the check box for Internet Information Services.

For Windows 7 the process is almost identical. The local installation will provide
you with a local web server, the IIS PowerShell cmdlets, and the graphical IIS manager
you'll need to try the labs in this book.

24.2 *Choosing a virtualization platform*

To build the server-based environments recommended for this book, you need access
to either a set of physical servers or a virtualization platform to create the server VMs. I
strongly recommend a virtualization platform because it's easier to carry the VMs on
your laptop and have them with you, easier to build new VMs, and easier to destroy
VMs as you experiment.

I assume you want to do this on a laptop. If not, if you're using a separate server,
then your options are fairly simple as you'll see. But let me explore all options in case
your laptop is your primary computer.

24.2.1 *Hyper-V on Windows 8*

If you are using Windows 8 as your client OS, then you already have a virtualization
platform called Hyper-V. Hyper-V permits you to build and run VMs locally. This is a
great feature for the IT pro and is the most affordable.

You can install Hyper-V from Control Panel > Programs > Turn Windows Features
on or off > Hyper-V. I cover more on working with Hyper-V and creating VMs in the
next section, but you can also check out http://mng.bz/J5o9.

24.2.2 *Hyper-V on Server 2008 R2 or Server 2012*

If you have Server 2008 R2 or Server 2012 on your laptop, you have Hyper-V available
as your virtualization platform, just like with Windows 8. You can also install the Server
operating system on a separate computer to use Hyper-V.

To install Hyper-V on the Server OS, open Server Manager, select Add new roles,
and choose Hyper-V. You can also use the PowerShell cmdlet `Add-WindowsFeature`
`HyperV`.

24.2.3 *Other options*

If you have Windows 7 or just want another option for a virtualization platform, consider using VMware workstation (for PC clients) or Fusion (for Mac clients) as your virtualization platform. If you choose VMware, the instructions in the next section will be

slightly different when creating a new VM, but both Hyper-V and VMware are simple to use. (I wrote this book and built the lab environments on a MacBook Pro using VMware Fusion.)

24.3 Single-server environment

The labs are designed for a minimum of two servers in chapters 1–12. It's possible to work through those first chapters on a single-server VM that's also a domain controller with DNS. If you only want one server VM, here's how to get started using Hyper-V:

1 Open Hyper-V Manager. Click Start > Administrative Tools > Hyper-V Manager.
2 From the actions pane, click New > Virtual Machine.
3 Proceed through the wizard to specify the custom settings you want to make. You can click Next to move through each page of the wizard or click the name of a page in the left pane to move directly to that page.
4 For a single server choose at least 1024 MB for memory.
5 Create a dynamic disk.
6 Attach the .iso file containing the server source files for the installation.
7 After you've finished configuring the virtual machine, click Finish.
8 Start the virtual machine and install Windows Server.

With the server installed, you'll want to install Active Directory, covered in the next section.

24.4 Two-server environment

The two-server environment is what I recommend for a much more realistic experience. Use the Hyper-V instructions from the single-server environment (the previous section) to create two VMs. One VM should be named DC (this will become the domain controller), and the other should be named Web1.

24.4.1 Building the domain controller

On the computer named DC, install Active Directory. I outline the process here, but for a complete, graphical, step-by-step guide, see http://mng.bz/SvP9.

1 In your virtual software, create a new computer and install Windows Server. You don't need much memory for this—512 MB to 1024 MB is sufficient. Name the computer DC and assign a password of your choosing to the Administrator account.
2 Install the ADDS role and a domain controller. You can do that in Server Manager for Windows Server 2008 R2 and Windows Server 2012.
3 Install Active Directory. When asked for a Fully Qualified Domain Name for your forest root domain, choose something simple. For this book I chose Company.loc.

4   Supply the Windows NetBIOS name for the domain; I'm using Company in my environment.

5   When prompted to choose the forest and domain functional level, choose the highest level, which is Windows Server 2008 R2 or Windows Server 2012.

6   When prompted for Additional Domain Controller Options, select the option to install DNS. Not only does Active Directory need DNS, but you'll also be using it for your websites.

NOTE If you set up your virtual computer with a dynamically assigned IP address, you'll receive a warning message saying that's not good practice. You can quit the installation and set the IP address, but this is only a test environment, so it's okay to select "Yes, the computer will use a dynamically assigned IP address." If you receive a warning about a DNS delegation creation problem, click Yes to continue.

7   When prompted for the file locations of the Active Directory files, accept the default locations.

8   When prompted for a Restore Mode password, use the same password you set for the Administrator account; it's okay because this is a test environment.

9   When the installation of Active Directory is complete, reboot.

10 Using Active Directory Users and Computers, create three or four users. Nothing special—it can be John Doe1, John Doe2, and so on. You'll need them in the security sections.

24.4.2 *Installing Active Directory Certificate Services (optional)*

Throughout the book, you may want to experiment in generating and using certificates for SSL. In the book I have you generate a self-signed certificate, and ADCS isn't required. But if you'd like the most realistic experience, install the ADCS role.

For complete instructions on installing ADCS on your domain controller, see http://mng.bz/2317.

24.4.3 *The remaining Web1 server*

The second server simply needs to start with a default installation of the server operating system. Chapter 2 takes you through the process of installing IIS, so the second server only needs to be the default installation. You should join the second computer to the domain you created when you made the domain controller.

I recommend that you run updates on both servers before beginning. You may consider copying the VMs to separate storage so you can quickly rebuild the environment in the future. At this point, you're ready to begin!

24.5 *The extended environment*

The extended environment is for the later chapters, starting with chapter 13. The extended environment contains additional web servers for the load balancing and

Application Request Routing labs. I encourage you to extend your environment to practice those concepts. Each additional VM only needs 512 MB of RAM and a basic server operating system installation, so not much disk space is required.

Using the instructions from section 24.4, the following section discusses two different environments I used in the book.

24.5.1 *Extended environment: basic*

The most basic extended environment to accomplish the load balancing and ARR labs contains a total of three VMs:

1 Install and configure the domain controller (DC).
2 Install and configure ADCS (optional) on the domain controller.
3 Install two additional servers, Web1 and Web2.
4 Join the web servers to the domain and run updates.

24.5.2 *Extended environment: advanced*

The advanced extended environment isn't really hard to build, it just requires several more VMs. For chapters 19 and 21—when working with the Web Farm Framework—it's best to have one or two additional web servers that will act as control servers. I prefer to load balance the control servers, so a total of four web servers is required, along with the domain controller. Here's what you'll need for the final chapters:

1 Install and configure the domain controller (DC).
2 Install and configure ADCS (optional) on the domain controller.
3 Install four additional servers, Control1, Control2, Web1, and Web2.
4 Join the web servers to the domain and run updates.

24.6 *Final notes*

Regardless of which lab environment you choose—from running IIS directly on your client operating system to building a large VM environment—I'm confident that you'll be successful in learning IIS from this book. You can reference back to chapters and concepts when you're challenged by a task in the real world.

Feel free to get started with the book using the most basic environment and then extend it as you go along. Don't let the complexity of the VMs slow you down.

index

Learn Windows PowerShell 3 in a Month of Lunches, Second Edition

by Don Jones
    Jeffery Hicks

ISBN: 978-1-617291-08-1
368 pages
$44.99
November 2012

Learn PowerShell Toolmaking in a Month of Lunches

by Don Jones
    Jeffery Hicks

ISBN: 978-1-617291-16-6
312 pages
$44.99
December 2012